Prentice Hall
LITERATURE
Timeless Voices, Timeless Themes

Selection Support:
Skills Development Workbook

PLATINUM

Prentice
Hall

Upper Saddle River, New Jersey
Glenview, Illinois
Needham, Massachusetts

ISBN 0-13-054827-8

15 16 17   10 09 08

CONTENTS

UNIT 1: ON THE EDGE

UNIT 2: STRIVING FOR SUCCESS

UNIT 3: CLASHING FORCES

UNIT 4: TURNING POINTS

UNIT 5: EXPANDING HORIZONS

UNIT 10: EPICS AND LEGENDS

"Contents of the Dead Man's Pocket" by Jack Finney

Build Vocabulary

Spelling Strategy   When adding a suffix beginning with a vowel to a word that ends in a silent *e*, drop the *e*, then add the suffix—for example, *convolute → convoluted*. There are a number of exceptions to this rule, such as *noticeable, mileage,* and *canoeing,* which must be memorized.

Using the Root *-term-*

A. DIRECTIONS: The Latin root *-term-*, meaning "end" or "boundary," occurs in a number of English words. Using what you know about *-term-* (along with some prefixes and suffixes), determine the meanings of the following words.

1. termination _____

2. termless _____

3. terminable _____

Using the Word Bank

convoluted	grimace	deftness
imperceptibly	reveling	interminable

B. DIRECTIONS: Match each word in the left column with its definition in the right column. Write the letter of the definition on the line next to the word it defines.

_____ 1. convoluted   a. skillfulness

_____ 2. grimace   b. seemingly endless

_____ 3. deftness   c. taking great pleasure in

_____ 4. imperceptibly   d. intricate; twisted

_____ 5. reveling   e. almost unnoticeably

_____ 6. interminable   f. twisted facial expression

Making Verbal Analogies

C. DIRECTIONS: Each item consists of a related pair of words in CAPITAL LETTERS followed by four lettered pairs of words. Choose the lettered pair that best expresses a relationship similar to that expressed in the pair in capital letters. Circle the letter of your choice.

____ 1. CONVOLUTED : SIMPLE ::
    a. texture : wavy
    b. pie : slice
    c. bumpy : smooth
    d. easy : difficult

____ 2. REVELING : ENJOYING ::
    a. hopeful : thrilled
    b. miserly : thrifty
    c. hidden : missing
    d. satisfied : contented

____ 3. BRIEF : INTERMINABLE ::
    a. inch : infinity
    b. lengthy : speech
    c. lawyer : professional
    d. shower : storm

Name _____ Date _____

Build Grammar Skills: Identifying Types of Nouns

A **noun** is a word that names a person, place, thing, or idea. **Concrete nouns** name specific people, places, or things that can be seen or recognized through any of the five senses. **Abstract nouns** name ideas, actions, conditions, and qualities that cannot be seen, heard, smelled, tasted, or touched. Below are examples of concrete and abstract nouns.

Concrete Nouns: desk, window, hallway, Tom, closet, wife, Wilshire Boulevard
Abstract Nouns: tomorrow, conscience, promotion, deceit, intention, impulse, fear

A. Practice: Read the following sentences from "Contents of the Dead Man's Pocket," and underline the nouns. Write *C* above each concrete noun and *A* above each abstract noun.

1. By a kind of instinct, he instantly began making his intention acceptable to himself by laughing at it.

2. The realization suddenly struck him that he might have to wait here till Clare came home, and for a moment the thought was funny.

3. Already his legs were cramped, his thigh muscles tired; his knees hurt, his feet felt numb and his hands were stiff.

4. In the inside pocket of his jacket he found a little sheaf of papers, and he pulled one out and looked at it in the light from the living room.

B. Writing Application: Write a brief paragraph summarizing Tom's experience on the apartment ledge. Use a combination of abstract and concrete nouns, including at least four of the following: terror, paper, strength, fingers, body, control, triumph.

_____

_____

_____

_____

_____

_____

_____

_____

_____

_____

_____

_____

"Contents of the Dead Man's Pocket" by Jack Finney

Reading Strategy: Reread or Read Ahead

Your primary goal in reading is to understand what the writer is saying. On a first reading, you may miss details or have questions about what is happening. It makes sense, then, to go back and reread a passage to clarify details. Sometimes you may need to read ahead to find answers to questions or to understand why an author is presenting certain information.

A diagram like this one can help you note when to reread or read ahead to find an answer.

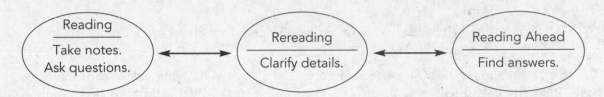

DIRECTIONS: Read the following passages from the story. Then, answer the questions.

1. Nothing, then, could ever be changed; and nothing more—no least experience or pleasure—could ever be added to his life. He wished, then, that he had not allowed his wife to go off by herself tonight—and on similar nights. He thought of all the evenings he had spent away from her, working; and he regretted them.

What details early in the story foreshadow Tom's realization that he should have spent more time with his wife? Reread to find at least two details.

_____

_____

_____

2. Now he placed the heels of his hands against the top edge of the lower window frame and shoved upward. But as usual the window didn't budge, and he had to lower his hands and then shoot them hard upward to jolt the window open a few inches.

Why is this detail about the window important later in the story? Read ahead to find the answer.

_____

_____

_____

3. He turned to pull the door closed and the warm air from the hall rushed through the narrow opening again. As he saw the yellow paper, the pencil flying, scooped off the desk and, unimpeded by the glassless window, sail out into the night and out of his life, Tom Benecke burst into laughter and then closed the door behind him.

What is the significance of the yellow paper, and why does Tom find it amusing when it sails out the window? Reread to find earlier details about the yellow paper.

_____

_____

_____

Name _____ Date _____

Literary Analysis: Suspense

The **suspense** of "Contents of the Dead Man's Pocket" begins the moment you read the title. You ask yourself, "What *are* the contents of the dead man's pocket?" or perhaps, "Who is the dead man?" When a writer causes questions to form in a reader's mind, that writer is creating suspense.

Finney adds to the suspense by including small details. The details make readers feel as if they are right out there on the ledge with Tom. Notice how the details of this passage add to the suspense.

> The fingers of his left hand clawlike on the little stripping, he drew back his other fist until his body began teetering backward.

The word *clawlike* gives you a perfect picture of how Tom is hanging on. As you read the phrase "his body began teetering backward," you might think, "Well, that's it. He's finally going to fall."

DIRECTIONS: Analyze the following passage from "Contents of the Dead Man's Pocket" and underline the suspenseful details. Then, on the lines provided, explain why those details build suspense.

> He waited, arm drawn back, fist balled, but in no hurry to strike; this pause, he knew, might be an extension of his life. And to live even a few seconds longer, he felt, even out here on this ledge in the night, was infinitely better than to die a moment earlier than he had to. His arm grew tired, and he brought it down and rested it.

> Then he knew that it was time to make the attempt. He could not kneel here hesitating indefinitely till he lost all courage to act, waiting till he slipped off the ledge. Again he drew back his arm, knowing this time that he would not bring it down till he struck. His elbow protruding over Lexington Avenue far below, the fingers of his other hand pressed down bloodlessly tight against the narrow stripping, he waited, feeling the sick tenseness and terrible excitement building. It grew and swelled toward the moment of action, his nerves tautening.

_____

_____

_____

_____

_____

_____

_____

_____

_____

_____

_____

_____

"**View From the Summit**" by Edmund Hillary
"**The Dream Comes True**" from *The Tiger of the Snows*
by Tenzing Norgay

Build Vocabulary

Spelling Strategy   The suffix *-able* is much more common than the suffix *-ible*. Memorizing words with the *-ible* suffix, such as *discernible, gullible, eligible,* and *fallible,* is the best way to avoid misspellings.

Using the Root *-voc-*

A. DIRECTIONS: The word root *-voc-* means "speak," "say" or "to call." Tell what the meaning of each of these words has to do with "speaking" or "calling."

1. evoke _____

2. vocation _____

3. invocation _____

4. vocalize _____

Using the Word Bank

ample	aperture	belay
laboriously	feasible	formidable

B. Directions: On the line, write the letter of the word or phrase most nearly *similar* in meaning to the Word Bank word.

_____ 1. ample
   a. bountiful
   b. bright
   c. meager
   d. lively
   e. kind

_____ 2. aperture
   a. photograph
   b. gorge
   c. opening
   d. light
   e. shutter speed

_____ 3 belay
   a. unexpected hold up
   b. foothold
   c. rope support
   d. summit
   e. ax

_____ 4. laboriously
   a. effortlessly
   b. painstakingly
   c. comfortably
   d. cautiously
   e. quickly

_____ 5. feasible
   a. hopeless
   b. unlikely
   c. timid
   d. possible
   e. questionable

_____ 6. formidable
   a. unforgivable
   b. harmless
   c. frightful
   d. lovable
   e. pleasant

"View From the Summit" by Edmund Hillary
"The Dream Comes True" from *The Tiger of the Snows*
by Tenzing Norgay

Build Grammar Skills: Noun Function

A **noun** is a word that names a person, place, thing, or idea. In a sentence, a noun can function as a subject, direct object, object of the preposition, or predicate nominative. In the following examples, each noun is labeled according to its function.

Example: *Mount Everest* is the world's highest *mountain*.

Example: *Hillary* took three *photographs* of *Norgay* on the *summit*.

A. Practice: Circle each noun in the sentences below, and label it according to its function. Write *S, DO, OP,* or *PN* above the noun.

1. Hillary and Norgay were partners in their climb to the top of Mount Everest.

2. Snow glasses protected their eyes from icy winds.

3. Hillary and Norgay ate warm soup and tinned apricots in their tent.

4. Their last big obstacle was a cliff of rock rising straight up out of the ridge.

5. Hillary was the first person ever to make it to the summit.

6. At the summit, Norgay unwound four flags from around his ax.

B. Writing Application: Follow the directions in parentheses to write five sentences about Hillary and Norgay's climb to the top of Mount Everest.

1. (Use a noun as a subject.) _____

_____

2 (Use a noun as a direct object.) _____

_____

3. (Use a noun as the object of a preposition.) _____

_____

4. (Use a noun as a predicate nominative.) _____

_____

5. (Use a noun as a direct object and another as the object of a preposition.) _____

_____

"View From the Summit" by Edmund Hillary
"The Dream Comes True" from *The Tiger of the Snows*
by Tenzing Norgay

Reading Strategy: Distinguish Fact From Opinion

A **fact** is an objective statement that can be proved true by historical records, experimentation, or direct observation; an **opinion,** on the other hand, is a subjective statement that cannot be objectively verified. In autobiographical writing, the writer attempts to present the events of his or her life as they are perceived by the writer. Subjective, felt impressions become an important part of what a writer has to communicate to readers, who, in turn, must be aware of what is objective fact and what is the writer's subjective, personal opinion.

DIRECTIONS: Decide whether each of the following quotations states a fact or an opinion. On the line at the right, write *fact* or *opinion*. Then write an explanation of each answer on the line below.

1. "It was impressive all right, but not impossible. . . ."   1. _____

   _____

2. "At 6:30 A.M. we crawled out of our tent and were ready to go."   2. _____

   _____

3. ". . . after each short stop we kept going, twisting always higher along the ridge. . . ."   3. _____

   _____

4. ". . . we each helped and were helped by the other in equal measure."   4. _____

   _____

5. "One scene was of particular interest."   5. _____

   _____

6. "When he came up to me I examined his oxygen equipment."   6. _____

7. ". . . we were not the leader and the led. We were partners."   7. _____

   _____

8. "Hillary stepped on top first. And I stepped up after him."   8. _____

   _____

"View From the Summit" by Edmund Hillary
"The Dream Comes True" from *The Tiger of the Snows*
by Tenzing Norgay

Literary Analysis: Author's Perspective

Newspaper articles, novels, and even poems contain the opinions, experiences, memories, or outright biases of the author. This is called the **author's perspective.** Reading Hillary's and Norgay's versions of the same events provides an opportunity to compare the authors' perspectives and to detect any attempts to sway readers to form certain opinions.

DIRECTIONS: Each pair of passages below describes the same event. Read the pair carefully. Then state your opinions about the author's perspective in each passage. Explain what details from the passages led you to your opinions.

1. **Hillary:** After I had covered several rope-lengths, I noticed to my surprise that Tenzing was moving rather slowly and seemed in some distress. When he came up to me I examined his oxygen equipment. The pressure seemed satisfactory but then I noticed that his face mask was choked up with ice. I squeezed the mask to dislodge the ice and was relieved to see Tenzing breathing freely again. I checked my own equipment—it, too, held some ice, but not enough to cause me concern, and I quickly cleared it away.

   Norgay: But every so often, as had happened all the way, we would have trouble breathing and have to stop and clear away the ice that kept forming in the tubes of our oxygen sets. In regard to this, I must say in all honesty that I do not think Hillary is quite fair in the story he later told, indicating that I had more trouble than he with breathing and that without his help I might have been in serious difficulty.

   _____

   _____

   _____

   _____

2. **Hillary:** Towering over our heads was the South Summit and running along from it to the right were the great menacing cornices overhanging the Kangshung Face. Ahead of me was a sharp narrow ridge, icy on the right and looking more manageable on the left. So it was to the left I went, at first making easy progress, but then experiencing one of the most unpleasant mountaineering conditions—breakable crust.

   Norgay: There are still the cornices on our right and the precipice on our left, but the ridge is now less steep. It is only a row of snowy humps, one beyond the other, one higher than the other. But we are still afraid of the cornices and, instead of following the ridge all the way, cut over to the left, where there is now a long snow slope above the precipice.

   _____

   _____

   _____

   _____

"The Monkey's Paw" by W. W. Jacobs
"The Bridegroom" by Alexander Pushkin

Build Vocabulary

Spelling Strategy   When adding a suffix that begins with a consonant to a word that ends in silent *e*, keep the *e*: *furtive* + *-ly* = *furtively*. If the suffix begins with a vowel, drop the silent *e*: *avarice* + *-ious* = *avaricious*.

Using the Root *-cred-*

A. DIRECTIONS: The word root *-cred-* means "believe" or "trust." The root *-cred-* comes from the Latin word *credo*, which means "I believe." Define each of the following words. In each of your definitions, use a form of the word *believe* or *trust* to show the connection with the root *-cred-*.

Example: incredible unbelievable _____

1. credential _____

2. credence _____

3. discredit _____

4. creed _____

Using the Word Bank

B. DIRECTIONS: Match each word in the left column with its definition in the right column.

____   1. fusillade   a. feeling that something bad will occur

____   2. credulity   b. commonplace; ordinary

____   3. doughty   c. spoken ill of

____   4. prosaic   d. noisy commotion

____   5. maligned   e. burst of fire from many guns

____   6. foreboding   f. brave; valiant

____   7. avaricious   g. tendency to believe too readily

____   8. tumult   h. greedy for riches

Identifying Antonyms

C. DIRECTIONS: Choose the word or phrase that is most nearly *opposite* in meaning to each numbered word. Write the letter of the correct answer on the line.

____   1. prosaic
     a. ordinary   b. pretty   c. commonplace   d. unique   e. verbose

____   2. avaricious
     a. wealthy   b. generous   c. greedy   d. modest   e. mean-spirited

____   3. doughty
     a. cowardly   b. stouthearted c. courageous   d. exhausted   e. sarcastic

The Monkey's Paw/The Bridegroom   **9**

"The Monkey's Paw" by W. W. Jacobs
"The Bridegroom" by Alexander Pushkin

Build Grammar Skills: Antecedents of Pronouns

Pronouns are words used in place of nouns. A pronoun's **antecedent** is the noun (or other pronoun) to which the pronoun refers. An antecedent can come before or after the pronoun, can be in another sentence, and might be more than one word. In order to make sense, a pronoun must agree with its antecedent in number and gender.

Example: *Mr. White* tried to distract *his* son during a chess game.

A. Practice: Complete the following sentences by filling in the blank with a pronoun that refers to the underlined antecedent.

1. <u>Sergeant Morris</u> told _____ hosts that the monkey paw was magical.

2. Though uncertain whether to believe _____ guest, <u>the Whites</u> listened eagerly.

3. The visitor brought bad news to <u>the Whites</u>; he told _____ their son was dead.

4. Though initially distressed by _____ fate, <u>Natasha</u> soon saw an opportunity for justice.

5. Natasha's <u>parents</u> heeded her wishes because _____ wanted to make her happy.

6. At the feast, <u>Natasha</u> told the bridegroom that _____ had had an evil dream.

B. Writing Application: Rewrite the following sentences, using pronouns to avoid repetition of nouns. Then, draw a line from each pronoun to its antecedent.

1. Mr. White took the paw from Herbert, looked at the paw, and placed the paw upon the table.

_____

2. When Herbert saw frightening faces in the fire, Herbert reached for a glass of water.

_____

3. With Mr. and Mrs. White's second wish, Mr. and Mrs. White wish for Herbert's return.

_____

4. Natasha devises a plan to catch the criminal during Natasha's wedding feast.

_____

Name _____ Date _____

"The Monkey's Paw" by W. W. Jacobs
"The Bridegroom" by Alexander Pushkin

Reading Strategy: Predict Outcomes

As you read a tale of suspense, you can make use of the author's foreshadowing—clues about future events—to **predict the outcome** of the story. As bizarre or frightening as it may be, the outcome should always make sense to the reader. For example, when Herbert sits up late at night gazing at the fire, he sees the horrible face of a monkey in the flames. Later, Herbert dies because of the wish his father has made with the monkey's paw.

The critic G. K. Chesterton said about W. W. Jacobs's horror stories: "His horror is wild, but it is a sane horror."

1. What do you think Chesterton meant by this statement? Explain your answer, giving examples from the story.

_____
_____
_____
_____
_____
_____

2. Based on the evidence in the story, what did you predict Mr. White's third wish would be? Were you correct? Explain your answer, using evidence from the story.

_____
_____
_____
_____
_____
_____

3. Describe the clues Pushkin provided to help the reader predict the outcome of "The Bridegroom"?

_____
_____
_____
_____
_____
_____

"The Monkey's Paw" by W. W. Jacobs
"The Bridegroom" by Alexander Pushkin

Literary Analysis: Foreshadowing

Foreshadowing is the use of hints or clues that suggest what events will happen later in a story. Writers use foreshadowing to create suspense, draw readers into the plot, or to prepare readers for the outcome of events.

DIRECTIONS: Read the following passages from "The Monkey's Paw" and "The Bridegroom." Identify what event each passage foreshadows.

1. "Hark at the wind," said Mr. White, who, having seen a fatal mistake after it was too late, was amiably desirous of preventing his son from seeing it.

   _____

   _____

2. "He wanted to show that fate ruled people's lives, and that those who interfered with it did so to their sorrow. He put a spell on it so that three separate men could each have three wishes from it."

   _____

   _____

3. "The first man had his three wishes, yes," was the reply; "I don't know what the first two were, but the third was for death."

   _____

   _____

4. Herbert sat alone in the darkness, gazing at the drying fire, and seeing faces in it. The last face was so horrible and so simian that he gazed at it in amazement.

   _____

   _____

5. Stricken with foreboding/They pleaded, got angry,/But still she was silent;

   _____

   _____

6. He gazed as he flew past,/And Natasha gazed./He flew on. Natasha froze.

   _____

   _____

7. "Your will be done. Call/My bridegroom to the feast,/Bake loaves for the whole world,/Brew sweet mead and call/The law to the feast."

   _____

   _____

8. "The eldest brother/Takes his knife and, whistling,/Sharpens it; seizing her by/The hair he kills her/And cuts off her right hand."

   _____

from "A Walk to the Jetty" from *Annie John* by Jamaica Kincaid

Build Vocabulary

Spelling Strategy   The prefix *ad-* means "to," "at," "toward," or "akin to." The prefix *ap-*, which is used in the word *apprenticed,* is a variation of *ad-* . Variations of *ad-* occur when it is added to words beginning with one of these nine consonants: *c* (*account*), *f* (*affront*), *g* (*aggressor*), *l* (*allot*), *n* (*annex*), *p* (*apprenticed*), *r* (*arrest*), *s* (*assign*), *t* (*attend*).

Using the Root *-stup-*

The word root *-stup-* means "stunned" or "amazed." Knowing what the root *-stup-* means can help you figure out that the word *stupor* means "a state in which the mind is stunned."

A. DIRECTIONS: The following words contain the root *-stup-*. Complete each sentence with the most appropriate word from the list.

stupid	stupefied	stupendous	stupefaction

1. When Annie presented her mother with the little basket containing senna and eucalyptus leaves and camphor, her mother acted as if Annie had done the most _____ task.

2. A feeling of _____ overcame Annie as she walked to the jetty, her heart swelled with gladness one moment and shriveled with sadness the next.

3. Miss Dulcie always found fault with Annie's work and treated Annie as if she were _____.

4. Annie walked past the doctor's office, grooming shop, and the library in a _____ state, as if she were in a dream.

Using the Word Bank

loomed	apprenticed	raked	stupor

B. DIRECTIONS: Match each word in the left column with its definition in the right column. Write the letter of the definition on the line next to the word it defines.

____ 1. apprenticed   a. scratched or scraped, as with a garden tool

____ 2. stupor   b. appeared in a large or threatening form

____ 3. raked   c. mental dullness, as if drugged

____ 4. loomed   d. worked a specified length of time in a craft or trade in return for instruction and, formerly, support

from "A Walk to the Jetty" from *Annie John* by Jamaica Kincaid

Build Grammar Skills: Pronoun Case

Pronouns help writers avoid unnecessary repetition. Always be sure to use the correct form of a pronoun. **Pronoun case** refers to the different forms that a pronoun takes to indicate its use in a sentence. Pronouns have three cases: *nominative*, *objective*, and *possessive*. The following chart shows the uses of each of these cases.

Case	Use in Sentence	Example
Nominative I, you, he, she, it, we, they	The pronoun is used as the subject or renames the subject.	*She* is a seamstress. The seamstress is *she*.
Objective me, you, him, her, it, us, them	The pronoun functions as an object.	I bought *them* yesterday. Miss Dulcie made *me* sweep. Annie loomed way above *him*.
Possessive my, mine, your, yours, his, her, hers, its, our, their, theirs	The pronoun indicates ownership.	*My* father talked to the watchman. The powder was *hers*, not *mine*.

A. Practice: Read the following sentences and determine whether the underlined pronoun uses the nominative, objective, or possessive case. Write N, O, or P on the line provided.

_____ 1. Despite a strong attachment to her mother, Annie longed for independence.

_____ 2. The doctor told Annie's father that he should take a walk every evening after dinner.

_____ 3. As Annie and her parents walked to the jetty, she noticed strangers staring at them.

_____ 4. Their walk took only half an hour, but Annie felt she was reliving the years of her life.

_____ 5. Annie recalled a large porcelain dog with a red satin ribbon around its neck.

_____ 6. The ship carried her away; she waved until her mother was just a dot on the launch.

B. Writing Application: Revise the following passage to correct errors in pronoun usage. Then, continue the passage with two more sentences that contain pronouns. Use at least two different pronoun cases in your sentences.

Annie was not interested in she father's talks with the night watchman. Them would talk about cricket and other topics that did not interest she. Her preferred more personal topics, such as family life, or likes and dislikes. When the two men laughed so hard that they laughter echoed out to sea and back, her could not understand what was so funny.

_____

_____

_____

_____

_____

Name _____ Date _____

from "A Walk to the Jetty" from _Annie John_ by Jamaica Kincaid

Reading Strategy: Draw Inferences

As an active reader, you can make inferences, or draw conclusions, about characters based on what they say and do, and what others say about them.

DIRECTIONS: Read each of the following passages from the story. Then answer each question.

1. Then she would send me to the store to buy buttons or thread, though I was only allowed to do this if I was given a sample of the button or thread, and then she would find fault even though they were an exact match of the samples she had given me. And all the while she said to me, "A girl like you will never learn to sew properly, you know."

What can you infer about the nature of Annie's relationship with Miss Dulcie?

_____

_____

_____

2. Once, a book she was reading had a large picture of a man in it, and when I asked her who he was she told me that he was Louis Pasteur and that the book was about his life. It stuck in my mind, because she said it was because of him that she boiled my milk to purify it before I was allowed to drink it, that it was his idea, and that that was why the process was called pasteurization.

What can you infer about the mother's character based on her behavior in this passage?

_____

_____

_____

3. My father kissed me goodbye and told me to be good and to write home often. After he said this, he looked at me, then looked at the floor and swung his left foot, then looked at me again. I could see that he wanted to say something else, something that he had never said to me before, but then he just turned and walked away.

What inference can you make about what Annie's father wanted to say?

_____

_____

_____

4. Big tears streamed down her face, and it must have been that—for I could not bear to see my mother cry—which started me crying, too. She then tightened her arms around me and held me to her close, so that I felt that I couldn't breathe.

What two contrasting inferences can you make about Annie's relationship with her mother?

_____

_____

_____

from "A Walk to the Jetty" from *Annie John* by Jamaica Kincaid

Literary Analysis: Flashback

A **flashback** is a part of a story that presents an event that happened at an earlier time. In this story from *Annie John*, Jamaica Kincaid uses a common flashback technique. She begins the story with a final event—Annie's arrival at the jetty—and then tells the rest of the story as a series of flashbacks that help explain Annie's departure from her island home. Kincaid organizes the flashbacks as a "narrative walk" from Annie's home to the jetty. These flashbacks reveal to the reader Annie's experiences and motivations.

DIRECTIONS: The following chart includes a number of visual clues that prompt flashbacks to experiences in Annie's life. Complete the chart. Describe the memory or experience prompted by each clue. Then explain what the flashback reveals about Annie, her relationships with others, or her motivations to leave home.

Visual clue	Flashback	What is revealed
Miss Dulcie's house	1. _____	2. _____
The road to school, church, choir	3. _____	4. _____
The library	5. _____	6. _____

"The Masque of the Red Death" by Edgar Allan Poe

Build Vocabulary

Spelling Strategy   The word ending -*que* indicates a word of French origin; this suffix is pronounced as /k/. For example, the word *masque* has the same pronunciation as *mask*.

Using the Suffix -*tion*

A. DIRECTIONS: The suffix -*tion* means "the act or quality of." Complete each sentence with one of the following -*tion* words.

fascination	devastation	celebration	isolation

1. Prince Prospero lived in _____, hiding from the plague-ridden world outside the abbey's walls.

2. He had a _____ with the bizarre.

3. He mistakenly believed that the plague's _____ could not reach him.

4. The masque was more an attempt to ward off death than a _____.

Using the Word Bank

august	arabesque	disapprobation
habiliments	cessation	piquancy

B. DIRECTIONS: Match each word in the left column with its definition in the right column. Write the letter of the definition on the line next to the word it defines.

____   1. august   a. a pleasantly sharp quality

____   2. piquancy   b. clothing

____   3. arabesque   c. stopping, either forever or for some time

____   4. disapprobation d. elaborately designed

____   5. habiliments   e. imposing and magnificent

____   6. cessation   f. disapproval

Recognizing Antonyms

C. DIRECTIONS: Choose the word that is most nearly the *opposite* of the word in CAPITAL LETTERS. Write the letter on the line next to the capitalized word.

_____   1. AUGUST:
    a. grand
    b. awesome
    c. approachable
    d. royal
    e. vain

_____   2. CESSATION:
    a. interrupted
    b. discontinuation
    c. arrest
    d. fluidity
    e. halting

Name _____ Date _____

"The Masque of the Red Death" by Edgar Allan Poe

Build Grammar Skills: Using Adjectives
and Adverbs Correctly

Sometimes, the same word can be either an adjective or an adverb, depending upon how it is used in a sentence. Remember that an **adjective** modifies a noun or pronoun. An **adverb** modifies a verb, an adjective, or another adverb. In the following examples, the word *straight* is used as an adjective to modify the noun *vista*, and then as an adverb to modify the verb *ran*.

> **Adjective:** In many palaces, the imperial suite forms a long, *straight* vista.
> **Adverb:** The prince ran *straight* across the room and through the six chambers.

In general, adverbs and adjectives have different forms. Many adverbs end in *-ly*. A few words ending in *-ly*, however, are adjectives.

> **Adjective:** The revelers anticipated a *lively* evening in the *stately* suite.
> **Adverb:** The waltzers danced *gaily* to the music.

A. Practice: Read the following sentences. On the line, write whether each underlined word is an *adverb* (adv.) or an *adjective* (adj.). Then, draw a line to the word it modifies.

_____ 1. The gates leading into the abbey were bolted and <u>firmly</u> sealed.

_____ 2. The prince entertained his <u>lighthearted</u> friends with poets, dancers, music, and food.

_____ 3. While the plague raged <u>furiously</u> abroad, the Prince held a magnificent masked ball.

_____ 4. The effect of the reddish light streaming into the seventh room was <u>ghastly</u>.

_____ 5. At the chime of the ebony clock, the revelers were still and <u>silent</u>.

_____ 6. <u>Unimpeded</u>, the masked figure passed within a yard of the prince.

B. Writing Application: Rewrite the following passage using adjectives and adverbs to add descriptive detail. Underline each added adjective once and each adverb twice.

> The partygoers had thought they were safe, but they could no longer deny the presence of the Red Death at their ball. It had entered the abbey and moved among them that night. One by one, they surrendered to the plague and fell to the floor.

_____

_____

_____

_____

"The Masque of the Red Death" by Edgar Allan Poe

Reading Strategy: Context Clues

When you read a story, you may come across an unfamiliar word. You can use **context clues**—the words, phrases, and sentences surrounding the word—to help you determine its meaning. For example, in the statement, "In spite of these things, it was a gay and magnificent *revel*," you can use the words around *revel* to determine that it means "party" or "celebration."

For each of the following sentences, use context clues to determine the meaning of the *italicized* word. Write the meaning of the word on the lines below.

1. "He had directed, in great part, the movable embellishments of the seven chambers, upon occasion of this great *fête*."

   _____

   _____

   _____

2. "There were sharp pains, and sudden dizziness, and then *profuse* bleeding at the pores."

   _____

   _____

   _____

3. "But to the chamber which lies most westwardly of the seven, there are now none of the maskers who venture; for the night is waning away; and there flows a *ruddier* light through the blood-colored panes."

   _____

   _____

   _____

4. "When the eyes of Prince Prospero fell upon this *spectral* image (which with a slow and solemn movement, as if more fully to sustain its role, stalked to and fro among the waltzers) he was seen to be convulsed."

   _____

   _____

   _____

5. "There was a sharp cry—and the dagger dropped gleaming upon the sable carpet, upon which, instantly afterwards, fell *prostrate* in death the Prince Prospero."

   _____

   _____

   _____

Unit 1: On the Edge

"The Masque of the Red Death" by Edgar Allan Poe

Literary Analysis: Symbols

A **symbol** is a character, place, object, or event that represents something else. An author often uses symbols in a story in order to teach a lesson.

Complete the following chart. Explain what you think each symbol in "The Masque of the Red Death" represents and how it helps teach the lesson of the story.

Symbol	What it represents	How it helps teach the lesson
Example: dreams	Masqueraders, fantasies	Shows us that life is fleeting; forebodes the grim ending to the story
1. the masked visitor		
2. the black chamber		
3. the music		
4. the tripods with the flames		

Name _____   Date _____

"**Fear**" by Gabriela Mistral
"**The street**" by Octavio Paz
"**Spring and All**" by William Carlos Williams

Build Vocabulary

Spelling Strategy   When you add the suffix -less to a word ending in a single *l*, simply add the suffix. Don't change the spelling of the original word. For example, *wheel* + *less* becomes *wheelless*. Note that with the suffix added, the new word has two *l*'s. Thus, *soul* + *less* becomes *soulless*.

Using the Suffix -*less*

The suffix -*less* means "without." *Less* is a word in its own right, of course, meaning "not as much," as in "less time," but when used as a suffix, -*less* means "absent." When William Carlos Williams refers to vines with no leaves, he says "leafless." One who has no fear at all is fearless.

A. DIRECTIONS: Select a word from the list and add the suffix -*less* to complete the sentence.

tail	tree	sail	point

1. The grass rippled as far as the eye could see on the _____ plain.

2. A _____ squirrel was likely a survivor of a near miss by a dog or cat.

3. The argument seemed _____ to those who didn't understand the issues.

4. Its masts ripped away in the storm, the _____ schooner was doomed to drift.

Using the Word Bank

contagious	lifeless	clarity	stark	profound

Recognizing Synonyms

B. DIRECTIONS: Circle the letter of the word that most closely matches the meaning of the Word Bank word.

____ 1. profound
    a. competent
    b. deep
    c. recovered
    d. certain

____ 2. clarity
    a. volume
    b. kindness
    c. clearness
    d. distance

____ 3. stark
    a. raw
    b. far
    c. thin
    d. fiery

____ 4. contagious
    a. enclosed
    b. adjacent
    c. communicable
    d. realistic

"**Fear**" by Gabriela Mistral
"**The street**" by Octavio Paz
"**Spring and All**" by William Carlos Williams

Build Grammar Skills: Coordinate Adjectives

Coordinate adjectives are adjectives of equal rank that modify the same noun and must be separated by commas. Adjectives are considered to be of equal rank if (1) the adjectives can be transposed and the sentence still sounds correct and (2) the adjectives can be separated by *and* without changing the meaning of the sentence. Adjectives that are not of equal rank cannot be separated by *and*, and must stay in the order in which they are written. They do not need commas.

Adjectives of equal rank	**Adjectives of unequal rank** (Only the first sentence is correct.)
The dead, brown leaves covered the ground.	The two talented poets read their work.
The dead and brown leaves covered the ground.	The two and talented poets read their work.
The brown, dead leaves covered the ground.	The talented two poets read their work.

A. Practice: Read the following sentences, and underline any series of two or more adjectives. If the adjectives are coordinate, separate them with commas.

1. The concerned protective mother cherished her young daughter.

2. Swallows nest in the eaves and fly far away into the wide blue sky.

3. The anxious man walked down the dark shadowy street.

4. He walked blindly, his feet stepping on silent stones and dry autumn leaves.

5. A scattering of tall evergreen trees lined the edge of the field.

6. As spring approaches, the dry prickly grass grows soft and moist.

B. Writing Application: Answer the following questions, using at least one set of coordinate adjectives.

1. How might the mother describe her little girl's hair in "Fear"?

_____

2. What type of clothing might the narrator be wearing in "The street"?

_____

3. How might the narrator describe the water in "Spring and All"?

_____

4. What other changes might spring reveal in "Spring and All"?

_____

"Fear" by Gabriela Mistral
"The street" by Octavio Paz
"Spring and All" by William Carlos Williams

Reading Strategy: Form a Mental Image

As we read, the words the poet uses create impressions in our minds. These images may be dark and possibly confusing, as in "The street," in which the narrator must ". . . walk in blackness and . . . stumble and fall." The image may be picturesque, as in "Fear," in which the little girl could turn into a swallow, a princess, or a queen—but not with a fairy-tale ending. Sometimes sensory language creates a physical sense, as does the raw, cold wind in "Spring and All."

You can learn to pay attention to specific images as you read to see how they reveal the poem's meaning. Use the following chart to help you as you read the poems in this group.

DIRECTIONS: Choose a poem. In the first column, write a word or phrase from the poem that creates a mental image for you. In the second column, describe the image that the word or phrase provides. In the third column, briefly explain how that image contributes to your understanding of the poem.

Sensory Word	Mental Image	Meaning to the Poem

"Fear" by Gabriela Mistral
"The street" by Octavio Paz
"Spring and All" by William Carlos Williams

Literary Analysis: Imagery

Much of poetry's impact and meaning comes from **imagery,** the descriptive language that re-creates sensory experience. Images may strengthen or shift or contrast in ways that help give a poem its power. They may also, however, perform so subtly that it's hard to tell where the over-all impression comes from, or where it changes, or how visual and physical images work to-gether.

As you read through a poem, try to decide to what sense the image appeals. Does it make you see? hear? feel? smell? taste? Then consider what effect the particular image has on your feelings or thoughts. You may see the imagery growing or changing, or even contrasting with previous images.

DIRECTIONS: For each line, note the senses appealed to by the imagery. Describe how the image invokes those senses. What are the pictures, or sounds, or physical sensations? In the third column, explain the effect or feeling produced by the image.

"Fear"

Lines 11–14	Senses and Descriptions	Effect or Feeling
In tiny golden slippers		
how could she play on the meadow?		
And when night came, no longer		
would she sleep at my side.		

"The street"

Lines 1–4	Senses and Descriptions	Effect or Feeling
A long and silent street.		
I walk in blackness and I stumble and fall		
and rise, and I walk blind, my feet		
stepping on silent stones and dry leaves.		

"Two Friends" by Guy de Maupassant
"Damon and Pythias" retold by William F. Russell

Build Vocabulary

Spelling Strategy   When adding a suffix to a word ending in *y* preceded by a consonant, change the *y* to *i* unless the suffix starts with an *i*. For example, when the suffix *-ness* is added to the word *jaunty*, the *y* changes to an *i* to form the Word Bank word *jauntiness*. However, when the suffix *-ing* is added to the word *ready*, it becomes *readying*.

Using the Root -tain-

Understanding that the word root *-tain-* means "to hold" will help you to define a variety of words that are formed using *-tain-*. For example, when you read in the story "Damon and Pythias" that Pythias is "detained," you can figure out, using your knowledge of the story and the root word *-tain-*, that he was "held back."

A. DIRECTIONS: Read the sentences below and define the italicized words.

1. The lunchbox *contains* a sandwich, an apple, crackers, and cookies.

   _____

2. Will you be able to *obtain* tickets to the outdoor concert next Saturday?

   _____

3. Plenty of water and sunlight will *sustain* the life of that plant.

   _____

Using the Word Bank

B. DIRECTIONS: Choose the letter of the word or phrase that best defines each numbered word.

____ 1. ardent
   a. enthusiastic
   b. dull
   c. sympathetic
   d. slow

____ 2. vernal
   a. old
   b. like summer
   c. like winter
   d. like spring

____ 3. jauntiness
   a. sloppiness
   b. harsh cruelty
   c. carefree gentleness
   d. simplicity

____ 4. impediments
   a. things standing in the way
   b. useful things
   c. equipment
   d. boots

____ 5. hindrances
   a. helpful people
   b. obstacles
   c. roads
   d. friends

____ 6. detained
   a. studied
   b. sent forth
   c. kept silent
   d. kept in custody

____ 7. dire
   a. unimportant
   b. silent
   c. urgent
   d. cold

____ 8. annals
   a. history
   b. illnesses
   c. family members
   d. weapons

"**Two Friends**" by Guy de Maupassant
"**Damon and Pythias**" retold by William F. Russell

Build Grammar Skills: Degrees of Modifiers

Most adjectives and adverbs have three forms, called **degrees**, that are used to make comparisons. The three degrees of comparison are the *positive*, the *comparative*, and the *superlative*. There are different ways to form the comparative and superlative degrees. For most one- and two-syllable modifiers, add *-er* to form the comparative degree and *-est* to form the superlative degree. In cases when adding *-er* and *-est* to one- and two-syllable modifiers would sound awkward, use *more* and *most* to form the comparative and superlative degrees. For adverbs ending in *-ly* and for all modifiers with three or more syllables, use *more* and *most* to form the comparative and superlative degrees.

DEGREES OF MODIFIERS

Positive	Comparative	Superlative
nice	nicer	nicest
brilliant	more brilliant	most brilliant
soon	sooner	soonest
slowly	more slowly	most slowly

Use the comparative form of a modifier to compare two things. Use the superlative form to compare three or more things.

A. Practice: Identify the degree of the underlined modifier in each sentence. Write *P*, *C*, or *S* on the line.

_____ 1. Morissot and Sauvage grew <u>bolder</u> as they drank absinthe.

_____ 2. Morissot <u>anxiously</u> watched his float bob up and down.

_____ 3. Damon and Pythias had the <u>truest</u> friendship in all of Syracuse.

_____ 4. Dionysius witnessed the <u>most devoted</u> display of loyalty he had ever seen.

B. Writing Application: Follow the directions below to write four sentences using different degrees of comparison.

1. Use the comparative form of *happy* to describe Morissot and Sauvage in "Two Friends."

_____

2. Use the positive form of *cruelly* to describe Dionysius's behavior in "Damon and Pythias."

_____

3. Use the superlative form of *swift* to describe Pythias's return to the palace in "Damon and Pythias."

_____

4. Use the comparative form of *peaceful* to compare life before and after the war in "Two Friends."

_____

Name _____ Date _____

"Two Friends" by Guy de Maupassant

"Damon and Pythias" retold by William F. Russell

Reading Strategy: Significant Details

When you read, always notice an author's precise details about characters, plot, and setting. These details are often significant and placed in the story to reveal key information about the characters or a particular situation. Significant details can also increase the tension of a story by hinting at its ending.

DIRECTIONS: Identify the significant details in the following passages from "Two Friends" and "Damon and Pythias." Then describe what these details reveal about situation, plot, or character.

> **Example:** Pointing up to the heights, M. Sauvage murmured, "The Prussians are up there!" And a feeling of uneasiness paralyzed the two friends as they faced this deserted region.

> **Answer:** Sauvage's observation that Prussians could emerge at any moment and the fact that they are in a deserted region are significant details. These details indicate that the characters are in danger, and that people are not around to protect them.

"Two Friends"

1. But suddenly a dull sound which seemed to come from under ground made the earth tremble. The cannons were beginning.

   _____

   _____

2. Then more followed, and time after time the mountain belched forth death-dealing breath, breathed out milky-white vapor which rose slowly in the calm sky and formed a cloud above the summit.

   _____

   _____

"Damon and Pythias"

3. Pythias immediately thought of his friend Damon, and he unhesitatingly sent for him in this hour of dire necessity, never thinking for a moment that his trusty companion would refuse his request. Nor did he, for Damon hastened straightaway to the palace—much to the amazement of King Dionysius—and gladly offered to be held hostage for his friend, in spite of the dangerous condition that had been attached to this favor.

   _____

   _____

4. In reply, however, Damon merely smiled, since, in spite of the fact that the eleventh hour had already arrived, he still believed that his lifelong companion would not fail him.

   _____

   _____

"Two Friends" by Guy de Maupassant
"Damon and Pythias" retold by William F. Russell

Literary Analysis: Climax

In many stories, you are introduced to characters and a central conflict that drive the story forward. The series of events related to the introduction, development, and resolution of this conflict is the plot, and the climax of a story is the moment in the plot at which the story's tension is the greatest. Writers build toward climaxes in different ways—some with a great deal of suspense, some with a more subtle style—but at the climax of any story, the reader knows that something important is about to happen and that the outcome of the story is near.

DIRECTIONS: Below are passages from "Two Friends" and "Damon and Pythias." Identify the sentences in the passages that express each story's climax.

1. **"Two Friends"**

Then he rose suddenly, approached the two Frenchmen, took Morissot by the arm, dragged him aside, whispered to him, "Quick, the password? Your friend won't know. I'll pretend to relent."

Morissot answered not a word.

The Prussian drew M. Sauvage aside and put the same question.

M. Sauvage did not answer.

They stood side by side again.

And the officer began to give commands. The soldiers raised their rifles.

_____

_____

_____

_____

_____

_____

2. **"Damon and Pythias"**

Great excitement stirred the crowd that had gathered to witness the execution, for all the people had heard of the bargain that had been struck between the two friends. There was much sobbing and cries of sympathy were heard all around as the captive was brought out, though he himself somehow retained complete composure even at this moment of darkest danger.

Presently the excitement grew more intense still as a swift runner could be seen approaching the palace courtyard at an astonishing speed, . . .

_____

_____

_____

_____

_____

_____

from *In Commemoration: One Million Volumes* by Rudolfo A. Anaya

Build Vocabulary

Spelling Strategy   If a word ends in *-ent*, its parallel forms end in *-ence* or *-ency: persistent* → *persistence, inherent* → *inherence, consistent* → *consistency.* If a word ends in *-ant*, the parallel forms end in *-ance* or *-ancy: abundant* → *abundance, poignant* → *poignancy, reliant* → *reliance.* Primarily adjectives, these words indicate state or condition in their noun forms.

Using the Prefix *in-*

The prefix *in-* has two primary purposes in English. One is to express the idea of "into," as in the Word Bank words *inherent,* meaning "inborn," and *induced,* meaning "led into." The other common use of the prefix *in-* is to express negation—to mean "not"—as in *invisible* or *inappropriate.*

A. DIRECTIONS: Determine the meaning of the italicized word in each sentence either from context or, if necessary, by checking a dictionary. Write the meaning in the space provided, and indicate whether the *in-* prefix means "not" or "into."

1. Anaya's speech helped *inaugurate* the new library.

   _____

2. As a child, he had an *insatiable* thirst for knowledge.

   _____

3. The few books in the little library had an *incendiary* effect on his imagination.

   _____

4. Anaya felt *indebted* to Miss Pansy, and remembered her in his speech.

   _____

Using Antonyms

B. DIRECTIONS: Write the letter of the word or phrase most nearly *opposite* in meaning.

____ 1. induced
   a. welcomed
   b. discouraged
   c. caused
   d. rejected

____ 2. inherent
   a. acquired
   b. inborn
   c. unnatural
   d. complete

____ 3. litany
   a. responsive
      readings
   b. monologue
   c. novel
   d. silence

____ 4. labyrinth
   a. maze
   b. canyon
   c. expressway
   d. path

____ 5. fomentation
   a. sour foam
   b. agitation
   c. peacefulness
   d. joy

____ 6. enthralls
   a. bores
   b. captivates
   c. excludes
   d. arrests

____ 7. poignant
   a. light
   b. unconscious
   c. trivial
   d. alone

____ 8. satiated
   a. overflowing
   b. slender
   c. conscious
   d. hungry

____ 9. dilapidated
   a. closed
   b. began
   c. neat
   d. fiery

from *In Commemoration: One Million Volumes* by Rudolfo A. Anaya

Build Grammar Skills: Action Verbs and Linking Verbs

Action verbs express action of some kind, either from the verb to an object, or on their own without reference to an object.

> **Action Verbs:** We *grow* flowers. The flowers *appear* in the spring.

In the first sentence, *flowers* is the object of the verb. In the second, the *flowers* "act" on their own without reference to an object.

Linking verbs express a state of being. Instead of transmitting an effect, a linking verb links the subject to a predicate adjective or predicate noun that further identifies or renames the subject.

> **Linking Verbs:** The music *grew* louder. The concert *was* a success.

In the first sentence, *louder* is a predicate adjective describing the music. In the second sentence, *success* is a predicate noun telling what the concert was.

The most common linking verbs are forms of the verb *to be: is, are, am, was, were, be, been.* Other verbs that often function as linking verbs include *seem, look, appear, smell, taste, feel, sound, become,* and *grow* (if it means *become*).

A. Practice: Circle the verb in each sentence. Write *A* on the line if the verb is an action verb or *L* if it is a linking verb.

_____ 1. The ancient stories taught Anaya to wonder.

_____ 2. In an old riddle, the stars were the coins of the Lord.

_____ 3. "Be as wise as your grandfather."

_____ 4. He spent many hours in the old library at Central and Edith Streets.

_____ 5. He felt safe and comfortable.

B. Writing Application: Follow the instructions for writing sentences that contain an action or linking verb.

> **Example:** Use a form of *feel* as an action verb in a sentence about his library card.
> He felt the tattered library card in his pocket as he ran back to his father's *ranchito*.

1. Use a form of *to be* to describe Anaya's occupation.

_____

2. Use a form of *look* as an action verb in a sentence about Anaya at the library as a child.

_____

3. Use a form of *look* as a linking verb in a sentence about the old library's appearance.

_____

4. Use a form of *appear* as an action verb in a sentence about the stars over New Mexico.

_____

5. Use a form of *appear* as a linking verb to describe the way the stars look.

_____

from *In Commemoration: One Million Volumes* by Rudolfo A. Anaya

Reading Strategy: Summarize

When you summarize, you use your own words to explain the main ideas presented in a piece of writing, a lecture, or a speech. Writing passages in your own words can help you better understand and remember the material. Written summaries are usually arranged in paragraphs. The chart below can help you summarize the main ideas in "One Million Volumes."

DIRECTIONS: Answer each question to help you summarize the main ideas. Write a response in the main idea box. Then, in the hanging boxes, support the main idea with one or two significant details or examples.

How did Anaya's childhood influence him?

MAIN IDEA

Details and Examples

How did Anaya nurture his love of words?

MAIN IDEA

Details and Examples

How does Anaya feel about books and libraries?

MAIN IDEA

Details and Examples

Unit 2: Striving for Success

Name _____ Date _____

from *In Commemoration: One Million Volumes* by Rudolfo A. Anaya

Literary Analysis: Author's Purpose

In *In Commemoration: One Million Volumes*, Rudolfo Anaya moves back and forth between lyrical recollection and personal opinion. He uses his memories to fulfill a larger purpose. His purpose is not only to evoke a particular place and time and to commemorate the acquisition of a library's one-millionth volume, but also to propose a personal definition of the word *library*.

DIRECTIONS: Classify each statement below under the purpose that it most clearly supports. Then find two other sentences from the essay that fit each purpose on the chart, and list them where they belong.

And now there are a million volumes for us to read here at the University of New Mexico library.

I clung to each syllable which lisped from his tobacco-stained lips.

With its storehouse of knowledge, it liberates, informs, teaches, and enthralls.

	PURPOSE	
evoke a time or place	commemorate an event	propose a definition

Name _____ Date _____

Build Vocabulary

Spelling Strategy   Place *i* before *e* except after *c*, or when it sounds like *a* as in *neighbor* and *weigh*. The word bank word *aggrieved* follows this rule.

Using Words in Other Contexts: Technical and Multiple-Meaning Words

Many words in English have different meanings. Three of the words in the Word Bank are technical words, or words used in a specific science, industry, or trade. For example, the words, *arable, fallow,* and *sheaf* are terms used in the farming industry. Two of these same words, however, have different meanings in a broader context. For instance, in the context of farming, *sheaf* means "a bundle of stalks," such as wheat. In a broader context, *sheaf* means "a collection of things gathered together," such as a sheaf of papers.

A. DIRECTIONS: Read the following sentence sets. Use context clues to determine the meaning of the underlined Word Bank word in each sentence. On the line below, explain the different meanings.

1. The school superintendent is in favor of year-round classes; he believes that, left unchallenged, students' minds go <u>fallow</u> over the course of the summer.

   The wheat farmer tilled the land but would allow it to lie <u>fallow</u> for a season before sowing.

   _____

2. The grain dealer carted his crop to the village, where he sold all but a single <u>sheaf</u> of rye.

   The harried musician dashed off to the recital with a <u>sheaf</u> of piano music tucked under her arm.

   _____

piqued	disparaged	forbore	aggrieved
sheaf	arable	fallow	

Using the Word Bank

B. DIRECTIONS: Match each word in the left column with its definition in the right column. Write the letter of the definition on the line next to the word it defines.

____	1. piqued	a. spoke slightly of; belittled
____	2. disparaged	b. plowed, but not planted
____	3. forbore	c. a bundle of grain
____	4. aggrieved	d. suitable for growing crops
____	5. sheaf	e. wronged
____	6. arable	f. offended
____	7. fallow	g. refrained from

Name _____ Date _____

Build Grammar Skills: Regular and Irregular Verb Forms

A verb has four principal parts: the present, the present participle, the past, and the past participle. All verbs form the present participle by adding *-ing* to the present form. Regular verbs form their past and past participle by adding *-d* or *-ed* to the present form.

Principal Parts of Regular Verbs			
Present	Present Participle	Past	Past Participle
disparage	disparaging	disparaged	(has/have) disparaged
change	changing	changed	(has/have) changed
till	tilling	tilled	(has/have) tilled

Other verbs are irregular. They form their past and past participles in some other way. It is important to learn the irregular forms so that you can use them correctly.

Principal Parts of Irregular Verbs			
Present	Present Participle	Past	Past Participle
am, is, are	being	was, were	(has/have) been
begin	beginning	began	(has/have) begun
buy	buying	bought	(has/have) bought
go	going	went	(has/have) gone
grow	growing	grew	(has/have) grown
sell	selling	sold	(has/have) sold

A. Practice: Use the correct form of the given verb to complete the sentence.

1. Now that Pahom had land of his own, he borrowed seed and sowed it on the land he had _____. (buy)

2. The time he spent _____ his land paid off; the harvest was a good one. (work)

3. The grass that grew and the flowers that bloomed there _____ unlike any that grew elsewhere. (be)

4. Everything would have _____ right, if the neighboring peasants would only not have trespassed on his wheatfields and meadows. (be)

B. Writing Application: Follow the directions below to write four sentences about events that take place in "How Much Land Does a Man Need."

1. Use the past form of *sell* to explain what the landowner did with her estate. _____

_____

2. Use the past participle form of *go* to explain the distance Pahom had traveled by the seventh day. _____

_____

3. Use the present participle form of *grow* to explain Pahom's reason for teaching the neighboring peasants a lesson in Part 3 of the story. _____

_____

Name _____ Date _____

"How Much Land Does a Man Need?" by Leo Tolstoy

Reading Strategy: Predict Outcome
Based on Character Traits

Characters reveal their traits through their words and actions. For example, the peasant Pahom boasts that if he owned enough land he wouldn't fear the Devil himself. Pahom's boastful trait helps you predict how he will act in the story. A character's traits can also help you predict a story's events and their outcome.

DIRECTIONS: As you read "How Much Land Does a Man Need?" answer the questions based on each of the following passages.

> "I wouldn't change my way of life for yours," said she. "We may live roughly, but at least we're free from worry. You live in better style than we do, but though you often earn more than you need, you're very likely to lose all you have. You know the proverb, 'Loss and gain are brothers twain.'"

1. What future event can be predicted from Pahom's wife's statement?

_____

> "Busy as we are from childhood tilling mother earth, we peasants have no time to let any nonsense settle in our heads. Our only trouble is that we haven't land enough. If I had plenty of land, I shouldn't fear the Devil himself!"

2. What lesson can you predict Pahom will learn?

_____

> "Why should I suffer in this narrow hole, if one can live so well elsewhere?" he thought. "I'll sell my land and my homestead here, and with the money I'll start afresh over there and get everything new. In this crowded place one is always having trouble. But I must first go and find out all about it myself."

3. What two other traits does Pahom reveal about himself?

_____

4. What event can you predict will recur throughout the story?

_____

> Hardly were his eyes closed when he had a dream. He thought he was lying in that same tent and heard somebody chuckling outside. He wondered who it could be, and rose and went out, and he saw the Bashkir chief sitting in front of the tent holding his sides and rolling about with laughter. Going nearer to the chief, Pahom asked: "What are you laughing at?" But he saw that it was no longer the chief but the grain dealer who had recently stopped at his house and had told him about the land. Just as Pahom was going to ask: "Have you been here long?" he saw that it was not the dealer, but the peasant who had come up from the Volga long ago, to Pahom's old home. Then he saw that it was not the peasant either, but the Devil himself. . . .

5. What is the true identity of the Bashkir chief? How is the identity revealed?

_____

6. What can you predict is the story's outcome?

_____

Name _____ Date _____

"How Much Land Does a Man Need?" Leo Tolstoy

Literary Analysis: Parable

A **parable** is a short, simple story that conveys a moral lesson about the way people should act or think. Generally, parables focus entirely on one or two characters and deal with a specific circumstance that motivates their actions. In addition, the outcome of a parable usually seems inevitable.

DIRECTIONS: Read the following parable. Then answer the questions that follow it.

A teenage boy discovered a wallet behind some bushes while he was walking to school one day. The wallet contained $80. The boy noticed an identification card in the wallet, but he decided not to return it to its owner. Instead, he hid the wallet in a dresser drawer and used the money to buy a movie and some CDs that he had wanted. He watched the movie that night but didn't really enjoy it. He listened to the CDs, but they didn't sound as good as he had thought they would. The next day, the boy took a job in a local supermarket. He put all of his first week's earnings—$80—into the wallet and returned the wallet to its owner. He even refused an offer of a reward for returning the wallet.

1. What characteristics of a parable does the story illustrate?

_____

_____

2. Why did the boy not return the wallet at first?

_____

_____

3. Why didn't the boy enjoy his purchases?

_____

_____

4. Why do you think he didn't return the empty wallet and tell the owner the money was already gone when he found it?

_____

_____

5. Why did the boy refuse a reward?

_____

_____

6. What is the moral of the parable?

_____

_____

7. What would be a good title for the parable?

_____

_____

"Success is counted sweetest" and "I dwell in Possibility—" by Emily Dickinson
"Uncoiling" by Pat Mora
"Columbus Dying" by Vassar Miller

Build Vocabulary

Spelling Strategy   The prefix *in-* becomes *il-* before *l* (*illegitimate*); *im-* before *m* and usually before *b* or *p* (*immaterial, important*); and *ir-* before *r* (*irregular*).

Using the Prefix *im-*

The prefix *im-*, which is a variation of the prefix *in-*, usually means "not."

A. DIRECTIONS: Use either *im-* or *in-* to create words whose meanings are opposite of those given. Write the antonyms on the blanks.

1. active _____   4. perfect _____

2. mature _____   5. balance _____

3. decisive _____   6. humane _____

Using the Word Bank

impregnable	thrall	vertigo

B. DIRECTIONS: Write your answers to the following questions, including a Word Bank word in each of your sentences. Use each word only once.

1. How might you feel at the end of a roller coaster ride?

_____

2. What type of hideout would soldiers strive to build?

_____

3. What type of laborer might have been used in transatlantic voyages?

_____

Identifying Antonyms

C. DIRECTIONS: Circle the letter of the word that is most nearly the *opposite* in meaning to the Word Bank word.

1. impregnable
   a. protected
   b. unconquerable
   c. strong
   d. vulnerable

2. thrall
   a. servant
   b. laborer
   c. lord
   d. captive

"Success is counted sweetest" and "I dwell in Possibility—" by Emily Dickinson
"Uncoiling" by Pat Mora
"Columbus Dying" by Vassar Miller

Build Grammar Skills: Subject-Verb Agreement

A verb changes form to agree in number (singular or plural) with its subject. However, the structure of some sentences may make you think twice about agreement choices. Keep these pointers in mind:

Distinguish between subjects and objects of prepositions.

A <u>basket</u> of flowers <u>was</u> on the table.

Here, *flowers* is the object of the preposition *of*. The singular subject *basket* takes the singular verb *was*.

Watch for compound subjects, which are joined by *and*, *or*, or *nor*.

The <u>brothers</u> and the family <u>dog</u> often <u>play</u> Frisbee. Neither the <u>mother</u> nor the <u>father</u> <u>likes</u> to play.

In the first sentence above, *brothers* and *dog* are a compound subject that takes the plural verb *play*. In the second sentence, *mother* and *father* are considered single elements in the compound subject and therefore take the singular verb *likes*.

A. Practice: Circle the correct verb form in each of the following sentences.

1. A thick bank of clouds (signals, signal) the coming storm.

2. Neither Columbus nor his men (knows, know) what lies ahead.

3. Distant strains of triumph (reaches, reach) the dying man.

4. Only seven of Emily Dickinson's poems (was, were) published in her lifetime.

5. Hunger, scabs, and fever (plagues, plague) Columbus' crew.

6. Every woman and child (startles, startle) at the wind's roar.

7. Both Vassar Miller and Pat Mora (is, are) contemporary poets.

8. Hawks and cholla (tangles, tangle) in the wind's dark hair.

B. Writing Application: Rewrite each of these sentences, correcting any errors in subject-verb agreement. If the subject and verb agree, write *Correct*.

1. Dickinson and Miller uses traditional rhyme schemes.

_____

2. Not one of Columbus' sailors are in good health.

_____

3. Women scurry to lock doors and close windows against the tornado.

_____

4. Neither success nor victory comfort the dying soldier.

_____

5. Hunger pains as well as fever torments the sailors.

_____

"Success is counted sweetest" and "I dwell in Possibility—" by Emily Dickinson
"Uncoiling" by Pat Mora
"Columbus Dying" by Vassar Miller

Reading Strategy: Draw Inferences

Poets often avoid stating the meaning of their poems directly. Instead, they craft images and words that you can use as evidence to figure out what the poem means. When you reach conclusions based on evidence, you **draw inferences**.

A. Practice: Draw inferences about the poems based on the evidence given. Write your conclusions on the lines.

1. The speaker in "Uncoiling" describes the women's songs as "lace lullabies." What can you infer about the effectiveness of the women's actions from this description?

   _____

   _____

2. What can you infer about the "House of Prose" from the images in "I dwell in Possibility—"?

   _____

   _____

3. What words and images help you infer that the speaker of "Columbus Dying" believes the explorer felt burdened by his discovery?

   _____

   _____

4 How does the speaker of "Success is counted sweetest" feel about "the purple Host"?

   _____

   _____

B. Practice: Read the passage. Write your answers to the questions that follow.

Although an exceptional student, Emily Dickinson received no advanced schooling beyond the required courses for young women—none existed. In keeping with the age, Emily's family did not encourage her intellectual abilities. It was thought improper for women to follow the same career paths as men. While her brothers were expected to pursue higher education and challenging careers, Emily received no such intellectual recognition. Instead, she kept house for her father for most of her adult years, quietly amassing the hundreds of poems that have become her legacy—and our national treasure.

1. What inferences can you draw about the writer's attitude toward Dickinson? What words and phrases do you use as evidence?

   _____

   _____

2. What can you infer about the level of equality that existed between men and women during Dickinson's lifetime?

   _____

   _____

"Success is counted sweetest" and "I dwell in Possibility—" by Emily Dickinson
"Uncoiling" by Pat Mora
"Columbus Dying" by Vassar Miller

Literary Analysis: Stated and Implied Theme in Poetry

The theme of a literary work is the central idea or insight into life presented in the work. Sometimes the theme is stated directly, as in "Success is counted sweetest." In most poems, however, the theme is not directly stated but is implied, as in the other poems listed above. To identify an implied theme, a reader must study the details given and then infer what is the most important thing being said by the sum of those details.

DIRECTIONS: The following poem by Emily Dickinson has an implied theme. Read the poem, and then answer the questions to help you identify the poem's implied theme.

> "Hope" is the thing with feathers—
>
> That perches in the soul—
>
> And sings the tune without the words—
>
> And never stops—at all—
>
> 5 And sweetest—in the Gale—is heard—
>
> And sore must be the storm—
>
> That could abash the little Bird
>
> That kept so many warm—
>
> I've heard it in the chillest land—
>
> 10 And on the strangest Sea—
>
> Yet, never, in Extremity,
>
> It asked a crumb—of Me.

1. What specific images are evoked?

_____

_____

2. What do these images suggest?

_____

_____

3. What is the poet's feeling toward "the little Bird"?

_____

_____

4. What would you say is the theme of the poem?

_____

_____

from *My Left Foot* by Christy Brown

Build Vocabulary

Spelling Strategy   When you hear a "shun" sound at the end of a word, it may be spelled in any one of four ways. The words *volition* and *contention* use *-tion* to make the "shun" sound. Look at how these other words make the "shun" sound: *suspicion, dimension, impression.*

Using the Root *-vol-*

A. DIRECTIONS: Determine the meaning of the italicized word in each sentence by using context clues. Remember that the root *-vol-* means "wish" or "will." Write your definition in the space provided.

1. The students *volunteered* their time to deliver meals to homebound elderly citizens.

   _____

2. An *involuntary* groan escaped my lips as I looked out the window and saw that it was beginning to pour.

   _____

B. Using the Word Bank

impertinence	conviction	inert
contention	volition	taut

B. DIRECTIONS: Replace each italicized word or group of words with a word from the Word Bank. Rewrite the sentence in the space provided.

1. Christy's nerves were *tense* as everyone watched his left foot.

   _____

2. Christy believes his mother's *strong belief* was perhaps the most powerful force in his life.

   _____

3. Many people would view disagreeing with a doctor as an *inappropriate action*.

   _____

4. Though Christy was not able to walk, he was not *inactive*.

   _____

5. Christy was dependent upon his family members and could not act of his own *free will*.

   _____

6. Her *statement for which she argued* was that Christy would be treated just like the rest of her children.

   _____

Name _____ Date _____

Build Grammar Skills: Past and Past Perfect Tenses

The **past tense** of a verb indicates that an action began and ended in the past. The **past perfect** tense indicates a past action that was completed before another past action took place. It is formed with *had* and the past participle of a verb (the form ending in *-ed* or an irregular ending such as *-n* or *-t*).

>   **Past Tense:** Christy's mother *rejected* the opinions of the doctors.
>   **Past Perfect Tense**: They *had told* her that nothing could be done.

In the first sentence, the verb *rejected* indicates something that happened in the past. In the second sentence, the past perfect *had told* indicates an action that took place before Christy's mother rejected the doctors' opinions.

A. Practice: Read each sentence. In the following sentences, circle the verbs in the past tense and underline the verbs in the past perfect tense.

1. In his family, Christy belonged to the middle group of children; nine others had been born before him.

2. After giving birth, his mother had been sent away to recuperate, so Christy was not baptized until later.

3. Christy was about four months old when his mother first noticed that something was wrong.

4. By the time Christy was a year old, his mother's concerns had grown to the point where she decided to seek medical advice.

5. Although the doctors had been unable to help, Christy's mother refused to give up hope.

B. Writing Application: Rewrite each of the following sentences, supplying the verb in the tense indicated.

1. Mrs. Brown [decide—past perfect] to treat Christy the same as her other children.

   _____

2. Knowing that she was on his side [give—past] him the strength to face his future.

   _____

3. She would spend many hours reading to him, but he could make no sign that he [understand—past perfect] her. _____

   _____

4. At age five, something amazing happened; Christy [use—past] his left foot to write the letter *A*.

   _____

5. It [happen—past perfect] so quickly; he had just reached out and snatched a piece of chalk from his sister's hand. _____

   _____

Name _____ Date _____

from *My Left Foot* by Christy Brown

Reading Strategy: Identify Author's Purpose

Writers of nonfiction always have a purpose for writing. As readers, we can't always be sure of what that purpose is. What we can be sure of, however, is how the words make us feel. From those feelings, then, we can suppose what the author's purpose is.

DIRECTIONS: Read each of the following passages from *My Left Foot*. Consider how the passage makes you feel. Then state what you think is the author's purpose behind the passage.

1. She refused to accept this truth, the inevitable truth—as it then seemed—that I was beyond cure, beyond saving, even beyond hope.

   _____

   _____

2. It was hard, heart-breaking work, for often all she got from me in return was a vague smile and perhaps a faint gurgle.

   _____

   _____

3. I used to lie on my back all the time in the kitchen or, on bright warm days, out in the garden, a little bundle of crooked muscles and twisted nerves, surrounded by a family that loved me and hoped for me and that made me part of their own warmth and humanity.

   _____

   _____

4. I was lonely, imprisoned in a world of my own, unable to communicate with others, cut off, separated from them as though a glass wall stood between my existence and theirs, thrusting me beyond the sphere of their lives and activities.

   _____

   _____

5. Then, suddenly, it happened! In a moment everything was changed, my future life molded into a definite shape, my mother's faith in me rewarded and her secret fear changed into open triumph.

   _____

   _____

6. That one letter, scrawled on the floor with a broken bit of yellow chalk gripped between my toes, was my road to a new world, my key to mental freedom.

   _____

   _____

from *My Left Foot* by Christy Brown

Literary Analysis: Epiphany

This portion of the autobiography *My Left Foot* describes the moment when Christy displays to his family that his mother was right. Up to this point, Christy's mother has had only her faith in her own belief that Christy would someday communicate. As he writes the letter *A* on the floor, Christy gives her proof that it *was* his body that was "shattered, not his mind." In the passage, there is no doubt about the effect that this epiphany had on Brown's life, as well as on his mother's.

DIRECTIONS: Answer the questions that follow to increase your understanding of Christy Brown's epiphany and how he develops the moment in his writing.

1. Identify one sentence from the selection that you think most closely describes what Christy's life would have been like if he had not shown that he could communicate. How does the information in the sentence contribute to the significant moment?

   _____

   _____

   _____

   _____

2. Christy devotes a lengthy paragraph to describing the doctors' opinions of his condition and his mother's reactions to those opinions. How does this contribute to the significant moment that Christy relates later in the passage?

   _____

   _____

   _____

3. Why does Christy relate the story about looking at the storybook for hours with his mother? What effect does this scene have on the significant moment?

   _____

   _____

   _____

4. Christy begins one paragraph with "Then, suddenly, it happened." Eighteen paragraphs later we discover what "it" is. Why did Christy take so long to reveal what he had done?

   _____

   _____

   _____

5. Re-read the paragraph that begins, "The stillness was profound." Why do you think Christy includes those details of setting here? What impact do these details have on the significant moment?

   _____

   _____

   _____

"A Visit to Grandmother" by William Melvin Kelley

Build Vocabulary

Spelling Strategy   When the suffix -ing is added to a word ending in -e, the -e is dropped; for example, *bake* becomes *baking*, and *grimace* becomes the Word Bank word *grimacing*. (Exceptions: *eyeing, dyeing*)

Using Word Origins

A word's *etymology* is its history, or origin. A dictionary presents a word's etymology in brackets following the word's pronunciation key and part of speech label or occasionally at the end of the definition. In most cases, the information in the brackets describes the language(s) from which the word originated, the original form of the word, and the original meaning of the word.

A. DIRECTIONS: Use a dictionary to look up the origin of each of the following words from "A Visit to Grandmother." Then fill in the appropriate information on the lines provided. As you look at the words, you will notice that some words have been part of many different languages. The last version listed within the set of brackets is the word's original version.

1. grimace

   Language of origin _____

   Original form _____

   Original meaning _____

2. indulge

   Language of origin _____

   Original form _____

   Original meaning _____

3. venture

   Language of origin _____

   Original form _____

   Original meaning _____

Using the Word Bank

B. DIRECTIONS: Match each word in the left column with its definition in the right column. Write the letter of the definition on the line next to the word it defines.

____ 1. indulgence   a. coated with a varnish made from shellac or resin

____ 2. grimacing   b. took the risk of

____ 3. lacquered   c. making a twisted or distorted facial expression

____ 4. ventured   d. leniency; forgiveness

"A Visit to Grandmother" by William Melvin Kelley

Build Grammar Skills: Progressive Verb Tenses

To name an action or condition that is taking place at the present time, use the **present progressive** tense of a verb. The present progressive tense is formed with *am*, *are*, or *is* and the present participle of a verb.

Present Progressive Tense: His brother *is smiling* broadly as he enters the room.

The **past progressive** tense names an action or condition that was taking place at some point in the past. It is formed with *was* or *were* and the present participle of a verb.

Past Progressive Tense: When I looked at his face, I saw that he *was grimacing*.

A. Practice: Complete the following sentences by filling in the blank with the present progressive or past progressive form of the verb indicated.

1. Last week, Chig's father decided that he _____ to his college class reunion in Nashville, Tennessee. (go)

2. Chig's brother and sister _____ for camp and besides were too young to go. (leave)

3. Chig and his dad _____ for home when Dad casually suggests that they visit Chig's grandmother. (pack)

4. The old lady looked up at Chig and asked "Who _____ there?" (stand)

5. The family _____ dinner when Aunt Rose suggested Mama tell them about the horse. (eat)

6. "I _____ to think," Mama replied, holding her fork halfway to her mouth. (try)

B. Writing Application: Revise the following sentences by changing verbs in the present tense to the present progressive form, and verbs in the past tense to the past progressive form.

1. Aunt Rose, over Chig's weak protest, spoons mashed potatoes onto his plate.

_____

2. Well, I look at this horse and notice how he looks more and more wide awake every minute.

_____

3. For a while there, I felt a little better about riding with GL behind that crazy-looking horse.

_____

4. Mama and Charles stared into each other's eyes; Grandma leaned toward him.

_____

"A Visit to Grandmother" by William Melvin Kelley

Reading Strategy: Clarify

To understand clearly the characters and events of a story, you should continually **clarify**—check your understanding of—any details of the story that are confusing to you. Clarify important details of a story by reading ahead to gather more information and by reviewing parts of the story you have already read. As you read, you can take notes, create charts or a family tree showing relationships among characters, and sketch out a timeline showing the order of events in a story or in a character's past. Using these techniques to clarify will help you to keep track of important details about setting, relationships, and key events.

DIRECTIONS: As you read, clarify the following situations from "A Visit to Grandmother."

1. Show how you would help someone to clarify the details of the story Grandmother tells about her adventure with GL's horse and buggy. What happened, and in what order did the events of the story occur?

   _____

   _____

   _____

   _____

2. Even before his father's outburst at the family dinner table, Chig senses that there is something tense and strange about his father's relationship with his family. Clarify the different clues that alert Chig to the fact that something is wrong with his father's relationship with Grandmother.

   _____

   _____

   _____

   _____

3. How might you clarify the details of GL's personality that make him different from Chig's father?

   _____

   _____

   _____

   _____

4. How might you clarify for someone the order of events described by Chig in "A Visit to Grandmother"? Describe Chig and his father's trip to Grandmother's house, what they do when they are there, and what happens when GL makes his entrance.

   _____

   _____

   _____

   _____

Name _____ Date _____

Literary Analysis: Characterization

An author reveals the personalities of characters in a story by using *direct* or *indirect charac-terization*. An author may make direct statements about a character, or he or she may describe the character's actions, thoughts, and appearance, as well as what other people in the story think of the character.

A. DIRECTIONS: Complete the following chart with examples from the story of direct and indirect characterization for each character listed.

Character	Examples of Direct Characterization	Examples of Indirect Characterization
Example: GL	GL is said to be part con man, part practical joker, and part Don Juan.	He was wearing brown-and-white two-tone shoes with very pointed toes and a white summer suit.
1. Charles		
2. Chig		
3. Mama		
4. Rose		

B. DIRECTIONS: In a brief essay, indicate whether direct or indirect characterization makes you feel you know a character better. Explain your answer.

_____

_____

_____

_____

_____

_____

_____

_____

_____

"Mowing" and "After Apple-Picking" by Robert Frost
"Style" and "At Harvesttime" by Maya Angelou

Build Vocabulary

Spelling Strategy   In many instances, the *ou* diphthong denotes a word that originated in Middle English; even today, British English uses the *ou* diphthong in many words that American English spells with *o*. For example: **flavour, flavor; candour, candor; savour, savor**

Using *-ough*

Words that contain the letter combination *-ough* are easily mispronounced because they have three possible pronunciations. Some rhyme with *now*, some rhyme with *off*, and some rhyme with *you*. The only way to be sure of the proper pronunciation is to memorize each word.

A. DIRECTIONS: Fill in each blank with an *-ough* word from the list below. The word you choose for each blank should rhyme with the end word in the line above it.

   bough   trough   through   enough   rough   cough

   Slushy, lazy snow piles are visiting now—
   Resting on roofs, on fields, on every _____.
   But soon leaves that are rested and new
   Will push forcefully _____
   And take their turn.
   And we hope that the lazy piles of white, although stubborn and tough
   will accept that their stay has been long _____

Using the Word Bank

bough	trough	manifestation	disparaging	potency
judicious	gibe	admonition	immutable	

B. DIRECTIONS: Fill in the blank with a synonym from the Word Bank for the italicized word in each sentence.

1. A swing hung from the maple tree's strongest *branch*. _____

2. The temperature dropped and ice formed in the horse's *feedbox*. _____

3. The elaborate parade was a *visible expression* of the town's holiday enthusiasm. _____

4. His feelings were hurt by that *belittling* remark. _____

5. Noticing dark, threatening clouds in the sky, the camp counselor made a *wise and careful* decision to postpone our hike. _____

6. The athlete was distracted by an unfriendly *jeer* from a spectator. _____

7. After his bike accident, he received a *warning* to ride more carefully. _____

8. We will not bother arguing; their decision seems *unchangeable*. _____

9. The storm's *power* caused damage to trees, roads, and buildings. _____

"Mowing" and "After Apple-Picking" by Robert Frost
"Style" and "At Harvesttime" by Maya Angelou

Build Grammar Skills: Adverb Function

An **adverb** is a word that modifies a verb, an adjective, or another adverb. An adverb answers one of four questions about the word it modifies: *Where? When? In what way?* or *To what extent?* An adverb modifying a verb can answer any of the four questions. An adverb modifying an adjective or another adverb answers only one question: *To what extent?*

Modifying Verb: Handle the apples *carefully*; do not let them fall. (in what way)
 I will *soon* be done with apple-picking. (when)

Modifying Adjective: Style is as *perfectly* personal as a fingerprint. (to what extent)

Modifying Adverb: He worked *more* slowly as the day went on. (to what extent)

A. Practice: Read the following sentences, and underline the adverbs. Then, draw a line from each adverb to the word it modifies. Write verb, adjective, or adverb over the modified words. On the line, write what question the adverbs answer.

1. The heat of the sun made the afternoon seem very long._____

2. One should watch very carefully the steady march of the human parade._____

3. Tangling with brutes will often result in an upset stomach._____

4. Societies range from the most privileged to the most needy._____

5. His scythe moved quickly over the low-lying marshland._____

6. From the cliff I could see the river below._____

B. Writing Application: Follow the directions below to write four sentences that use adverbs to modify verbs, adjectives, and other adverbs.

1. Write a sentence about "Style," using an adverb that answers the question *When?*

 _____

2. Write a sentence about "Mowing," using an adverb that modifies another adverb.

 _____

3. Write a sentence about "Style," using an adverb that modifies an adjective.

 _____

4. Write a sentence about "Apple-Picking," using adverbs that answer the questions *When*

 and *To what extent?* _____

"Mowing" and "After Apple-Picking" by Robert Frost
"Style" and "At Harvesttime" by Maya Angelou

Reading Strategy: Interpret

Poets choose the words of their poems carefully in order to create particular images for their readers. The sense impressions created by a poet help the reader to *interpret* the theme of the poem.

DIRECTIONS: Read the following poem by Robert Frost, "Nothing Gold Can Stay." Then answer the questions that follow.

Nature's first green is gold,

Her hardest hue to hold.

Her early leaf's a flower;

But only so an hour.

5 Then leaf subsides to leaf.

So Eden sank to grief.

So dawn goes down to day.

Nothing gold can stay.

1. What is the image presented in the first line?

_____

_____

2. What image do lines 3–5 create?

_____

_____

3. What image is suggested by the reference to "Eden" in line 6?

_____

_____

4. How does the last line summarize the images, and the theme, of the poem?

_____

_____

5. How is this poem similar to "Mowing" and "After Apple-Picking"?

_____

_____

"Mowing" and "After Apple-Picking" by Robert Frost
"Style" and "At Harvesttime" by Maya Angelou

Literary Analysis: Tone

In a literary work, a writer carefully chooses words and phrases to convey a particular feeling or attitude toward his or her subject. This attitude is called **tone**. The tone of a work may be, among other things, serious, casual, distant, personal, sad, or humorous. For example, when the speaker in Frost's "After Apple-Picking" says, "But I am done with apple-picking now./Essence of winter sleep is on the night,/The scent of apples: I am drowsing off," the reader can sense the speaker's exhaustion and his wish to put thoughts of work out of his mind and allow rest to consume him. When Maya Angelou writes, "Content is of great importance, but we must not underrate the value of style. That is, attention must be paid to not only what is said but how it is said," the reader can sense a confident, instructional tone.

DIRECTIONS: Read "Fire and Ice" by Robert Frost. As you read, identify the tone of the poem and think about how it relates to the poem's message. Then answer the questions that follow.

Fire and Ice

Some say the world will end in fire,

Some say in ice.

From what I've tasted of desire

I hold with those who favor fire.

5 But if it had to perish twice,

I think I know enough of hate

To say that for destruction ice

Is also great

And would suffice.

1. What is the tone of "Fire and Ice"?

_____

2. What specific phrases create this tone?

_____

3. What is the poem's message? In what way does its tone relate to its message?

_____

_____

4. Is the tone of this poem similar to or different from the tones of "Mowing" or "After Apple-Picking"? Explain your response.

_____

_____

Build Vocabulary

Spelling Strategy   A compound word is a two-part word that functions as a single unit. The parts of a compound word may be written separately (*fruit trees*), hyphenated (*half-moon*), or closed up (*windfall*). Consult a dictionary or style manual when you are unsure about how to spell an unfamiliar compound.

Using Words From Myths

A. DIRECTIONS: Many words in common use owe their origin to various Greek and Roman myths. Use a dictionary to learn the meaning of each word. On the line, write the definition and an explanation of each word's relation to a myth or to a Greek or Roman god or goddess.

1. nemesis _____
   _____

2. cereal _____
   _____

3. atlas _____
   _____

4. mercurial _____
   _____

5. arachnophobia _____
   _____

Using the Word Bank

paddocks	jovial	exquisite	bouquet

B. DIRECTIONS: Use each of the Word Bank words in a sentence according to the instructions given.

1. Use the word *paddocks* in a description of the paddocks that are next to the orchard in the story.

   _____

2. Use *jovial* in a sentence about a relative.

   _____

3. Use *exquisite* in a sentence in which you describe your idea of the perfect piece of fruit.

   _____

4. Use *bouquet* in a sentence about the smell of your perfect piece of fruit.

   _____

"The Apple Tree" by Katherine Mansfield

Build Grammar Skills: Commonly Confused Words: *Lie* and *Lay*

Like all languages, English contains a number of confusing expressions. Two frequently misused words in speaking and writing are the words **lie** and **lay**. Although the words seem similar, having to do with things at rest, they actually have different meanings. The verb *lie* means "to recline." Its principal parts—*lie, lying, lay,* and *lain*—are never followed by a direct object. The verb *lay* means "to put or set (something) down." Its principal parts—*lay, laying, laid,* and *laid*—are usually followed by a direct object.

The following chart compares the principal parts of the two verbs.

Verb form	Lie (recline)	Lay (set or put)
Present	The apple basket *lies* on the table.	She *lays* the basket on the table.
Present Participle	The basket is *lying* on the table.	She is *laying* the basket on the table.
Past	Yesterday, the basket *lay* in the same place.	Yesterday, she *laid* the basket in the same place.
Past participle	The basket *has lain* there all week.	She *has laid* it there so we can reach it.

A. Practice: Circle the word that correctly completes each sentence.

1. We had two orchards; one (lay, laid) at the foot of a little hill and stretched to the paddocks.

2. When apples fall to the ground, they might (lie, lay) tangled in the grass for days.

3. Apples found (lying, laying) on the ground, are made into apple cider.

4. We walked to a stump under the wattles, where Father had (lain, laid) the apple.

5. When we got home, Mother was (lying, laying) a warm apple pie on the table.

6. After eating it, we felt so full that we had to (lie, lay) down on the couch.

B. Writing Application: Follow the directions to write six sentences using a form of the words *lie* or *lay*.

1. Use the present form of *lie*. _____

_____

2. Use the past form of *lie*. _____

_____

3. Use the present participle form of *lie*. _____

_____

4. Use the present form of *lay*. _____

_____

5. Use the past participal form of *lie*. _____

_____

6. Use the past form of *lay*. _____

_____

"The Apple Tree" by Katherine Mansfield

Reading Strategy: Question

When you read news articles, poems, or short stories, questions probably spring to mind about what is happening, why things happen, or why the writer expresses something in a particular way. Do you pay attention, or do you just read on? If you do pay attention to the questions in your mind, you may gain fuller understanding of what you are reading. Here are some general types of questions to think about as you read a short story.

- Ask questions about the setting. Where and when does the action or story take place? How does the setting affect the story's action? the story's mood?

- Ask questions about the characters' actions. Why do they do what they do? What are the consequences of their actions?

- Ask questions about the characters' speech. Why do they speak the way they do? Why do they say what they say?

DIRECTIONS: As you read "The Apple Tree," ask yourself these questions. The answers are probably not stated in the story. It is possible that you may not be able to answer the questions right away. You may have to piece together information or clues to come up with the answers after you finish the story.

1. Why does the author spend so much time describing both the "wild" orchard as well as the "other" orchard?

   _____
   _____
   _____

2. On the way to the apple tree, the children don't seem to walk *with* their father. They are described as "tailing after" or "with Bogey and me stumbling after." What does this say about the children's relationship with their father?

   _____
   _____
   _____

3. Why don't the children reveal to their father how awful the apple is?

   _____
   _____
   _____

4. What does their lying say about their relationship with their father?

   _____
   _____
   _____

"The Apple Tree" by Katherine Mansfield

Literary Analysis: Allusion

An **allusion** is a literary reference to a person, place, or event mentioned in other works of literature, in history, in religion, or in mythology. (In "The Apple Tree," the author makes an allusion to the Biblical story of Adam and Eve.) An allusion adds a level of meaning that is not apparent to the reader who is unfamiliar with the allusion. Likewise, the reader sometimes is aware that an allusion exists but that research must be done to determine its meaning.

DIRECTIONS: Each of the following allusions includes a brief explanation of the idea the allusion most often expresses. On the lines below each one, briefly tell the story behind the allusion or explain how the allusion represents the idea. You may wish to use a dictionary or other reference books for help.

1. *Mythological allusion:* Odysseus
    Idea: urge to wander; inclusion in series of unusual events

    _____

    _____

2. *Religious allusion:* Job
    Idea: patience; faithfulness despite great suffering

    _____

    _____

3. *Mythological allusion:* Valhalla
    Idea: honor for heroes

    _____

    _____

4. *Historical allusion:* Lincoln
    Idea: honesty and humility

    _____

    _____

5. *Religious allusion:* Nirvana
    Idea: peacefulness; complete happiness

    _____

    _____

6. *Literary allusion:* Lilliput; Lilliputian
    Idea: tininess; narrow-mindedness

    _____

    _____

"Africa" by David Diop
"Old Song" Traditional
from *The Analects* by Confucius
"All" by Bei Dao
"Also All" by Shu Ting

Build Vocabulary

Spelling Strategy   In the word *lamentation, -ti-* produces the sound |sh|. Other letter combinations that also may produce the |sh| sound include *ce* (ocean), *ch* (machine), *ci* (social), *sch* (schnauzer), *sci* (conscious), *si* (dimension), *ssi* (expression), *su* (sugar), and *xi* (anxious).

Using the Suffix *-ment*

The suffix *-ment* indicates "the state of or condition of." Thus, the Word Bank word *chastisements* means "the condition of being chastised, or punished." The suffix is usually added to a verb to create a noun that names the condition of, or explains a concrete result of, the verb. For example, the state defined by the verb *excite* is *excitement.*

A. DIRECTIONS: Write a sentence, changing each of the following verbs to a noun with the *-ment* suffix. Remember that the *-ment* suffix indicates the state of, or the concrete result of, the verb form.

1. nourish _____

2. engage _____

3. involve _____

4. entertain _____

5. bewilder _____

Using the Word Bank

B. DIRECTIONS: Match each word in the left column with its definition in the right column. Write the letter of the definition on the line next to the word it defines.

____ 1. impetuous   a. punishments

____ 2. chastisements   b. the act of crying out in grief; wailing

____ 3. lamentation   c. impulsive; passionate

Making Verbal Analogies

C. DIRECTIONS: Each item consists of a related pair of words in CAPITAL LETTERS, followed by four lettered pairs of words. Choose the pair that best expresses a relationship similar to that expressed in the pair in capital letters. Circle the letter of your choice.

1. IMPETUOUS : HASTY ::
   a. full : slow
   b. courageous : accurate
   c. accident : plan
   d. cautious : careful

2. ERRORS :
   CHASTISEMENTS ::
   a. mistakes : scoldings
   b. punishments : crimes
   c. faults : forgiveness
   d. battles : triumphs

3. GRIEF : LAMENTATION ::
   a. anger : tears
   b. humor : laughter
   c. writing : pen
   d. tragedy : destiny

"Africa" by David Diop
"Old Song" Traditional
from *The Analects* by Confucius
"All" by Bei Dao
"Also All" by Shu Ting

Build Grammar Skills: Active Voice and Passive Voice

A verb is in the **active voice** when the subject of the sentence performs the action. A verb is in the **passive voice** when the subject of the sentence receives the action. The passive voice uses a form of *to be* together with a past participle.

Active Voice: Confucius *emphasized* the importance of moral conduct.
Passive Voice: The importance of moral conduct *was emphasized by* Confucius.

Use the active voice whenever possible. It is livelier and more direct than the passive voice. Use the passive voice if the person or thing performing an action is unknown or unimportant.

A. Practice: Read each sentence and write *A* above any verbs in the active voice and *P* above any verbs in the passive voice.

1. When the treatment of parents was asked about by Meng Wu Po, the Master said, "Behave in such a way that your parents have no anxiety about you."

2. Many African societies did not preserve their wisdom and stories on paper; instead, a rich oral tradition was developed by them.

3. Solemnly a voice answers me.

4. High office is held by men with narrow views.

B. Writing Application: Rewrite the following sentences, changing all verbs in the passive voice to the active voice.

1. Only one volume of poetry was published by David Diop before his life was tragically taken by a plane crash.

   _____

   _____

2. To remain unsoured even though one's merits are unrecognized by others is expected of a gentleman. _____

   _____

3. The reputation of being slow in word but prompt in deed is coveted by a gentleman.

   _____

   _____

4. Shu Ting was forced by political events to leave Beijing and live in a small peasant village.

   _____

   _____

"**Africa**" by David Diop
"**Old Song**" Traditional
from *The Analects* by Confucius
"**All**" by Bei Dao
"**Also All**" by Shu Ting

Reading Strategy: Relate to What You Know

Although the subject matter of these selections may seem remote, you can learn important lessons from them by conducting the ideas they present to your own knowledge and experiences.

DIRECTIONS: In the first column, write lines from the selections that contain advice, a principle, or an idea that the author is trying to express in one of the selections. In the second column, note a specific situation from your life to which you might apply the author's advice, principle, or idea. Finally, in the third column, note how to apply or interpret the situation in a way that relates the idea from the selection to what you know. One example appears.

Advice, Principle, or Idea	Concrete Situation From My Life	Application or Interpretation
Govern the people by regulations and chastisements, and they will flee from you…	I know more about some subjects than my friends, and I feel they should be informed.	If I tell people what to do or criticize them a lot, they probably won't respond.

Africa/Song/Analects/All/Also All **59**

Unit 2: Striving for Success

"Africa" by David Diop
"Old Song" Traditional
from *The Analects* by Confucius
"All" by Bei Dao
"Also All" by Shu Ting

Literary Analysis: Aphorisms

An **aphorism** is a short, concise statement expressing a wise or clever observation or a general truth. In order to fully understand an aphorism, it is a good idea to paraphrase it—to state the meaning of the statement in your own words.

DIRECTIONS: Use your own words to paraphrase each of the following aphorisms from the poems listed above.

1. "Do not seek too much fame, but do not seek obscurity."

   _____

   _____

2. "A gentleman is ashamed to let his words outrun his deeds."

   _____

   _____

3. "Not every seed finds barren soil."

   _____

   _____

4. "You can blow out a candle but you can't blow out a fire."

   _____

   _____

5. "Today is heavy with tomorrow—the future was planted yesterday."

   _____

   _____

6. "A gentleman covets the reputation of being slow in word but prompt in deed."

   _____

   _____

7. "Excel when you must, but do not excel the world."

   _____

   _____

"Through the Tunnel" by Doris Lessing

Build Vocabulary

Spelling Strategy   When adding a suffix to a word that ends in *y* preceded by a consonant, change the *y* to *i*; for example, *promontory* becomes *promontories*.

Using the Root -*lum*-

A. DIRECTIONS: The root -*lum*- means "light." Complete each sentence with a -*lum*- word from the following list.

luminous   luminescence   illuminating

1. First-time listeners found the knowledgeable speaker's lecture _____.

2. Some deep-sea fish are characterized by _____, which makes them visible in the dark, murky waters.

3. The _____ planet Venus sometimes has been mistaken for a UFO.

Using the Word Bank

contrition	promontories	luminous	supplication
frond	convulsive	gout	

B. DIRECTIONS: Match each word in the left column with its definition in the right column. Write the letter of the definition on the line next to the word it defines.

_____ 1. contrition   a. giving off light

_____ 2. promontories   b. a leaflike shoot

_____ 3. luminous   c. feeling of remorse for having done something wrong

_____ 4. supplication   d. marked by an involuntary muscular contraction

_____ 5. frond   e. the act of asking humbly and earnestly

_____ 6. convulsive   f. a spurt, splash; a glob

_____ 7. gout   g. high places extending out over a body of water

Understanding Sentence Completions

C. DIRECTIONS: Circle the letter of the word that best completes each sentence.

_____ 1. Hoping for a royal blessing, the peasant knelt in _____ before the king.
    a. contrition   c. supplication
    b. confusion   d. defiance

_____ 2. Darting fireflies created a _____ nighttime display.
    a. desirable   c. faint
    b. convulsive   d. luminous

_____ 3. The gently waving _____ brushed the swimmer's face.
    a. promontories   c. gout
    b. frond   d. contrition

Unit 3: Clashing Forces

"Through the Tunnel" by Doris Lessing

Build Grammar Skills: Complete Subject

A **complete subject** includes the essential noun, pronoun, or group of words acting as a noun that names the person, place, or thing that a sentence is about. A complete subject may consist of a single essential word. Often, however, it includes many other words that modify the essential words. In the examples that follow, the complete subject is italicized and the essential word is underlined.

> **Complete Subject** (single word): _They_ began diving again and again.
> **Complete Subject** (many words): Soon _the biggest of the boys_ poised himself.

A. Practice: Underline the complete subject in each of the following sentences. Then, circle the essential word or words in the complete subject.

1. The young English boy stopped at a turning of the path.

2. His mother walked on in front of him, carrying a bright striped bag in one hand.

3. Above them, some boys were stripping off their clothes.

4. All of them were burned smooth dark brown.

5. He grabbed the goggles from her hand.

6. The water beyond the rock was full of boys blowing like brown whales.

7. Myriads of minute fish were drifting through the water.

8. The great rock rose sheer out of the white sand.

B. Writing Application: Write complete sentences to answer the following questions about events that take place in "Through the Tunnel." Then, underline the complete subject in each sentence.

1. Why does Jerry go to the beach with his mother on the first morning?

_____

2. What is it about the bay that appeals to Jerry?

_____

3. What happens that makes Jerry swim over to the group of local boys?

_____

4. Who dove through the tunnel first?

_____

5. What happened the first time Jerry adjusted his goggles and dove?

_____

6. What unpleasant side effect does Jerry suffer when he holds his breath for long periods?

_____

Name _____ Date _____

"Through the Tunnel" by Doris Lessing

Reading Strategy: Question

Writers rarely spell out the significance of each detail or action in a story. Instead, readers must ask questions and then look for answers by piecing together details that offer insight and understanding. For example, you might gather information about a character's background that will help you answer a question about his or her behavior. Keeping questions in mind as you read helps you to gain a fuller understanding of what you are reading.

DIRECTIONS: Use the following chart to write three questions that come to mind as you read "Through the Tunnel." Then, record the details that prompted those questions and the details that provide the answers. For instance, the ominous details about the wildness of the bay and the mother "worrying off to the beach" may cause you to question whether something bad is going to happen to Jerry. Later in the story, other details provide an answer to that question.

Question:	
Details That Prompted the Question:	
Details That Provide an Answer:	

Question:	
Details That Prompted the Question:	
Details That Provide an Answer:	

Question:	
Details That Prompted the Question:	
Details That Provide an Answer:	

Unit 3: Clashing Forces

Name _____ Date _____

"**Through the Tunnel**" by Doris Lessing

Literary Analysis: Internal Conflict

A good story presents an intriguing struggle, or conflict. Sometimes the struggle is an **internal conflict,** or a struggle within a character over opposing feelings, beliefs, or needs. People face conflicting feelings about making significant life changes and, often, these feelings focus on facing and conquering one's fears. In "Through the Tunnel," Jerry struggles to make the transition from the world of childhood to the world of adolescence.

DIRECTIONS: Answer the following questions about Jerry's internal conflict. Write your answers on the lines.

1. With what opposing forces does Jerry struggle?

_____
_____
_____
_____

2. At the beginning of the story, what childish behavior does Jerry demonstrate?

_____
_____
_____
_____

3. What physical challenges does Jerry face?

_____
_____
_____
_____

4. What mental challenges does Jerry meet?

_____
_____
_____
_____

5. By the end of the story, what behavior shows that Jerry has passed from the world of childhood to the world of adolescence?

_____
_____
_____
_____

"The Dog That Bit People" by James Thurber

Build Vocabulary

Spelling Strategy   When adding -ly to a word ending in a consonant + le, drop the le; for example, irascib*le* becomes irascib*ly*, and jang*le* becomes jang*ly*.

Using the Prefix epi-

The prefix epi-, which can mean "upon" or "above," has its origins in both Latin and Greek. Consequently, many medical terms that come from Latin and Greek incorporate the prefix epi-.

A. DIRECTIONS: Using clues within the sentences, write definitions for the epi- words.

1. The pathologist removed the *epicardium* to reveal the heart.

_____

2. Next, she pulled back the *epiglottis* to reveal the glottis lying beneath it.

_____

Using the Word Bank

incredulity	choleric	irascible
jangle	indignant	epitaph

B. DIRECTIONS: Match each word in the left column with its definition in the right column. Write the letter of the definition on the line next to the word it defines.

____ 1. incredulity   a. grumpy; irritable

____ 2. choleric   b. discord; harsh sounds

____ 3. irascible   c. inscription on a tomb or gravestone

____ 4. jangle   d. feeling or expressing anger or scorn, especially an injustice

____ 5. indignant   e. unwillingness or inability to believe

____ 6. epitaph   f. quick-tempered

Identifying Antonyms

C. DIRECTIONS: Each of the following questions consists of a word in CAPITAL LETTERS followed by four lettered words. Circle the letter of the word that is most nearly *opposite* in meaning to the word in capital letters. Because some of the choices are close in meaning, consider all the choices before deciding which is best.

____ 1. CHOLERIC: ____ 2. IRASCIBLE: ____ 3. INCREDULITY:
   a. feisty   a. even-tempered
   b. calm   b. annoying
   c. disturbed   c. unpredictable
   d. happy   d. amusing

"The Dog That Bit People" by James Thurber

Build Grammar Skills: Complete Predicate

A **complete predicate** includes the essential verb or verb phrase that tells something about the subject of a sentence. Often it includes many other words that modify the verb or verb phrase or help it complete the meaning of the sentence. In the examples that follow, the complete predicate is italicized and the essential verb is underlined.

Complete Predicate (single word): The intolerant garage man *sneered*.
Complete Predicate (many words): He *stopped* and *came over to see what we wanted*.

A. Practice: Underline the complete predicate in each of the following sentences. Then, circle the essential verb or verb phrase in the complete predicate.

1. Jeannie had six puppies in the clothes closet of a fourth floor apartment in New York.

2. Muggs came wandering into the room like Hamlet following his father's ghost.

3. Muggs stayed out in the pantry with the mice.

4. Lots of people reported our Airedale to the police.

5. I carried him into the kitchen and flung him onto the floor and shut the door.

6. Muggs died quite suddenly one night.

7. He didn't like to stay in the house for some reason or other.

8. Mother was holding the thought the very next day.

B. Writing Application: Write a paragraph describing the events that took place after Thurber grabbed Muggs by the tail and tossed him into the kitchen. When you have finished writing, go back and underline the complete predicate in each sentence that you wrote.

_____

_____

_____

_____

_____

_____

_____

_____

_____

_____

_____

"The Dog That Bit People" by James Thurber

Reading Strategy: Form Mental Images

As a comic writer, James Thurber creates vivid and amusing pictures of his experiences. As readers, we can best appreciate his tales when we form mental images, or pictures in our mind, of what he describes. For example, Thurber doesn't just tell us that he once had a dog get sick in his car. He vividly describes his prize-winning giant poodle wearing a red rubber bib and sitting beneath a small green umbrella that was held by the writer himself.

As you read, picture colors, shapes, and sizes. Hear the sounds. Imagine the characters' emotions and expressions on their faces.

DIRECTIONS: Write your answers to the following questions.

1. How does the title "The Dog That Bit People" help you establish mental images?

   _____

   _____

   _____

   _____

2. How is Thurber's description of the mice almost cartoonish?

   _____

   _____

   _____

   _____

3. List three details that help you form a mental picture of the scene in which the mantelpiece falls to the floor.

   _____

   _____

   _____

   _____

4. Which of Muggs' actions seems most comic to you? Explain.

   _____

   _____

   _____

5. Which reaction to Muggs seems most comic to you? Explain.

   _____

   _____

   _____

   _____

© Prentice-Hall, Inc.

Unit 3: Clashing Forces

"The Dog That Bit People" by James Thurber

Literary Analysis: Humorous Essay

In "The Dog That Bit People," James Thurber links several stories about his dogs, and one dog in particular, to create an entertaining humorous essay. A **humorous essay** is a nonfiction composition that presents the author's thoughts on a subject in an amusing way.

These are some key elements used in humorous essays:

- **Exaggeration** treats something with more importance than it deserves.

- An **odd juxtaposition** connects dissimilar words or ideas for comic effect; for example, " . . . a prizewinning French poodle surrounded by garage men . . . "

- An **understatement** treats an important subject as if it were not important.

- An **anecdote** briefly recounts a humorous or strange event.

- **Irony** is the difference between appearance and reality; for example, "Mother persuaded herself it was all for the best that the dog had bitten him, even though father lost an important business association because of it."

DIRECTIONS: Write a quotation from Thurber's essay that demonstrates each of the following elements of writing used in a humorous essay.

1. exaggeration

   _____

   _____

   _____

2. odd juxtaposition

   _____

   _____

   _____

3. understatement

   _____

   _____

   _____

4. anecdote

   _____

   _____

   _____

5. irony

   _____

   _____

   _____

"Conscientious Objector" by Edna St. Vincent Millay
"A Man" by Nina Cassian
"The Weary Blues" by Langston Hughes
"Jazz Fantasia" by Carl Sandburg

Build Vocabulary

Spelling Strategy   In the Word Bank word *melancholy*, the letters *c* and *h* combine to produce a hard k sound, rather than a soft sound as in *choose*. English uses a number of spellings to produce the hard k sound: *c* (*cost*), *k* (*king*), *ck* (*back*), and even *qu* (*physique*).

Using the Root -chol-

The word root -*chol*- probably comes from the Greek word for bile, a yellow-greenish fluid secreted by the liver for the digestion of fats. In ancient physiology (the science of living organisms), bile was believed to be one of four fluids that determined mental health. Today, -*chol*- carries a medical implication, as well as the old reference to mood. Determining whether the use of the root -*chol*- is physiological or psychological helps in understanding a word's meaning.

A. DIRECTIONS: For each of the following words, indicate whether the modern meaning of the word refers to a physical or a mental condition. If you do not know a word, check a dictionary.

1. cholera _____

2. choler _____

3. cholesterol _____

4. choleric _____

Using the Word Bank

B. DIRECTIONS: Use context and your knowledge of the words to respond to the following items.

1. Give reasons why someone's face might indicate pallor.

_____

2. Describe a person who wore a melancholy expression.

_____

3. Explain the maxim "As you sow, so shall you reap."

_____

Identifying Synonyms

C. DIRECTIONS: Circle the letter of the word that most closely matches the meaning of the Word Bank word.

____ 1. melancholy	____ 2. pallor	____ 3. reap
a. mixed	a. blemish	a. issue
b. despondent	b. vigor	b. assault
c. contagious	c. expression	c. harvest
d. ecstatic	d. paleness	d. recur

"Conscientious Objector" by Edna St. Vincent Millay
"A Man" by Nina Cassian
"The Weary Blues" by Langston Hughes
"Jazz Fantasia" by Carl Sandburg

Build Grammar Skills: Subjects in Inverted Sentences

In some sentences, the usual subject-verb order is **inverted,** or reversed. Sentences in the English language that may be inverted include questions, sentences beginning with *there* or *here*, and sentences that have been inverted for emphasis. To find the subject in an inverted sentence, mentally rephrase the sentence. Then, the subject and verb will fall into the usual order.

Inverted Sentence	Subject Placement	Begins with	Example
Question	subject often follows the verb	a verb, a helping verb, or *how*, *what*, *when*, *where*, *who*, *whose*, or *why*	Am *I* a spy in the land of of the living? Where is *he* living? What is *it* about?
Sentence beginning with *there* or *here*	subject usually follows the verb	*there* or *here*	There will be *things* I cannot do at all.
Inverted for emphasis	subject always follows the verb	often begins with a preposition	In the clearing stood the *soldier*.

A. Practice: In the following sentences, underline the subject once and the verb twice.

1. What does the speaker refuse to do in "Conscientious Objector"?

2. There are some wonderful images in "Jazz Fantasia."

3. Where the soldier's arm had once been grew a wing.

4. Why did Langston Hughes write a poem about the blues?

5. Here is my favorite collection of jazz poems.

6. Do you have a favorite jazz musician?.

B. Writing Application: Revise the following sentences, changing them from inverted order to subject-verb order.

1. There is a powerful message of hope and determination in "A Man."

_____

2. In the corner of the smoke-filled room, crooned the jazzman.

_____

3. Can you hear him crooning far into the night?

_____

4. Never through me shall you be overcome.

_____

"Conscientious Objector" by Edna St. Vincent Millay
"A Man" by Nina Cassian
"The Weary Blues" by Langston Hughes
"Jazz Fantasia" by Carl Sandburg

Reading Strategy: Respond to Images and Ideas

One of the powers of poetry is the way it stimulates our imagination as we read. Analyzing your responses to a poem helps make you an alert and appreciative reader.

DIRECTIONS: Use the graphic organizer to analyze your responses to images and ideas from these selections. In the left column, write an image or idea for consideration (four are suggested for you). In the center column, write whether the image or idea appeals to your intellect, emotions, or senses. In the third column, write about your response to the image or idea.

Image/Idea	Appeals to	Response
"A Man" "There will be things I cannot do at all,/applaud for example,/at shows where everyone applauds."		
"Conscientious Objector" "I will not tell him/which way the fox ran."		
"The Weary Blues" "In a deep song voice with a melancholy tone"		
"Jazz Fantasia" ". . . the green lanterns calling to the high soft stars . . ."		

© Prentice-Hall, Inc.

Unit 3: Clashing Forces

"Conscientious Objector" by Edna St. Vincent Millay

"A Man" by Nina Cassian

"The Weary Blues" by Langston Hughes

"Jazz Fantasia" by Carl Sandburg

Literary Analysis: Tone

Writers choose words that create a **tone** in order to help us "hear" their poems the way they wish. For example, a hundred-year-old tree could be a "stately giant, silent witness to a century" or a "lightning-slashed hulk, gnarled, nearing the last fall."

As you read, ask yourself questions like these: Why did the poet select this particular word? Would another word do as well? What change would occur in the tone if I changed a word?

DIRECTIONS: In each passage, change the underlined word or words to reflect the shift in tone indicated in the instructions, then rewrite the line.

1. Change the suggested tone from vulnerable to hostile.

   While fighting for his country, he lost an arm and was suddenly <u>afraid</u>.

   _____

   _____

2. Change the suggested tone from brisk to bloodthirsty.

   He is in <u>haste</u>; he has <u>business</u> in Cuba, <u>business</u> in the

   Balkans, many <u>calls</u> to make this morning.

   _____

   _____

3. Change the suggested tone from sluggish to brisk.

   <u>Droning</u> a <u>drowsy</u> syncopated tune,

   _____

   _____

4. Change the suggested tone from dim to bright.

   By the <u>pale</u> <u>dull</u> <u>pallor</u> of an <u>old</u> gas light

   _____

   _____

5. Change the suggested tone from exhaustion to nervousness.

   He slept like a <u>rock</u> or a man that's <u>dead</u>.

   _____

   _____

6. Change the suggested tone from mournful to vibrant.

   <u>sob</u> on the <u>long</u> <u>cool</u> <u>winding</u> saxophones.

   _____

   _____

"Like the Sun" by R. K. Narayan
"Tell all the Truth but tell it slant—" by Emily Dickinson

Build Vocabulary

Spelling Strategy   When writing the adjective forms of most words ending in the letters -ence or -ance, change -ce to -tial. For example, the adjective form of the noun sequence is sequential. The two exceptions to this rule are the words province and finance, whose adjective forms are provincial and financial.

Using the Root -gratis-

In "Like the Sun," Sekhar is treated in an ingratiating way by his headmaster. The root -gratis- comes from a Latin word meaning "pleasing" or "a favor." The word ingratiating—which means "trying to please or bring into favor"—is one of several English words containing a variation of the root -gratis-.

A. DIRECTIONS: The words in the following list are related to the root -gratis-. Read the sentences and fill in each blank with the most appropriate word from the list.

congratulate   gratify   grateful   gratuity

1. Remember to _____ Joyce on her achievements this year.

2. Give the waiter a generous _____ for his skill and hard work in serving us.

3. They are _____ for your assistance and good advice.

4. The movie is so well made it will _____ even the toughest critics.

Using the Word Bank

B. DIRECTIONS: Choose the letter of the word that most closely matches the meaning of the Word Bank word. Write the letters on the lines provided.

_____ 1. incessantly
    a. quickly
    b. hopelessly
    c. endlessly
    d. carelessly

_____ 2. stupefied
    a. stunned
    b. confused
    c. ignorant
    d. old

_____ 3. ingratiating
    a. grateful
    b. bringing into favor
    c. treating with cruelty
    d. helpful

_____ 4. essence
    a. frightening element
    b. courage
    c. crucial element
    d. insignificant element

_____ 5. shirked
    a. neglected
    b. shortened
    c. bullied
    d. assisted

_____ 6. scrutinized
    a. frightened
    b. opened
    c. examined closely
    d. handled carelessly

_____ 7. tempering
    a. melting
    b. adjusting
    c. making someone angry
    d. painting

"Like the Sun" by R. K. Narayan
"Tell all the Truth but tell it slant—" by Emily Dickinson

Build Grammar Skills: Direct and Indirect Objects

A **direct object** is a noun or pronoun that receives the action of a transitive action verb. To find a direct object, ask *Whom?* or *What?* after an action verb. In the following examples, subjects are underlined once, action verbs twice, and direct objects are italicized and labeled.

                                              DO

Examples: The headmaster called *Sekhar* to his office.

An **indirect object** is a noun or pronoun that appears with a direct object and names the person or thing that something is given to or done for. To find an indirect object, check to see if the sentence has a direct object. If so, ask *To or for whom?* or *To or for what?* after the action verb.

                                     IO   **DO**

Examples: The headmaster asked *him* his *opinion.*

Do not confuse an indirect object with an object of a preposition. An indirect object is never preceded by the word *to* or *for.*

A. Practice: In the following sentences, underline the direct objects once and circle the indirect objects. If the sentence has no indirect object, write *no IO* on the line.

_____ 1. No human being can look truth straight in the face without blinking or being dazed.

_____ 2. Dickinson gives readers advice about the need to "dazzle gradually."

_____ 3. Sekhar's wife served him his morning meal.

_____ 4. God hasn't given me a child, but at least let him not deny me the consolation of music.

_____ 5. Sekhar felt the greatest pity for him.

_____ 6. No one would tell me the truth about my music all these days.

B. Writing Application: Write a description of a time when a decision you made had unexpected consequences. Include and label two direct objects and two indirect objects in your description.

_____

_____

_____

_____

_____

_____

_____

_____

_____

"Like the Sun" by R. K. Narayan
"Tell all the Truth but tell it slant—" by Emily Dickinson

Reading Strategy: Analyze Causes and Effects

A **cause-and-effect** sequence is one in which something is caused by one or more events that occurred before it. Identifying causes and effects is a part of daily life. Making decisions based on predicted outcomes, taking safety precautions when traveling, and coming up with solutions to problems show an awareness of cause-and-effect relationships.

Cause-and-effect relationships are also explored in writing. "Like the Sun" provides a perfect example of clear cause-and-effect relationships. As the story begins, Sekhar makes a decision that leads to a series of consequences. Use the following graphic organizer to connect Sekhar's actions and their results.

DIRECTIONS: Complete the organizer by filling in the boxes with the actions that resulted from Sekhar's decision. On the lines that follow, describe two future effects that may have resulted had Sekhar continued to tell the truth. Explain your reasoning.

Cause

> Sekhar decides to tell the truth.

Effect 1

Effect 2

_____

_____

_____

_____

_____

"Like the Sun" by R. K. Narayan
"Tell all the Truth but tell it slant—" by Emily Dickinson

Literary Analysis: Irony

Irony is a literary technique that involves the use of surprising or amusing contradictions. These contradictions often result from differences between what a character believes and what is actually the case, or from differences between what a character expects and what actually happens. There are three types of irony—**verbal irony, dramatic irony,** and **irony of situation.** In **verbal irony,** a statement is made that means one thing but implies something else. In **dramatic irony,** something unknown to the characters in a story or play is known by the reader or audience. In **irony of situation,** something happens that goes against the expectations of certain characters, the reader, or the audience.

DIRECTIONS: Explain what is ironic in each of the following passages from "Like the Sun" and "Tell all the Truth but tell it slant—." Then identify the type of irony in each passage.

"Like the Sun"

1. She asked, "Why, isn't it good?" At other times he would have said, considering her feelings in the matter, "I feel full up, that's all." But today he said, "It isn't good. I'm unable to swallow it."

_____

_____

Type of irony: _____

2. "No. I want it immediately—your frank opinion. Was it good?"
   "No, sir. . ." Sekhar replied.

_____

_____

Type of irony: _____

3. He received a call from the headmaster in his classroom next day. He went up apprehensively. "Your suggestion was useful. I have paid off the music master. No one would tell me the truth about my music all these days."

_____

_____

Type of irony: _____

"Tell all the Truth but tell it slant—"

4. The Truth must dazzle gradually/Or every man be blind—

_____

_____

Type of irony: _____

"Hearts and Hands" by O. Henry
"The Fish" by Elizabeth Bishop

Build Vocabulary

Spelling Strategy   To form the plural of nouns ending in *ch, s, sh, ss,* and *x,* you usually add *-es* to the end of the word. For example, the plural of *influx* is *influxes,* and that of *coach* is *coaches.*

Using the Prefix *counter-*

A. DIRECTIONS: Each of the following words contains the prefix *counter-*, which means "in opposition" or "contrary to." Use each word in a sentence. Be sure the context of the sentence hints at the meaning of the word.

1. counterattack _____

_____

2. counterculture _____

_____

3. countermand _____

_____

4. counterproposal _____

_____

Using the Word Bank

B. DIRECTIONS: Complete each of the following sentences.

1. The passengers are described as an *"influx"* because they are _____

_____ .

2. The glum-faced man *forestalled* Mr. Easton by _____

_____ .

3. *Counterfeiting* is illegal because _____

_____ .

4. The marshal and his prisoner *sidled* down the aisle of the train because _____

_____ .

5. The fish is *venerable* because _____

_____ .

6. The word *infested* used in connection with the white sea-lice indicates that _____

_____ .

7. The fish's *"sullen face"* made the narrator think the fish was _____

_____ .

Hearts and Hands/The Fish   **77**

"Hearts and Hands" by O. Henry
"The Fish" by Elizabeth Bishop

Build Grammar Skills: Compound Predicates

A **compound predicate** consists of two or more verbs or verb phrases that share the same subject in a sentence. The verbs or verb phrases are joined by a conjunction such as *and*, *but*, *or*, or *nor*. In the following example, the parts of the compound predicate are underlined twice and the subject is underlined once.

> The younger man roused himself sharply at the sound of her voice, struggled with a slight embarrassment, and then clasped her fingers with his left hand.

When a compound predicate consists of two or more verb phrases with the same helping verb, the helping verb is often used only with the first verb in order to avoid awkward repetition.

Awkward: When I arrived, the fisherwoman was sitting in her boat, was reeling in her line, and was hauling up the hugest fish I'd ever seen.

Better: When I arrived, the fisherwoman was sitting in her boat, reeling in her line, and hauling up the hugest fish I'd ever seen.

A. Practice: In each sentence, underline the verbs or verb phrases that make up the compound predicate. Circle the conjunction that joins the verbs.

1. Mr. Easton is either leading the glum-faced man through the train or being led by him.

2. The two men passed down the aisle of the coach and seated themselves across from an attractive young woman.

3. You ride and shoot and go into all kinds of dangers.

4. I caught a tremendous fish and held him beside the boat, half out of water, with my hook fast in a corner of his mouth.

5. I admired his sullen face and saw that from his lower lip hung five old pieces of fish-line.

B. Writing Application: Revise each pair of sentences by combining information to form a compound predicate.

1. The men excused themselves. They went to the smoking car.

   _____

2. The young woman looked out the car window. She began speaking truly and simply.

   _____

3. The battered fish was speckled with barnacles. It was infested with tiny white sea-lice.

   _____

4. I stared and stared. Finally I let the fish go.

   _____

"Hearts and Hands" by O. Henry
"The Fish" by Elizabeth Bishop

Reading Strategy: Predict Story Events

As you get to know the characters and the situation in a story, you develop expectations. Based on those expectations, you begin to predict what might happen next, and you begin to anticipate how the characters will probably react to events. Similarly, the thoughts or ideas expressed in the poem might lead you to expect, or predict, how the poet or speaker of the poem will treat the poem's subject. As you read, it is natural to change your predictions based on new information.

DIRECTIONS: Read each of the following sentences or passages. Then predict a probable development or outcome, or make a prediction about the character based on the information in the passage.

1. As they passed down the aisle of the coach, the only vacant seat offered was a reversed one facing the attractive young woman.

   _____

   _____

2. When she spoke her voice, full, sweet, and deliberate, proclaimed that its owner was accustomed to speak and be heard.

   _____

   _____

3. He slightly raised his right hand, bound at the wrist by the shining "bracelet" to the left one of his companion.

   _____

   _____

4. I caught a tremendous fish/and held him beside the boat/half out of the water, with my hook/fast in a corner of his mouth.

   _____

   _____

5. and then I saw/that from his lower lip . . ./hung five old pieces of fish-line, . . ./with all their five big hooks/grown firmly in his mouth.

   _____

   _____

6. I stared and stared/and victory filled up/the little rented boat, . . .

   _____

   _____

Unit 3: Clashing Forces

"Hearts and Hands" by O. Henry

"The Fish" by Elizabeth Bishop

Literary Analysis: Surprise Ending

The endings of "Hearts and Hands" and "The Fish" may be surprises, but the writers didn't just pull them out of thin air. The endings are believable, reasonable developments, even if they aren't exactly what readers expect. Now that you have encountered the surprise endings in "Hearts and Hands" and "The Fish," perhaps you can think of some details or clues that should have made you suspect that the situations were not completely predictable.

A. Identifying Clues

DIRECTIONS: Use the questions that follow to analyze the clues in "Hearts and Hands" and "The Fish."

1. Experienced readers of O. Henry's stories have learned to *expect* an unexpected ending. List three details about Mr. Easton or his actions that indicate that his situation might be different from the way it is represented.

   _____

2. The glum-faced "criminal" who is with Mr. Easton says he is being taken to prison for counterfeiting. Why is this ironic?

   _____

3. In "The Fish," Bishop uses the words *tremendous, venerable, admired, medals,* and *wisdom.* How do these words serve as clues that the speaker might not eat the fish?

   _____

4. What makes the ending of "The Fish" ironic?

   _____

B. Reacting to Surprise Endings

DIRECTIONS: Answer the following questions to increase your understanding of the surprise endings and your reaction to them.

1. How did you *expect* "Hearts and Hands" to end? Explain why.

   _____

2. How did you react as you read the conversation between the two passengers at the end of the story? Why?

   _____

3. Was O. Henry's ending more satisfying or less satisfying than the one you had in mind? Explain your answer.

   _____

4. As you read the last line of "The Fish"—"And I let the fish go."—how did you feel? Explain why.

   _____

from *Desert Exile* by Yoshiko Uchida
"Speech on Japanese American Internment" by Gerald Ford

Build Vocabulary

Spelling Strategy   In the Word Bank word *euphemism*, the letters *ph* spell the sound of *f*. Other spellings of *f* are *ff* (*stuff*) and *gh* (*rough*).

Using the Root *-curs-*

A. Directions: Explain the meaning of the italicized word in each sentence. Keep in mind that the root *-curs-* means "to run." Some English words contain *-cours-*, a variation of *-curs-*.

1. After the race I could feel the blood *coursing* in my veins.

   _____

2. First I printed my name, then frowned, erased, and rewrote it *cursively*.

   _____

Using the Word Bank

cursory	euphemism	adept	destitute
unwieldy	communal	conspicuous	assuage

B. Directions: Rewrite each sentence, replacing the italicized word or words with the appropriate word from the Word Bank.

1. Soon, some people became *highly skilled* at finding ways to make life more bearable.

   _____

2. The Uchida family's friends helped *pacify* their fears and discomforts.

   _____

3. The word "barrack" was a *less offensive word for* "stable," which is where we were to live.

   _____

4. Having been allowed to bring more belongings would have been *hard to manage* given the small quarters.

   _____

5. One *superficial* glance around the mess hall told Yoshiko everything she needed to know.

   _____

6. Living in the stable was *shared by the community*; there was little or no privacy.

   _____

7. The makeshift nature of the camp made it seem as if the internees were *living in poverty*.

   _____

8. The haste with which the camp had been prepared was *easy to see*.

   _____

from *Desert Exile* by Yoshiko Uchida
"Speech on Japanese American Internment" by Gerald Ford

Build Grammar Skills: Compound Subjects

A **compound subject** consists of two or more subjects that share the same verb and are joined by a conjunction such as *and* or *or*. In the following example, the parts of the compound subject are underlined once and the verb is underlined twice.

My <u>family</u> and the other new <u>arrivals</u> <u>stepped</u> off the bus.

A. Practice: In each sentence, underline the words that make up the compound subject. Circle the conjunction that joins the subjects.

1. Dust, dirt, and wood shavings covered the linoleum that had been laid over manure-covered boards.

2. Canned sausages, boiled potatoes, and butterless bread made up our first meal.

3. An elderly man and a young family with two crying babies shared our table.

4. My sister and I worried about Mama, for she wasn't strong and had recently been troubled with neuralgia, which could easily be aggravated by the cold.

5. Our blankets, pillows, sheets, tea kettle, and most welcome of all, our electric hot plate helped us to feel more at home.

6. Mama and Kay made up the army cots with our bedding.

7. Twenty-five stalls facing north and an equal number facing south comprised our stable.

8. An artist, my father's barber and his wife, a dentist and his wife, an elderly retired couple, a group of Kibei bachelors, an insurance salesman and his wife, and a widow with two daughters lived in our stable.

B. Writing Application: Revise each pair of sentences by combining information to form a compound subject.

1. Our neighbors argued with their teenage son. Our teenage neighbor argued with his parents.

_____

2. Shelves and a crude table filled our makeshift living room. Two benches filled it, too.

_____

3. The evacuation of Japanese Americans during World War II was an unfortunate and historically embarrassing error. Their subsequent neglect was also unfortunate and embarrassing.

_____

4. The contributions made by Japanese Americans helped ensure the well-being of our common nation. The sacrifices made by Japanese Americans helped ensure the well-being of our common nation.

_____

from *Desert Exile* by Yoshiko Uchida
"Speech on Japanese American Internment" by Gerald Ford

Reading Strategy: Background Knowledge

You may or may not know much about Japanese internment camps, but you do know about people's need for privacy. That bit of knowledge will help you understand the feelings Uchida expresses about living *without* privacy. Using background knowledge will help you get more out of what you read.

A. Putting Events in Context

When you read a nonfiction account of an historical event, you can use your background knowledge to place the event in *context*. This means considering the time and place of the event's occurrence. For example, the excerpts from both *Desert Exile* and Gerald Ford's speech fit into the context of World War II. Almost anything you know about World War II will help you relate to and more fully understand these selections.

DIRECTIONS: Being aware of what you know and what you don't know is the first step. Before you read the two selections, answer these questions. Following the questions is some additional background for the selections. Read the background, and then read the selections.

1. What do you know about what was going on in the world in 1942?

_____

2. What was going on in the United States in 1942?

_____

Additional Background

On December 8, 1941, the day after a devastating Japanese attack on Pearl Harbor, the United States Congress declared war on Japan. A month after the attack on Pearl Harbor, the American government, fearing that Japanese Americans would aid Japan, made plans to move all Americans of Japanese descent, even full U.S. citizens, from their West Coast homes to temporary inland sites. Executive Order 9066 effectively suspended the civil liberties of Japanese Americans by means of relocation and internment.

B. After You Read

DIRECTIONS: Answer the following questions about the excerpts from *Desert Exile* and Gerald Ford's speech based on the prior knowledge you had or the knowledge you gained from the background information on this page.

1. How did knowing that the United States was at war with Japan affect your attitude toward the internment of Japanese Americans?

_____

2. How did knowing that U.S. citizens had no choice but to leave their homes affect your reading of Uchida's account?

_____

3. How do your own experiences of eating in the school cafeteria help you relate to Uchida's description of the main mess hall?

_____

Name _____ Date _____

from *Desert Exile* by Yoshiko Uchida
"Speech on Japanese American Internment" by Gerald Ford

Literary Analysis: Writer's Purpose

Whenever an author writes, he or she has a purpose. Yoshiko Uchida writes to tell the story of her own experience as a Japanese American internee during World War II. Gerald Ford is performing an official governmental act. His formal words and language were to become a historical document. To convey his or her purpose, an author may include specific details—a moving or humorous description, or moving or persuasive passages, for example. Recognizing the importance of certain language and details will help you to understand an author's purpose.

DIRECTIONS: Identify Uchida's or Ford's purpose for including the details in the following passages.

from *Desert Exile*

1. It had rained the day before, and the hundreds of people who had trampled on the track had turned it into a miserable mass of slippery mud.

   _____
   _____

2. The stall was about ten by twenty feet and empty except for three folded army cots lying on the floor.

   _____
   _____

3. I wrote to my non-Japanese friends in Berkeley shamelessly asking them to send us food, and they obliged with large cartons of cookies, nuts, dried fruit, and jams.

   _____
   _____

4. The wonderful news had come like an unexpected gift, but even as we hugged each other in joy, we didn't quite dare believe it until we actually saw him.

   _____
   _____

from Gerald Ford's speech, February 19, 1976

5. It was on that date in 1942 that Executive Order 9066 was issued resulting in the uprooting of many, many loyal Americans.

   _____
   _____

6. The proclamation [4417] that I am signing here today should remove all doubt on that matter.

   _____
   _____

"The Cabuliwallah" by Rabindranath Tagore

Build Vocabulary

Spelling Strategy   The *j* sound in *judicious* can be produced by a number of different spellings: *g* (gem), *dg* (fudge), *di* (soldier), and *du* (gradual).

Using the Root *-jud-*

The word root *-jud-* means "judge." Knowing this can help you see how *-jud-* is related to the meaning of the Word Bank word *judicious*— "showing good judgment or common sense."

A. DIRECTIONS: Define the italicized word in each sentence by using context clues. Remember that the root *-jud-* means "judge."

1. The three branches of government include executive, legislative, and *judicial*.

   _____

2. Even as he aged, his *judgment* remained sound and fair.

   _____

3. Gina's habit of *prejudging* people severely limited her ability to form friendships.

   _____

4. The speaker challenged the audience to live their lives without *prejudice* toward others.

   _____

Using the Word Bank

B. DIRECTIONS: Follow each set of directions.

1. Write a sentence describing an event in the story, using the word *impending*.

   _____

2. Describing the Cabuliwallah's position in Indian society, using the word *precarious*.

   _____

3. Write a sentence describing Mini's father, using the word *judicious*.

   _____

4. Write a sentence about the phrase "father-in-law's house" using the word *euphemism*.

   _____

5. Use the word *imploring* in a sentence about a dialogue between Mini's mother and father.

   _____

6. Write a sentence about the Cabuliwallah's arrest, using the word *fettered*.

   _____

7. Write a sentence describing Calcutta's streets, using the word *sordid*.

   _____

8. Write a sentence about Mini's wedding day, using the word *pervaded*.

   _____

Unit 3: Clashing Forces

"**The Cabuliwallah**" by Rabindranath Tagore

Build Grammar Skills: Predicate Nominatives and Predicate Adjectives

A **predicate nominative** is a noun or pronoun that appears with a linking verb and re-names, identifies, or explains the subject of a sentence. A subject and a predicate nominative are two different words for the same person, place, or thing. In the following example, the sub-ject and predicate nominative are underlined and labeled, and the linking verb is underlined twice.

                                S   PN

Example: The <u>Cabuliwallah</u> in this story <u>is</u> a <u>salesman</u> from Cabul.

A **predicate adjective** is an adjective that appears with a linking verb and describes the subject of the sentence. In the following example, you can see that the linking verb joins the subject to a word that describes the subject. This descriptive word is a predicate adjective.

                                S   PA

Example: The <u>position</u> of Tagore's hero <u>was</u> <u>precarious</u>.

A. Practice: Underline and label the predicate nominatives or predicate adjectives in each sentence.

1. Tagore's conversations with Mini are always lively.

2. The Cabuliwallah was a patient listener, equaled only by Mini's own father.

3. The two were now great friends, with many quaint jokes which afforded them a great deal of amusement.

4. The words "father-in-law" are a euphemism for jail, the place where we are well cared for at no expense.

5. Unfortunately, Mini's mother is a very timid and fearful lady.

6. Her suspicions were unfounded; it did not seem right to forbid the man to come to the house.

B. Writing Application: Revise each sentence below so that it has a predicate nominative or a predicate adjective.

    Example: Mini had a delightful conversation with the Cabuliwallah.
    Answer: Mini's conversation with the Cabuliwallah was delightful.

1. His bribe consisted of almonds and raisins.

    _____

2. The tall loose-garmented man seemed to be an amusing friend.

    _____

3. To Tangore's wife, the Cabuliwallah's friendship with her daughter had a suspicious quality.

    _____

4. He had a joyful reunion with his only child.

    _____

"The Cabuliwallah" by Rabindranath Tagore

Reading Strategy: Engage Your Senses

Sensory details tell what can be seen, heard, tasted, felt, or smelled. By using details that engage readers' senses, a writer draws his or her readers into the story—much as Tagore does by using sensory details to create a rich setting and vivid characters. For example, instead of merely stating, "Mini laughed," Tagore appeals to your senses of sight and sound by writing, "Mini would ripple her face with laughter and begin 'O Cabuliwallah! Cabuliwallah! What have you got in your bag?'"

A. DIRECTIONS: Complete the following chart by listing details of sight, sound, taste, touch, and smell that help evoke an image of each character.

	Sight	**Sound**	**Taste**	**Touch**	**Smell**
Mini					
Rahmun the Cabuliwallah					
Mini's father					

B. DIRECTIONS: Summarize in one or two sentences your impression of each character, based upon the sensory details you have identified.

1. Mini: _____

_____

2. Rahmùn the Cabuliwallah:_____

_____

3. Mini's father: _____

_____

"The Cabuliwallah" by Rabindranath Tagore

Literary Analysis: Relationships Between Characters

In a short story, you can learn many things about a character by what he or she says and does. A character's relationship with another character, however, can be even more revealing because relationships never stay the same. As interactions and feelings pass between characters, their relationships change, grow, stagnate, and sometimes end. Tagore's short story explores three different relationships: the relationship between Mini and her father, Mini and the Cabuliwallah, and Mini's father and the Cabuliwallah.

DIRECTIONS: Answer each of the following questions.

1. How would you describe the relationship between Mini and her father at the beginning of the story? What details support your description?

_____

_____

_____

2. Why do Mini and the Cabuliwallah develop such a close relationship?

_____

_____

_____

3. How does Mini react to the Cabuliwallah when he returns on her wedding day? What does their interaction reveal about the changes in their relationship?

_____

_____

_____

4. How would you describe the relationship between Mini's father and the Cabuliwallah before his arrest?

_____

_____

_____

5. How does the relationship between Mini's father and the Cabuliwallah change on Mini's wedding day? What causes this change?

_____

_____

_____

6. Do you think the changes in the relationships between Mini, Mini's father, and the Cabuliwallah were caused by personality changes or maturity and experience? Explain your answer.

_____

_____

_____

from *Speak, Memory* by Vladimir Nabokov

Build Vocabulary

Spelling Strategy   The sound *shun* in a suffix is usually spelled *sion, tion,* or *ssion.* For example, *ssion* in the word *procession* is pronounced as *shun.*

Using the Prefix *pro-*

The prefix *pro-* means "before in place or time," or "moving forward." For example, the Word Bank word *procession* is formed from the Latin word *procedere,* with *pro-* meaning "forward" and *cedere* meaning "to go."

A. DIRECTIONS: Using what you know about the prefix *pro-*, determine the meanings of the following words. In some form, use the word *forward* in your definitions.

1. proclamation _____

2. procrastinate _____

3. proffer _____

Using the Word Bank

B. DIRECTIONS: Replace each italicized word or group of words with a word from the Word Bank. Rewrite the sentence in the space provided.

1. Nabokov cannot remember the *clear, transparent* beauty of his mother's ruby and diamond ring without recalling the émigré life for which it later paid.

   _____

   _____

2. Nabokov organizes and presents his memories in a *formal, orderly way,* as if they were dutiful toy soldiers, marching forward in his imagination.

   _____

   _____

3. Nabokov's favorite book characters involve themselves in *difficult* yet admirable tasks, such as damsel rescues and solo airship flights.

   _____

   _____

4. Nabokov fondly recalls how his mother would slow and lower her voice, *ominously* creeping up on a story's dramatic moment.

   _____

   _____

5. At a young age, Nabokov exhibited *expertise* with language.

   _____

   _____

from *Speak, Memory* by Vladimir Nabokov

Build Grammar Skills: Clauses

A **clause** is a group of words with its own subject and verb. There are two basic kinds of clauses: the *independent* clause and the *subordinate* clause. An independent clause can stand by itself as a complete sentence. It can also be used with another independent clause or with a subordinate clause.

Standing Alone	**With Another Independent Clause**	**With a Subordinate Clause**
Nabokov wrote an autobiography.	His narrative recalls childhood memories, *and he describes them fondly.*	Some critics have said *that Nabokov treated words like butterflies.*

A subordinate clause cannot stand by itself as a complete sentence; it can only be part of a sentence. It can appear before, after, or in the middle of an independent clause.

Before an Independent Clause	**In the Middle of an Independent Clause**	**After an Independent Clause**
By the time he was fifteen years old, he had published a volume of verse.	Nabokov, *who wrote in both Russian and English,* treated words like butterflies.	Nabokov learned to read English *before he could read Russian.*

Subordinate clauses can function as adjectives, adverbs, and nouns in sentences.

A. Practice: In the following sentences, underline subordinate clauses once and independent clauses twice.

1. Although it all remained rather stiff and patchy, my imagination somehow managed to obtain the necessary data.

2. The schoolroom was drenched with sunlight.

3. I was thrilled by the thought that some day I might attain such proficiency.

4. The happy days when they would be cleaning streets and digging canals for the State were still beyond the horizon.

5. A rude jack-in-the-box shoots out, and that picture I heartily disliked.

B. Writing Application: Answer the following questions, using independent and subordinate clauses as indicated in parentheses.

1. How old was Nabokov when his family was forced to leave Russia? (independent followed by subordinate) _____

_____

2. What would Nabokov's mother do with Nabokov in the drawing room of their country cottage? (subordinate followed by independent) _____

_____

3. How would Nabokov's mother read a particularly dramatic passage? (independent with another independent)

_____

from *Speak, Memory* by Vladimir Nabokov

Reading Strategy: Author's Purpose

The **author's purpose** is his or her reason for writing, such as to inform, to entertain, or to persuade. In *Speak, Memory*, Nabokov has a dual purpose—to preserve treasured childhood memories and to inform you about the pleasure and satisfaction he took in learning to read. As with many writers, Nabokov's point of view is influenced by his experience. For example, Nabokov's privileged upbringing clearly influenced his attitude toward the Russian Revolution. Understanding the background of an author can help you better understand his or her perspective and purpose for writing.

DIRECTIONS: Following are some passages from *Speak, Memory*. Read each passage. Then, explain Nabokov's purpose for including that information. Point out any details that reflect Nabokov's privileged upbringing.

1. Ned lumbered past the window in a fair impersonation of the gardener's mate Ivan. . . . On later pages longer words appeared; and at the very end of the brown, inkstained volume, a real, sensible story unfolded its adult sentences . . . the little reader's ultimate triumph and reward. I was thrilled by the thought that some day I might attain such proficiency. The magic has endured, and whenever a grammar book comes my way, I instantly turn to the last page to enjoy a forbidden glimpse of the laborious student's future, of that promised land where, at last, words are meant to mean what they mean.

   _____

   _____

   _____

2. In the drawing room of our country house, before going to bed, I would often be read to in English by my mother. As she came to a particularly dramatic passage, where the hero was about to encounter some strange, perhaps fatal danger, her voice would slow down, her words would be spaced portentously, and before turning the page she would place upon it her hand, with its familiar pigeon-blood ruby and diamond ring. . . .

   _____

   _____

   _____

3. There were tales about knights whose terrific but wonderfully aseptic wounds were bathed by damsels in grottoes. From a windswept clifftop, a medieval maiden with flying hair and a youth in hose gazed at the round Isles of the Blessed. In "Misunderstood," the fate of Humphrey used to bring a more specialized lump to one's throat than anything in Dickens or Daudet (great devisers of lumps), while a shamelessly allegorical story, "Beyond the Blue Mountains," dealing with two pairs of little travelers—good Clover and Cowslip, bad Buttercup and Daisy—contained enough exciting details to make one forget its "message."

   _____

   _____

   _____

   _____

Name _____ Date _____

from *Speak, Memory* by Vladimir Nabokov

Literary Analysis: Personal Narrative

A **personal narrative** is a true story about a memorable person, event, or situation in a writer's life. Such a narrative is written from the first-person point of view. This episode from *Speak, Memory* is a personal narrative in which Nabokov recalls his childhood reading experiences and, in so doing, reveals what those experiences meant to him. With precise descriptions, figurative language, and sensory details, Nabokov brings his past alive for the reader as well. For example, Nabokov could have flatly said that money from the sale of his mother's ruby ring paid for years of émigré life. Instead, Nabokov creates the metaphor of the ring as a crystal ball (with himself as the crystal gazer), making the reader *see* the ring and the future it holds for Nabokov and his family.

> . . . and before turning the page she would place upon it her hand, with its familiar pigeon-blood ruby and diamond ring (within the limpid facets of which, had I been a better crystal-gazer, I might have seen a room, people, lights, trees in the rain—a whole period of émigré life for which that ring was to pay).

DIRECTIONS: Read each of the following passages from *Speak, Memory*, and then answer each question.

> The kind of Russian family to which I belonged—a kind now extinct—had, among other virtues, a traditional leaning toward the comfortable products of Anglo-Saxon civilization.

1. What two elements indicate that this sentence belongs to a personal narrative?

   _____

2. To what kind of family does Nabokov belong? What key words or phrases emphasize the description?

   _____

> The schoolroom was drenched with sunlight. In a sweating glass jar, several spiny caterpillars were feeding on nettle leaves (and ejecting interesting, barrel-shaped pellets of olive-green grass). The oilcloth that covered the round table smelled of glue. Miss Clayton smelled of Miss Clayton. Fantastically, gloriously, the blood-colored alcohol of the outside thermometer had risen to 24° Réaumur (86° Fahrenheit) in the shade. . . . Golden orioles in the greenery emitted their four brilliant notes: dee-del-dee-O!

3. What senses does Nabokov engage in the reader with his description of the schoolroom?

   _____

4. What do you think those days in the schoolroom mean to Nabokov? How does Nabokov's use of sensory details help you to draw your conclusion?

   _____

> And, yes—the airship. Yards and yards of yellow silk went to make it, and an additional tiny balloon was provided for the sole use of the fortunate Midget. At the immense altitude to which the ship reached, the aeronauts huddled together for warmth while the lost little soloist, still the object of my intense envy notwithstanding his plight, drifted into an abyss of frost and stars—alone.

5. Why do you think Nabokov responds with envy and empathy to Midget's plight?

   _____

"Games at Twilight" by Anita Desai

Build Vocabulary

Spelling Strategy   The suffix -*ious* is pronounced "e-us" and means "having or characterized by." Words ending in -*ious*—such as *supercilious*—are adjectives. You can distinguish between -*ious* and -*ous* words by pronunciation. However, it is difficult to know whether a word is spelled -*ious* or -*eous*. These words will have to be memorized.

Using the Prefix *super-*

A. DIRECTIONS: The prefix *super-* means "over," "above," or "on top of." Complete each sentence with the one of the following *super-* words.

   supervise   superb   superficial

1. Manu stumbled over the hosepipe and fell, but his wounds were only _____.

2. Ravi's older brother Raghu is a _____ football player.

3. When the children began to bicker, motherly Mira stepped in to _____ their games.

Using the Word Bank

B. DIRECTIONS: In the blank, write the letter of the definition next to the word it defines.

_____ 1. superciliously   a. no longer living

_____ 2. dogged   b. move sideways

_____ 3. sidle   c. persistent; stubborn

_____ 4. defunct   d. disdainfully; contemptuously

Using Synonyms

C. DIRECTIONS: In the blank, write the letter of the word that is most similar in meaning to the word from the Word Bank.

_____ 1. dogged
   a. exhausted
   b. controlling
   c. unyielding
   d. submissive

_____ 2. defunct
   a. useless
   b. expired
   c. thriving
   d. empty

_____ 3. superciliously
   a. arrogantly
   b. respectfully
   c. angrily
   d. passionately

_____ 4. sidle
   a. move back
   b. move sideways
   c. slip
   d. stumble

Unit 4: Turning Points

"Games at Twilight" by Anita Desai

Build Grammar Skills: Subordination

Writers use **subordination** when they connect unequal but related ideas in a complex sentence. The subordinate (less important) idea limits, develops, describes, or adds meaning to the main idea. In the following sentence from the story, italics indicate a related but unequal idea.

There was no one to hear *when he called out.*

The subordinating conjunction *when* introduces the less important idea. Other subordinating conjunctions include *because, while, though, after, if,* and *than* and relative pronouns like *who, which,* and *that.*

A. Practice: Underline the subordinate clause in each sentence. Then, write an explanation of why the idea in the subordinate clause is less important than the idea in the main clause.

1. Only small Manu suddenly reappeared, as if he had dropped out of an invisible cloud.

   _____

2. Raghu charged after him with such a bloodcurdling yell that Manu stumbled over the hosepipe.

   _____

3. The garage was locked with a great heavy lock to which the driver had the key in his room.

   _____

4. The shed wasn't opened more than once a year when Ma turned out all the old broken bits of furniture and rolls of matting, and leaking buckets.

   _____

B. Writing Application: Combine each set of sentences below to create a new sentence. Include a subordinate clause in your sentence.

1. Ravi sat dejectedly on the flower pot. The flower pot was cut to his own size.

   _____

2. Ravi felt as if he could reach up and touch the roof with his finger tips. Ravi felt this way even though he was small.

   _____

3. The parents would sit out on the lawn on cane basket chairs and watch the children. The children would tear around the garden.

   _____

4. It then occurred to him. He could have slipped out long ago, dashed across the yard to the veranda and touched the "den."

   _____

"Games at Twilight" by Anita Desai

Reading Strategy: Evaluate a Character's Decision

As a reader, you can **evaluate a character's decision** to better understand the character and his or her motives. When you evaluate a character's decision, you look at the problem or situation that demanded a decision. Then, you try to figure out what motivated the character to act the way he or she did. For example, you might ask why Ravi is so determined to win the game of hide-and-seek in "Games at Twilight." Does the narrator of the story give reasons, or do you have to infer them from the story? You might also ask why Ravi remained in the shed for so long. Was he too young to estimate how much time had passed? Next, you look at the decision the character made and the consequences of that decision. You also consider other choices the character could have made. Finally, you judge whether the character's decision was the best one he or she could have made.

DIRECTIONS: Answer the following questions to evaluate Ravi's decisions in "Games at Twilight."

1. What reasons are given in the story for Ravi's wanting to win so badly?

_____

_____

_____

2. What are his options? What are the pros and cons of each option?

_____

_____

_____

3. What option does Ravi choose? Is his choice effective?

_____

_____

_____

4. What are the ultimate consequences of Ravi's decision?

_____

_____

_____

5. Do you think Ravi made the right choice? What might he have done differently?

_____

_____

_____

"Games at Twilight" by Anita Desai

Literary Analysis: Motivation

The reason for a character's actions or words is called **motivation.** Understanding why characters act as they do will help you make sense of story events. For instance, in "Games at Twilight," Ravi sits alone in a dusty, dark, and scary shed for a long time. If you consider that Ravi wants to show the older children that he can outsmart them, you can better understand his behavior. As you read, use the following chart to explore the reasons for Ravi's actions.

DIRECTIONS: Listed in the left-hand column of the chart are some of Ravi's actions. Complete the chart by writing possible motivations for each action in the column labeled Motivation.

Action	Motivation
Ravi slips off the flower pot and into the shed.	
Ravi considers leaving the shed and half-rises from the bathtub.	
Ravi decides to hold out a bit longer and remains in the shed.	
Ravi charges at the other children, crying, "I won, I won, I won!"	

"The Bridge" by Leopold Staff
"The Old Stoic" by Emily Brontë
"I Am Not One of Those Who Left the Land" by Anna Akhmatova
"Speech During the Invasion of Constantinople" by Empress Theodora

Build Vocabulary

Spelling Strategy   The suffix -ous is pronounced "us" and means "full of," "by the nature of," or "having the quality of." Words ending in -ous are always adjectives, such as *timorous*.

Using the Root *-dom-*

The Word Bank word *indomitable* comes from the Latin root *-dom-*, meaning "to rule." In English, the root suggests control, power, or mastery.

A. DIRECTIONS: Use your knowledge of the root *-dom-*, your knowledge of English, and a dictionary to answer the following questions.

1. How is the meaning of *dominate* different from the meaning of *dominance*?

   _____

2. How is the meaning of *domineering* different from the meaning of *dominant*?

   _____

Using the Word Bank

B. DIRECTIONS: Write your response to the following items in the space provided.

1. When Brontë feels the need to *implore* in her poem, what is she doing?

   _____

2. Describe Emperor Justinian's *timorous* advisers.

   _____

3. Why was Empress Theodora *indomitable*?

   _____

Using Synonyms

C. DIRECTIONS: Circle the word most similar in meaning to the Word Bank word.

1. implore
   a. contemplate
   b. believe
   c. discover
   d. appeal

2. timorous
   a. apprehensive
   b. noisy
   c. prompt
   d. foreign

3. indomitable
   a. certain
   b. unvarying
   c. unconquerable
   d. faultless

Unit 4: Turning Points

"The Bridge" by Leopold Staff
"The Old Stoic" by Emily Brontë
"I Am Not One of Those Who Left the Land" by Anna Akhmatova
"Speech During the Invasion of Constantinople" by Empress Theodora

Build Grammar Skills: Adjective Clauses

An **adjective clause** is a subordinate clause that modifies a noun or pronoun by telling *what kind* or *which one*. Most adjective clauses begin with relative pronouns: *that, which, who, whom,* and *whose*. Often, *that, who,* and *whom* are understood—not written or spoken—as in this example:

The Brontë sisters are three women [whom] I would have liked to meet.

A. Practice: In each sentence, underline the adjective clause and circle the word it modifies.

1. I didn't believe, standing on the bank of a river which was wide and swift, that I would cross that bridge.

2. Lust of fame was but a dream that vanished with the morn.

3. And if I pray, the only prayer that moves my lips for me is, "Leave the heart that I now bear, and give me liberty!"

4. I am not one of those who left the land to the mercy of its enemies.

5. The present occasion is too serious to allow me to follow the convention that a woman should not speak in a man's council.

6. May I never see the day when those who meet me do not call me empress.

B. Writing Application: Combine each of the following pairs of sentences to make a single sentence that includes an adjective clause. Use the relative pronoun in parentheses, and add commas where necessary.

1. Leopold Staff kept true to the themes of history and nature despite the times in which he lived. He loved the quiet moments of life. (who)

   _____

   _____

2. *Wuthering Heights* was a classic story of love and revenge. Emily Brontë published it at age twenty. (which)

   _____

   _____

3. Anna Akhmatova published her first poetry at the age of seventeen. She survived the most tumultuous events of modern times. (who)

   _____

   _____

4. Empress Theodora delivered a brief speech. It convinced her husband to defend their palace in Constantinople, rather than try to escape. (that)

   _____

   _____

"The Bridge" by Leopold Staff
"The Old Stoic" by Emily Brontë
"I Am Not One of Those Who Left the Land" by Anna Akhmatova
"Speech During the Invasion of Constantinople" by Empress Theodora

Reading Strategy: Author's Perspective

In fine art, perspective is a way of arranging lines so that they appear to the eye as they do in reality. In literature, the author also arranges lines so that they portray a reality. The lines the author uses, of course, are words, but the idea is the same. The view presented depends on the **perspective** of the author, just as an artist draws a picture from a particular place.

Authors reveal their perspective in details. Sometimes these details are clear statements of attitudes, as in Brontë's poem, or sometimes subtle descriptions. It might seem odd to describe a conflagration, or fire, as "murky," until you consider smoke rising from smoldering villages as Anna Akhmatova sees it.

DIRECTIONS: Use the following chart to help you analyze the author's perspective. Choose one of the poems, and under the "Line" heading, copy a detail or line from the poem. Under the "Perspective" heading, describe what that line tells you about the author's perspective.

Line	Perspective
_____	_____
_____	_____
_____	_____
Line	**Perspective**
_____	_____
_____	_____
_____	_____
Line	**Perspective**
_____	_____
_____	_____
_____	_____
Line	**Perspective**
_____	_____
_____	_____
_____	_____

© Prentice-Hall, Inc.

Unit 4: Turning Points

"The Bridge" by Leopold Staff
"The Old Stoic" by Emily Brontë
"I Am Not One of Those Who Left the Land" by Anna Akhmatova
"Speech During the Invasion of Constantinople" by Empress Theodora

Literary Analysis: Dramatic Situation

Circumstances and conflicts provide the ground from which a writer's material grows. Writers respond to the particular world around them, just as you do. In some instances, as in Empress Theodora's case, the situation is dramatic and easily grasped. Her life is in danger. Should she stay or flee? Some **dramatic situations** may be less obvious, or may take place in the mind and heart. Emily Brontë cares passionately about how she wants to live, and expresses her thoughts in her poem. Leopold Staff writes of the difficulty of doing—or even under-standing—what he must do.

A dramatic situation often calls for a choice. As you read each selection, consider what choices are available to the speaker. What evidence in the work do you see of a dramatic situation? What choice is finally made?

DIRECTIONS: Use these graphic organizers to consider dramatic situations and choices in one or more of the poems. In the first column, write what you think is the dramatic situation to which the speaker must respond. In the second column, note words, images, or ideas that show what that situation is. In the third column, list the choices that you think could be made in that situation. In the last column, write the choice made by the speaker.

Title of Poem:

Dramatic Situation	Evidence of Situation	Choices Available	Choice Made

Title of Poem:

Dramatic Situation	Evidence of Situation	Choices Available	Choice Made

Name _____ Date _____

"The Good Deed" by Pearl S. Buck

Build Vocabulary

Spelling Strategy   For words ending in two consonants, keep both consonants when adding a suffix starting with either a vowel or a consonant. For example, when the suffix -ed is added to the words *repress* and *abash*, the Word Bank words *repressed* and *abashed* are formed.

Using the Root -*pel*-

The character of Lili Yang is able to communicate with Mrs. Pan because she was *compelled* by her parents to learn Chinese, her family's native language. The verb *compel* contains the root -*pel*-, which means "drive" or "push," so *compel* means "force or drive to do something."

A. Directions: Read the following sentences and fill in each blank with the most appropriate word from the list.

propel   repellent   impel

1. Her powerful speech should _____ people to take action.

2. Ivan asked the teacher, "What type of fuel is used to _____ a rocket"?

3. The strong scent of that candle is an effective insect _____.

Using the Word Bank

B. Directions: In the blank, write the Word Bank word that would best replace the italicized word or phrase.

1. Scholars *deeply respect* the writings of that philosopher. _____

2. Ken walked away with an *embarrassed* look on his face. _____

3. I *restrained* my urge to laugh out loud. _____

4. The new laws *force* all residents to recycle bottles and cans. _____

5. She reacted *angrily* to their ungratefulness. _____

C. Directions: Each question below consists of a word in CAPITAL LETTERS followed by four lettered words and phrases. In the blank, write the letter of the word or phrase that is most nearly opposite in meaning to the word in capital letters. Because some of the choices are close in meaning, consider all the choices before deciding which is best.

____ 1. CONTEMPLATIVELY: ____ 2. ASSAIL: ____ 3. REVERE:
   a. mistakenly   a. attack   a. disrespect
   b. rudely   b. protect   b. admire
   c. quickly   c. assist   c. anger
   d. thoughtlessly   d. correct   d. enjoy

"The Good Deed" by Pearl S. Buck

Build Grammar Skills: Adverb Clauses

A subordinate clause is a group of words that contains a subject and a verb but cannot stand by itself as a complete sentence. An **adverb clause** is a type of subordinate clause that modifies a verb, an adjective, or an adverb and is introduced by a subordinating conjunction such as *when, whenever, where, wherever, because, since, if, as,* or *why*. Adverb clauses make sentences clearer and more specific by explaining where, when, why, how, to what extent, or under what conditions actions occur. Review the following sentences from "The Good Deed".

main clause   adverb clause
Here in America the children are not taught <u>as we were in China</u>.

main clause   adverb clause
Nevertheless, she thought over what he had said <u>when she went back to the window</u>.

A. Practice: In each of the following sentences, underline the adverb clause and circle the word it modifies.

1. Mrs. Pan missed China because it was her birthplace and home.

2. She felt homesick whenever she thought of China's beauty and traditions.

3. Mrs. Pan's son worried since his mother seemed so unhappy.

4. Lili Yang, a family friend, impressed Mrs. Pan when she spoke Chinese and took an interest in China.

5. Mrs. Pan liked Lili as soon as she met her.

B. Writing Application: Rewrite each of the following sentences, adding one or more adverb clauses to make each sentence more specific and informative.

1. Mr. Pan moved his mother to America.

_____

_____

2. Mrs. Pan observed her grandchildren.

_____

_____

3. Mrs. Pan took a special interest in Lili Yang.

_____

_____

4. Lili spoke Chinese.

_____

_____

5. Mrs. Pan visited Mr. Lim.

_____

_____

"The Good Deed" by Pearl S. Buck

Reading Strategy: Draw Inferences

In real life, people do not always state directly their beliefs or their feelings. By observing the words, actions, and interactions of people, we can then **draw inferences** based on these observations. When you read a story, you should use this same technique to gain a better understanding of fictional characters. Writers do not always state directly the feelings or beliefs of their characters, but they provide details about the words, actions, and thoughts of their characters. As a reader you should carefully observe these details and use them to draw inferences about characters.

DIRECTIONS: As you read, use the following chart to record details that help you to draw inferences about characters.

Character's Actions	Character's Words	Inference
Young Mrs. Pan treats old Mrs. Pan with kindness.		Young Mrs. Pan respects old Mrs. Pan and feels compassion for her.
	"How is it . . . that the children do not . . . obey?"	Old Mrs. Pan is concerned about her grandchildren.

Name _____ Date _____

"**The Good Deed**" by Pearl S. Buck

Literary Analysis: Static and Dynamic Characters

Most people change and grow as a result of their choices and experiences. In fiction, a **dynamic character** is one who changes during the course of a story, while a static character is one who does not change at all. Details of a character's thoughts, words, and actions indicate whether or not a character experiences change during the course of a literary work.

DIRECTIONS: In "The Good Deed," the character of Old Mrs. Pan is a good example of a dynamic character. Use the following chart to record details that show how she changes during the course of the story.

Old Mrs. Pan as a Dynamic Character

Attitude at the beginning of the story	
Specific details showing this attitude	
Actions that indicate a change	
Attitude at the end of the story	
Specific details showing this attitude	

"Thoughts of Hanoi" by Nguyen Thi Vinh
"Pride" by Dahlia Ravikovitch
"Auto Wreck" by Karl Shapiro
"Before the Law" by Franz Kafka

Build Vocabulary

Spelling Strategy   The prefix *in-*, meaning either "not" or "into," changes form when attached to words that start with certain letters. It becomes *il-* before *l* *(illegible)*; *im-* before *b*, *m*, or *p* *(imbalance, immature, importunity)*; and *ir-* before *r* *(irregular)*. The prefix remains *in-* before words that start with all other letters, as in *inappropriate* and *insatiable*.

Using the Root *-sat-*

The root *-sat-* comes from a Latin word that means "full" or "enough." The root in English has come to mean "completely" or "completely full."

A. DIRECTIONS: Apply what you know about the root *-sat-* to define these words.

1. sate _____

2. satisfaction _____

3. unsatisfactory _____

Using the Word Bank

B. DIRECTIONS: In the blank, write the letter of the definition next to the word it defines.

____ 1. importunity   a. cannot be satisfied; constantly wanting more

____ 2. contemplation   b. unsettled

____ 3. insatiable   c. dull or stale because of overuse

____ 4. deranged   d. persistence in requesting or demanding

____ 5. convalescents   e. convenient

____ 6. banal   f. people who are recovering from illness

____ 7. expedient   g. thoughtful inspection; study

Using Verbal Analogies

C. DIRECTIONS: Each question consists of a related pair of words in CAPITAL LETTERS, followed by four lettered pairs of words. Choose the lettered pair that best expresses a relationship similar to that expressed in the pair in capital letters. In the blank, write the letter of your choice.

____ 1. BANAL : EXCITING ::   ____ 2. EXPEDIENT : SUITABLE ::
     a. tired : weak   a. warped : straight
     b. familiar : new   b. matched : paired
     c. old : young   c. timely : late
     d. cold : warm   d. ill-advised : inappropriate

Unit 4: Turning Points

"Thoughts of Hanoi" by Nguyen Thi Vinh
"Pride" by Dahlia Ravikovitch
"Auto Wreck" by Karl Shapiro
"Before the Law" by Franz Kafka

Build Grammar Skills: Noun Clauses

A **noun clause** is a subordinate clause that is used as a noun in a sentence. It can function as a subject, predicate noun, direct object, indirect object, or object of a preposition. The following examples show noun clauses with different functions.

Subject: *Whoever is going to shatter them* hasn't come yet.

Predicate Noun: The man's wish is *that he gain admittance to the law.*

Direct Object: The doorkeeper says *that he cannot grant admittance at the moment.*

Indirect Object: The story offers *whoever reads it* a meaningful message.

Object of a Preposition: The message is clear for *whoever wishes to reflect upon it.*

A. Practice: Underline the noun clause in each of the following sentences. Then, identify the function of the clause by writing *subject, predicate noun, direct object, indirect object,* or *object of preposition* on the line below each sentence.

1. Nguyen Thi Vinh's hope is that life in her hometown has not changed too much.

   _____

2. I fear that one day I'll be with the March-North Army meeting you on your way to the South.

   _____

3. That wounds develop gradually and then one day emerge is the theme of "Pride."

   _____

4. The onlookers watch the accident scene and wonder for whom the ambulance bell tolls.

   _____

B. Writing Application: Use each of the following noun clauses in a complete sentence. The words in parentheses describe the function each noun clause should have in the sentence.

1. that Nguyen Thi Vinh longs for the familiarity of her hometown (subject)

   _____

   _____

2. that her friend will forget their roots and look at her with hatred (predicate nominative)

   _____

   _____

3. that dying in an auto accident defies explanation (direct object)

   _____

   _____

4. what they could not control (object of preposition *about*)

   _____

   _____

"Thoughts of Hanoi" by Nguyen Thi Vinh
"Pride" by Dahlia Ravikovitch
"Auto Wreck" by Karl Shapiro
"Before the Law" by Franz Kafka

Reading Strategy: Evaluate Writer's Message

Everything you read has a message. For advertisements, the message is easy to figure out: "Buy me." For poems and fiction, the message may lie hidden in the fabric of the poem or story. Readers must ask themselves what it is that the writer wants them to take away from the poem or story. What does this writer want to communicate through this work? It might be a renewed faith in the goodness of people, or it might be a confirmation that evil never wins.

Once you identify it, you can **evaluate the writer's message.** Is the message logical? Is it valid? Does the author support the message well? How? You may or may not agree with the message, but you can still evaluate its validity.

DIRECTIONS: Answer the questions that follow to evaluate the message in each poem.

"Pride" by Dahlia Ravikovitch

1. What is Ravikovitch's message in "Pride"?

   _____

   _____

2. What image or images does Ravikovitch use to support her message?

   _____

   _____

3. Given her support of the message, is the message logical or valid? Explain why or why not.

   _____

   _____

   _____

"Before the Law" by Franz Kafka

4. What idea does Kafka want to communicate to readers in "Before the Law"?

   _____

   _____

5. Cite at least two lines from the work that particularly convey or support Kafka's message.

   _____

   _____

   _____

6. How valid is Kafka's message? Has he supported it sufficiently to make it believable? Explain your answer.

   _____

   _____

   _____

Unit 4: Turning Points

"Thoughts of Hanoi" by Nguyen Thi Vinh
"Pride" by Dahlia Ravikovitch
"Auto Wreck" by Karl Shapiro
"Before the Law" by Franz Kafka

Literary Analysis: Theme

What does this poem say about human life and values? This is a question you can ask yourself to discover the **theme** of a poem. The theme of a poem or of any literary work is its central meaning. In many literary works, the theme is not stated directly; writers often express their themes indirectly.

DIRECTIONS: Examine how two poets convey the themes of their poems through descriptions, images, and ideas.

"Thoughts of Hanoi" by Nguyen Thi Vinh

What is the theme of "Thoughts of Hanoi"?	
How does Nguyen Thi Vinh reveal the theme in this poem?	
What words or phrases does the poet use to convey the theme?	

"Auto Wreck" by Karl Shapiro

What is the theme of "Auto Wreck"?	
In what particular lines does Shapiro come closest to expressing the theme?	
What other words or phrases does Shapiro use to convey his theme?	

"The Widow and the Parrot" by Virginia Woolf

Build Vocabulary

Spelling Strategy   The rule of placing *i* before *e* except after *c* or when sounded like *a* as in *neighbor* or *weigh* has some exceptions. For instance, *ei* in *sovereigns* is not sounded like *a*; however, *i* is placed after *e*, not before.

Using Forms of *sagacity*

The Latin word *sagax*, which means "keen" or "acute," is the source for *sagacity* and its related words. *Sagacity* means "wisdom," or "keen judgment."

A. DIRECTIONS: Knowing what *sagacity* means, write a definition for each related word in the following sentences.

1. The sagacious judge could see through the prosecutor's ploy to admit unlawful evidence.

   sagacious: _____

2. Years of experience have made my grandmother the family sage.

   sage: _____

3. The parrot *sagaciously* observed Joseph and later led Mrs. Gage to the old miser's fortune.

   sagaciously: _____

Using the Word Bank

B. DIRECTIONS: Fill in the chart with a noun, a verb, and an adjective that has a close relationship to each Word Bank word.

	Noun	Verb	Adjective
1. ford			
2. dilapidated			
3. sovereigns			
4. sagacity			

Understanding Antonyms

C. DIRECTIONS: Each of the following questions consists of a word in CAPITAL LETTERS followed by four lettered words or phrases. Circle the letter of the word or phrase that is most nearly opposite in meaning to the word in capital letters.

1. DILAPIDATED:
   a. neglected   b. tidy   c. maintained   d. new
2. FORD:
   a. bridge   b. deep   c. rapids   d. gully

"The Widow and the Parrot" by Virginia Woolf

Build Grammar Skills: Appositives

Appositives are nouns or pronouns that are placed near other nouns or pronouns to identify, rename, or explain them. By using appositives, a writer can include more details without adding extra sentences. For example, look at the following:

> Mr. Stacey, *the farmer,* was going to Rodmell in his cart.

> We have the honor to inform you of the death of your brother, *Mr. Joseph Brand.*

Appositive phrases are nouns or pronouns with modifiers, placed next to a noun or pronoun to add information and details. The modifiers within an appositive phrase can be adjectives, adjective phrases, or other groups of words functioning as adjectives.

> Mrs. Gage, *an elderly widow,* was sitting in her cottage.

Notice how appositives or appositive phrases may help the writer avoid using too many short, choppy sentences.

> **Two sentences:** The parrot would have to be sold to pay her fare. The parrot was James.

> **Combined using an appositive:** The parrot *James* would have to be sold to pay her fare.

A. Practice: Underline the appositives or appositive phrases in the following sentences.

1. The village clergyman, the Rev. Samuel Tallboys, lent her two pound ten,

2. The dog Shag died some years previously.

3. She was determined to set off to Lewes the next day in order to claim her money from Messrs. Stagg and Beetle, the solicitors, and then to return home as quick as she could.

4. Mr. Beetle, my partner, went himself to Rodmell and searched the premises with the utmost care.

5. There is no house or cottage on that side of the river nearer than Asheham House, lately the seat of Mr. Leonard Woolf.

B. Writing Application: Combine each pair of sentences by using an appositive.

1. The coins were buried in the kitchen. It was the miser's hiding place. _____

   _____

2. Mrs. Ford took Mrs. Gage by the hand and led her off to her own cottage, where she was to sleep the night. Mrs. Ford was an old village woman. _____

   _____

3. The next day, she returned to Yorkshire. Yorkshire is a county in northern England. _____

   _____

4. Mrs. Gage uncovered long rolls of yellow stones. They were an amazing sight.

   _____

   _____

"The Widow and the Parrot" by Virginia Woolf

Reading Strategy: Drawing Inferences

Writers do not always state their ideas directly. As an active reader, you can **draw inferences,** or make assumptions, about a writer's ideas by observing what the characters in a story say and do, and what others say about them. Consider the details that the writer chooses to include or omit. Sometimes you must look beyond the literal meaning of the words to determine the author's full meaning.

DIRECTIONS: Read the following passages from the story. Then, answer the questions.

1. Mrs. Gage opened it and read: Dear Madam: We have the honor to inform you of the death of your brother Mr. Joseph Brand.
   Lawk a mussy, said Mrs. Gage. Old brother Joseph gone at last!

What can you infer about the nature of Mr. Sage's relationship with her brother based on her words?

_____

_____

2. Taking a lantern she next went round the house to see what sort of property her brother had left her. It was a bitter disappointment. There were holes in all the carpets. The bottoms of the chairs had fallen out. Rats ran along the mantelpiece. There were large toadstools growing through the kitchen floor. There was not a stick of furniture worth seven pence half-penny.

Based on this passage, what might you infer about her brother's manner of living?

_____

_____

3. Mrs. Gage stood still in amazement while James hopped about, pecking here and there, as if he were testing the bricks with his beak. It was a very uncanny sight, and had not Mrs. Gage been in the habit of living with animals, she would have lost her head, very likely, and hobbled back home.

From the passage, what can you infer about Mrs. Sage's attitude toward animals in general and toward James in particular?

_____

_____

4. It was not until she lay on her deathbed that she told the clergyman (the son of the Reverend Samuel Tallboys) the whole story, adding that she was quite sure that the house had been burnt on purpose by the parrot James, who, being aware of her danger on the river bank, flew into the scullery, and upset the oil stove which was keeping some scraps warm for her dinner.

What can you infer about Mrs. Gage's state of mind from this passage?

_____

_____

"The Widow and the Parrot" by Virginia Woolf

Literary Analysis: Motivation

The reason for a character's actions or words is called *motivation*. Understanding why characters act as they do will help you make sense of story events. For instance, in "The Widow and the Parrot," Mrs. Gage continues to send Christmas cards to her brother, even though he never acknowledges them. If you consider that Mrs. Gage is an elderly widow with no other living family, you can better understand her attempts to remain in touch with her brother, despite his indifference.

DIRECTIONS: Explore the motivations of characters in "The Widow and the Parrot" by answering the following questions.

1. What might have motivated Joseph Brand to treat the parrot well?

   _____

   _____

2. Although Mrs. Gage seems like a kind woman, she complains about her brother as she walks along the river bank. What motivates her negative words?

   _____

   _____

3. Suggest two motivations the parrot might have for burning the house.

   _____

   _____

4. What motivates Mrs. Gage to keep the secret of the recovered gold to herself?

   _____

   _____

5. What do you think finally motivates Mrs. Gage to reveal her secret?

   _____

   _____

6. Why do you think the parrot dies immediately after Mrs. Gage dies?

   _____

   _____

7. How does understanding Mrs. Gage's motivations early on help you predict her actions later in the story?

   _____

   _____

"Civil Peace" by Chinua Achebe

Build Vocabulary

Spelling Strategy   Many words in English end in -ible or -able. Fewer words end in -able. The words inestimable, amenable, and disreputable are among the words with the -able ending. Words ending in -ible include sensible, impossible, and flexible.

Using the Word Root -reput-

The word root -reput-, which means "to be regarded," anchors the meaning of words such as disreputable.

A. DIRECTIONS: Knowing that disreputable means "not respectable," rewrite each sentence, replacing the italicized words with disreptutable, reputation, or reputed.

1. The newspaper criticized the *man reported to be a* gangster.

   _____

2. He felt his *public image* had been tarnished.

   _____

3. Most people dismissed the *not highly regarded* paper's claims.

   _____

Using the Word Bank

B. DIRECTIONS: Match each word in the left column with its definition in the right column. In the blank, write the letter of the definition next to the word it defines.

____ 1. inestimable   a. poverty-stricken; in great need

____ 2. disreputable   b. building

____ 3. amenable   c. commanding; powerful

____ 4. edifice   d. responsive; open

____ 5. destitute   e. priceless; beyond reckoning

____ 6. imperious   f. sympathize; share suffering

____ 7. commiserate   g. not respectable

Understanding Antonyms

C. DIRECTIONS: Each question below consists of a word in CAPITAL LETTERS followed by four lettered words. Circle the letter of the word that is most nearly *opposite* in meaning to the word in capital letters.

1. AMENABLE:
   a. hesitant   b. attentive   c. remote   d. uncertain

2. IMPERIOUS:
   a. law-abiding   b. authoritative   c. friendly   d. frightened

"Civil Peace" by Chinua Achebe

Build Grammar Skills: Present Participial Phrases

A present participle is a verb form that ends in *-ing* and serves as an adjective. In a **present participial phrase,** a present participle is modified by an adverb or adverb phrase or accompanied by a complement (words that complete the meaning of a verb). The entire phrase functions as an adjective to modify a noun or pronoun.

Present Participle: Jonathan's *sobbing* children were paralyzed by fear.

In this sentence, the present participle *sobbing* acts alone to modify the noun *children.* It is not a participial phrase.

Present Participial Phrase: I am coming, said Jonathan *fumbling in the darkness.*

In this sentence, *in the darkness* is an adverb phrase that modifies the participle *fumbling.* The entire present participial phrase *fumbling in the darkness* modifies the noun *Jonathan.*

A. Practice: Underline each present participial phrase. Then circle the word it modifies.

1. It wasn't his disreputable rags, nor the toes peeping out of one blue and one brown canvas shoe, nor yet the two stars of his rank done obviously in a hurry in biro that troubled Jonathan.

2. Then he made the journey to Enugu and found another miracle waiting for him.

3. He had returned to Enugu early enough to pick up bits of old zinc and wood and soggy sheets of cardboard lying around the neighborhood.

4. Soon thousands more came out of their forest holes looking for the same things.

5. He paid the pounds, and moved in with his overjoyed family carrying five heads on their shoulders.

B. Writing Application: Use the verb in parentheses to develop a present participial phrase that modifies the italicized noun in each of the following sentences. Make sure that your phrase functions as an adjective that modifies the specified noun. Write your phrase in the space provided.

1. "Who is knocking?" whispered his *wife* (lie) _____.

2. (tremble) _____, *he* asked the nighttime visitors to identify themselves.

3. *Maria* and the *children,* (weep) _____, shrank into the corner.

4. His *wife,* (sweat) _____, was turning over akara balls in a wide clay bowl of boiling oil.

"**Civil Peace**" by Chinua Achebe

Reading Strategy: Prior Background Knowledge

Whether or not you have lived through a war, you can use your **prior knowledge,** or what you already know and can relate to, to help you understand Jonathan's experiences and reactions in "Civil Peace."

For instance, Jonathan doubts the genuineness of the officer who commandeers his bicycle. While you may not be familiar with military officers and how they look and behave, you probably have felt uncertain about the truthfulness of another person's actions or words. You can use this prior knowledge to understand Jonathan's reaction to the suspicious officer.

DIRECTIONS: For each story detail, list one example of prior knowledge that can aid your understanding.

Story Detail	Prior Knowledge
1. Jonathan earns money by taking people across the border on his bicycle.	
2. Jonathan feels astonished and grateful to find his house intact after the war.	
3. As he walks home, Jonathan grips his egg-rasher money tightly in his pocket.	
4. When thieves come in the middle of the night, Jonathan and his family fear for their lives.	
5. Despite losing his money, Jonathan feels lucky that he and his family escaped unharmed.	

"Civil Peace" by Chinua Achebe

Literary Analysis: Key Statement

A **key statement** reveals the central meaning of a story. Several times in Achebe's "Civil Peace" Jonathan thinks or says "Nothing puzzles God." By examining the instances in which the key statement appears, you can unlock the meaning of Achebe's story.

A. DIRECTIONS: Complete the following chart. Under Key Statement, copy the exact line from "Civil Peace" in which the statement "Nothing puzzles God" appears. Under Situation, describe the instance in which the statement is used.

Key Statement	Situation
1.	
2.	
3.	
4.	

B. DIRECTIONS: Use the completed chart and details from the story to answer the following questions.

1. By saying "Nothing puzzles God," what does Jonathan reveal about his own thinking?

_____

2. How do the situations in which Jonathan says or thinks "Nothing puzzles God" compare? Are they positive or negative? Explain.

_____

3. What significance does the statement have for Jonathan?

_____

4. How does the key statement "Nothing puzzles God" unlock the meaning of "Civil Peace"?

_____

"The Bean Eaters" by Gwendolyn Brooks
"How to React to Familiar Faces" by Umberto Eco

Build Vocabulary

Spelling Strategy   The difficulty of pronouncing certain letters when they occur next to each other causes the spelling of some prefixes to change. The *n* in the prefix *syn-* changes to *m* when the prefix is attached to a word that begins with *b, m,* or *p.* The words *symbiosis, symmetry,* and *symposium* are examples.

Using the Root -ami-

The word root *-ami-* means "friend." The root *-ami-* appears in the Word Bank word *amiably,* which means "in a friendly way."

A. DIRECTIONS: Complete each of the following sentences with one of the words in the list. Use context clues and what you know about the root *-ami-* to choose the correct word.

amiability   amicably   amities

1. The co-workers resolved their differences _____ .

2. The _____ between the two nations and their citizens have existed for centuries.

3. Friendly and easygoing, Jack easily won the _____ contest.

Using the Word Bank

B. DIRECTIONS: Answer each of the following questions to demonstrate your understanding of the Word Bank words. Circle the letter of your choice.

1. Which of the following describes a syndrome?
   a. Michelle fell into the habit of napping after school, then staying up past midnight to finish her homework. During the day, she felt tired and out of sorts. She couldn't wait to get home from school so she could sleep.
   b. Steven caught four colds last winter. Each one seemed more severe than the last.

2. Which of the following is an example of a speaker who is expounding?
   a. a teacher gives a 15-minute overview of a novel
   b. a teacher spends an hour explaining the events in Europe that led up to World War I

3. Which of the following describes someone who is behaving amiably?
   a. Mr. Martin nods to most of the students he meets in the hall, and greets those whom he knows by name.
   b. Mrs. Petrill is walking down to the corner market. She takes her time and stays along the edge of the sidewalk. She purchases a few items, thanks the clerk with a nod, and walks slowly home.

Recognizing Synonyms

C. DIRECTIONS: Circle the word or phrase that is closest in meaning to the Word Bank word.

1. amiably
   a. capably
   b. in a disagreeable manner
   c. accurately
   d. with friendliness

2. expound
   a. marvel
   b. clarify
   c. hammer
   d. concentrate

Name _____ Date _____

Build Grammar Skills: Verb or Participle?

It is easy to confuse a participle acting as part of a verb phrase with a participle acting as an adjective because they share the endings *-ing* and *-ed*. To help determine the difference, remember that a **verb** shows an action, a condition, or the fact that something exists. A **participle** acting as an adjective modifies a noun or a pronoun.

> **Verb:** They are *remembering* their past. (*Remembering* describes an action.)
> **Participle:** *Remembering*, they reflect on their past. (*Remembering* modifies *they*.)
>
> **Verb:** They rented the back room of the house. (*Rented* describes an action.)
> **Participle:** They live in the rented back room of the house. (*Rented* modifies *back room*.)

A. Practice: Identify each underlined word as a verb or a participle. Write *verb* or *participle* on the line provided. If the word is a participle, write the word it modifies.

_____ 1. A few months ago, as I was <u>strolling</u> in New York, I saw, at a distance, a man I knew very well.

_____ 2. I was just about to smile, when suddenly, I <u>recognized</u> him as Anthony Quinn.

_____ 3. Once a <u>stereotyped</u> actor, Quinn had achieved international fame.

_____ 4. He gave me a <u>telling</u> look; it said, "Keep your distance."

_____ 5. <u>Agitated</u>, I quickly turned the corner.

_____ 6. Once before, in a restaurant, I had <u>glimpsed</u> Charlton Heston.

_____ 7. I followed the <u>recommended</u> course of action and minded my own business.

_____ 8. Still, it was a <u>thrilling</u> experience.

B. Writing Application: Write two sentences for each of the given words. In the first sentence use the word as a verb. In the second sentence, use the verb as a participle.

1. cornered

_____

_____

2. strolling

_____

_____

3. creaking

_____

_____

"The Bean Eaters" by Gwendolyn Brooks
"How to React to Familiar Faces" by Umberto Eco

Reading Strategy: Responding to Connotations

When you work on building your vocabulary, you work on the denotation of words—the meaning given in the dictionary. When you write, or when you read what others have written, you need to consider the connotations of words. **Connotations** are the emotions or feelings associated with a word. For example, the words *hurry* and *race* both mean "to go quickly." The word *race*, however, has the added connotation of "with determination" or "frantically."

Words can have negative or positive connotations, or they can be neutral. Words such as *desk, pencil,* and *paper* are neutral; they don't cause emotional responses in readers. Now think about the words *hurry* and *race* again. Do you prefer to hurry through a day, or to race through a day? In this context, *race* has negative connotations because it connotes tension or stress.

The connotations you associate with words affect how you respond when you see them. This, in turn, affects your overall reaction to what you read. Watch for words that have positive or negative connotations as you read. Identifying them will help you understand how you feel about what you are reading.

A. DIRECTIONS: Indicate whether each of the following words has positive connotations, negative connotations, or is neutral.

1. strolling _____

2. insist _____

3. dragged _____

4. casual _____

5. confusion _____

6. amiably _____

7. dinner _____

8. clothes _____

B. DIRECTIONS: Explain the connotations of each word in the following groups of words.

1. hot, stifling _____

2. staring, meditating _____

3. gossip, chat _____

4. straightforward, blunt, curt _____

5. idle, lazy _____

C. DIRECTIONS: Review the first two sentences of Umberto Eco's essay. Explain your response to the image he creates. Note any words that have particular positive or negative connotations in those sentences.

_____

_____

_____

_____

_____

_____

"The Bean Eaters" by Gwendolyn Brooks
"How to React to Familiar Faces" by Umberto Eco

Literary Analysis: Tone

As readers, we respond to what we read with a variety of emotions. The attitudes and feelings that the writer expresses about the subject make up the **tone** of a literary work. Writers express their attitudes—that is, they create the tone—by means of word choice, the type of language they use, and the details they choose to relate. Consider how these two descriptions of a rainy day differ in tone.

The day and everything about it was sodden, gray to the core.
The puddle washed my boots just as the rain had cleansed every leaf and blade of grass.

By relating different details about the day and by careful word choice, two completely different attitudes are revealed in these sentences.

DIRECTIONS: Answer the following questions to help you analyze the tone of "The Bean Eaters" and "How to React to Familiar Faces."

1. Would you say that Gwendolyn Brooks is revolted by the two characters in her poem, or respectful of them? What words or details in the poem support your answer?

_____

_____

_____

_____

2. By what means does Umberto Eco establish a friendly, comfortable tone in his essay? Cite examples from the essay to support your answer.

_____

_____

_____

_____

3. Reading this essay, a reader can tell that Eco is amused by the behavior of people who meet celebrities. What if, instead of being amused, he were disgusted or outraged by this behavior? What would have to change in the essay to convey a tone of outrage?

_____

_____

_____

_____

"A Picture From the Past: Emily Dickinson" by Reynolds Price
"What Makes a Degas a Degas?" by Richard Mühlberger

Build Vocabulary

Spelling Strategy   The Word Bank word *austere* ends in a silent *e*. Depending on what suffix you are adding to the word *austere*, the silent *e* may or may not be dropped. To form the noun *austerity*, the silent *e* is dropped because the suffix *-ity* begins with a vowel. To form the adverb *austerely*, the silent *e* remains because the suffix *-ly* begins with a consonant.

Using the Root *-cent-*

A. DIRECTIONS: The word root *-cent-*, which means "hundred," appears in a number of English words. Using what you know about *-cent-*, determine the meaning of the following words.

1. centenary _____

2. centiliter _____

3. centigram _____

Using the Word Bank

B. DIRECTIONS: Replace each italicized word or group of words with a word from the Word Bank. Rewrite the sentence in the space provided.

1. For many poets, Emily Dickinson's work is a *huge and powerful* influence.

_____

_____

2. If Walt Whitman were still alive, he would be a *one-hundred-year-old person.*

_____

_____

3. Emily Dickinson's father was a *severe* man who took little interest in his daughter's life.

_____

_____

4. Paintings that are *covered in tough varnish* are sometimes difficult to restore.

_____

_____

Using Antonyms

C. DIRECTIONS: In the blank, write the letter of the word or phrase that is most nearly *opposite* in meaning to the Word Bank word.

____ 1. titanic
    a. powerful
    b. colossal
    c. trivial
    d. huge

____ 2. lacquered
    a. unprotected
    b. picturesque
    c. varnished
    d. covered

____ 3. austere
    a. severe
    b. harsh
    c. frugal
    d. moderate

"A Picture From the Past: Emily Dickinson" by Reynolds Price
"What Makes a Degas a Degas?" by Richard Mühlberger

Build Grammar Skills: Infinitives and Infinitive Phrases

Infinitives are the base forms of verbs that express existence or action. In English, the word *to* usually appears as a marker in front of the verb to indicate the infinitive form. Infinitives may function in sentences as nouns, adjectives, or adverbs.

> **Noun:** *To paint* requires attention to detail. (*To paint* is the subject of the sentence.)
> **Adjective:** Degas showed a willingness *to experiment*. (The infinitive *to experiment* modifies the noun *willingness*.)
> **Adverb:** Spontaneity is what he hoped *to convey*. (The infinitive *to convey* modifies the verb *hoped*.)

Infinitive phrases include an infinitive and modifiers or complements (words that complete the meaning). The entire phrase acts as a single part of speech in the same way that the infinitive does.

> **Infinitive phrase acting as a noun:** *To bring viewers into the moment* was part of his lifelong quest. (*To bring viewers into the moment* is the subject of the sentence.)

A. Practice: Underline the infinitive or infinitive phrase in each of the following sentences and indicate its function. Write *noun, adjective,* or *adverb* above the infinitive or infinitive phrase. If it is an adjective or an adverb, draw an arrow to the word it modifies.

1. Using his keen perception of characters, Reynolds Price is able to analyze the character of the very private American author Emily Dickinson.

2. The photograph has no name, no date, no indication of why it has been saved to turn up now like a pebble from Mars in the glare of our world.

3. Degas wanted to make paint look spontaneous.

4. *Dancers, Pink and Green* took the same amount of time to finish as many of his other paintings.

B. Writing Application: Follow the directions in parentheses to write four sentences using infinitives and infinitive phrases.

1. (Use the infinitive phrase *to go on the stage.*)

_____

2. (Use the infinitive phrase *to increase the feeling of movement.*)

_____

3. (Use the infinitive phrase *to paint.*)

_____

4. (Use the infinitive phrase *to keep out of the way.*)

_____

"A Picture From the Past: Emily Dickinson" by Reynolds Price
"What Makes a Degas a Degas?" by Richard Mühlberger

Reading Strategy: Relating Text and Pictures

In Reynolds Price's essay, Price carefully examines in words an anonymous daguerreotype of the poet Emily Dickinson. In Richard Mühlberger's essay, Mühlberger analyzes the theme, technique, style, and composition of two of Edgar Degas' paintings. In both cases, the writers acquire information from specific visual sources. As readers, we gain a deeper understanding of the authors' words and of the respective images by relating the images to the text. Together, words and images sometimes convey a meaning that neither can convey alone. You **relate images to text** by carefully studying the images as you read each author's descriptions and interpretations. For example, when Price describes Emily Dickinson's "sensible rough-knuckled hands," you should be able to look at the daguerreotype and actually see her hands. What makes the author conclude that they are "sensible"?

DIRECTIONS: For one or both essays, complete the following chart, identifying three of the author's descriptions of, and conclusions about, a visual image. In the third column, explain your interpretation of the image. If you agree with the author's interpretation, state that as well.

Essay title: _____

Author's Description	Author's Conclusion	Your Interpretation
1.		
2.		
3.		

"A Picture From the Past: Emily Dickinson" by Reynolds Price
"What Makes a Degas a Degas?" by Richard Mühlberger

Literary Analysis: Analytical Essay

Analysis is the act of dividing a subject into parts and then determining how the parts are related. In an **analytical essay,** a large idea is broken down into its smaller parts. By closely examining these parts, a writer helps the reader understand how the parts fit together and what they mean as a whole. For example, in "What Makes a Degas a Degas?" Mühlberger examines characteristics of two of Degas' paintings. Collectively, the parts of Mühlberger's essay create an overall impression of Degas' work and his approach to it.

DIRECTIONS: Answer each of the following questions about the two essays.

1. On what details about the daguerreotype of Dickinson does Price focus in his opening paragraph?

   _____

   _____

2. How does Price relate these details to the life of Emily Dickinson? Which does Price mean by saying, "such a picture and a face"?

   _____

   _____

3. What overall impression of Emily Dickinson does Price create? Which parts or details create this impression?

   _____

   _____

   _____

   _____

4. Into what parts, or categories, does Mühlberger divide his analysis of Degas' two paintings?

   _____

   _____

5. What overall impression of Degas' approach to his work do you gain from Mühlberger's analysis of Degas' technique?

   _____

   _____

6. What details support Mühlberger's general point that Degas sought to achieve a sense of spontaneity or immediacy in his work?

   _____

   _____

"The Orphan Boy and the Elk Dog," a Blackfeet Myth

Build Vocabulary

Spelling Strategy   When writing words ending in silent *e*, drop the *e* before adding a suffix beginning with a vowel. For example, the suffix *-ing* added to the word *emanate* forms the Word Bank word *emanating*.

Using Homographs

At the beginning of "The Orphan Boy and the Elk Dog," Long Arrow is forced to eat food scraps he finds in refuse heaps. The word *refuse* is a **homograph,** a word with the same spelling as at least one other word but with a different meaning and a different pronunciation. In this story, *refuse* (ref'yoos) is a noun meaning "garbage." The word *refuse* (ri fyooz') is a verb meaning "to reject." You can figure out the meaning of a homograph from its context in the sentence, and you can use a dictionary to verify its correct pronunciation.

A. DIRECTIONS: Consult a dictionary to confirm the two meanings and pronunciations of each of the following homographs. Then write two sentences for each word, showing its two different meanings.

1. lead

_____

_____

2. slough

_____

_____

Using the Word Bank

B. DIRECTIONS: Rewrite the following sentences, replacing the italicized phrase with a Word Bank word.

1. Long Arrow ate with *great pleasure* the food given to him by the holy man.

_____

2. Power seemed to be *coming forth* from the holy man.

_____

C. DIRECTIONS: Each question below consists of a related pair of words in CAPITAL LETTERS followed by four lettered pairs of words. Circle the letter of the pair that best expresses a relationship *similar* to that expressed in the pair in capital letters.

1. EMANATING : NOISE ::
   a. smile : laugh
   b. rising : fall
   c. glowing : light
   d. walking : run

2. RELISH : DISGUST ::
   a. simple : complex
   b. love : hate
   c. enjoy : like
   d. enormous : big

3. STIFLE : SMOTHER ::
   a. encourage : cultivate
   b. quiet : silence
   c. shout : whisper
   d. happily : joyfully

Build Grammar Skills: Commonly Confused Words: *accept* and *except*

Although the words *accept* and *except* have a similar look and sound, they have completely different meanings. The word *accept* is a verb meaning "to receive" or "to agree with." The word *except* is usually a preposition meaning "not including," and sometimes a verb meaning "to leave out." Notice the correct use of *accept* and *except* in the following sentences:

Many villagers did not *accept* the chief's decision to welcome the orphan boy.

People continued to *except* Long Arrow from the community.

Everyone *except* Long Arrow failed in trying to find Elk Dogs.

A. Practice: For each of the following sentences, circle the correct word in parentheses.

1. The chief was surprised when Long Arrow (accepted/excepted) the difficult challenge.

2. Long Arrow felt that his people might finally (accept/except) him if he found the Elk Dogs.

3. The boy left, and no one (accept/except) his grandfather knew where he was going.

4. Long Arrow (accepted, excepted) Good Running's advice and traveled south.

5. Throughout his journey, Long Arrow tried to be brave and (accept/except) fear from his mind.

6. Long Arrow gave away all (accept/except) two of the Elk Dogs to his grandparents.

B. Writing Application: Write a short paragraph describing a character or scene from the myth "The Orphan Boy and the Elk Dog." In your paragraph, correctly use the word *accept* twice and the word *except* twice. You may change the forms of the words by adding suffixes. For example, *acceptance, excepted,* and so on.

_____
_____
_____
_____
_____
_____
_____
_____
_____
_____
_____
_____

"The Orphan Boy and the Elk Dog," Native American (Blackfeet)

Reading Strategy: Interpreting

When you **interpret** what you read, you explain its meaning or significance. Part of the job of a reader is to examine the writer's words and to decide how they contribute to the mood and meaning of the work. As you read, ask yourself what point or message the writer is trying to convey beyond the literal words. Keeping this question in mind will help you interpret the underlying meanings of the selections you read.

DIRECTIONS: Read each of the following passages from "The Orphan Boy and the Elk Dog." Then, answer the questions.

1. Now he was like a beaten, mangy dog, the kind who hungrily roams outside a camp, circling it from afar, smelling the good meat boiling in the kettles but never coming close for fear of being kicked.

   In this passage, what does the image of the "beaten, mangy dog" suggest about Orphan Boy's relationship with the people in the camp?

   _____
   _____
   _____

2. "This boy," the chief said to himself, "is neither stupid nor crazy." He gave the orphan a piece of the hump meat, then a piece of liver, then a piece of raw kidney, and at last the very best kind of meat—a slice of tongue.

   What do the chief's actions tell you about his attitude toward Long Arrow? What is the significance of his offering Long Arrow "a slice of tongue"?

   _____
   _____
   _____

3. Afraid, Long Arrow thought, "How can I follow him and not be drowned?" But then he said to himself, "I knew all the time that this would not be easy. In setting out to find the Elk Dog, I already threw my life away." And he boldly jumped into the water.

   What is the author telling us about Long Arrow through his words and actions?

   _____
   _____
   _____

4. Long Arrow said, "My grandfather and grandmother who adopted me, I can never repay you for your kindness. Accept these wonderful Elk Dogs as my gift."

   What is the significance of Long Arrow's gift to his adopted family?

   _____
   _____
   _____

"The Orphan Boy and the Elk Dog," a Blackfeet Myth

Literary Analysis: Myth

Most cultures throughout the world have created their own **myths,** or traditional stories that attempt to explain the mysteries of nature, the origin of humans, or the behaviors and customs of a people. Myths generally involve mysterious, immortal, or larger-than-life characters, and the details of a myth often reveal the values, customs, and beliefs of a particular culture.

DIRECTIONS: Explore the ways in which "The Orphan Boy and the Elk Dog" fits the definition of a myth by rereading the following passages from the story. Explain how each passage presents details typical of a myth, such as details related to mysterious, larger-than-life characters or details that indirectly reveal the values, customs, and beliefs of Blackfeet culture.

1. Eventually the game was hunted out near the camp that the boy regarded as his, and the people decided to move. The lodges were taken down, belongings were packed into rawhide bags and put on dog travois, and the village departed.

   _____

   _____

   _____

2. He had to learn to speak and to understand well, and to catch up on all the things a boy should know. He was a fast learner and soon surpassed other boys his age in knowledge and skills. . . . He grew up into a fine young hunter, tall and good-looking in the quilled buckskin outfit the chief's wife made for him.

   _____

   _____

   _____

3. Long Arrow wandered on, walking for long hours and taking little time for rest. Through deep canyons and over high mountains he went, wearing out his moccasins and enduring cold and heat, hunger and thirst.

   Finally Long Arrow came face to face with a tall man, fierce and scowling and twice the height of most humans.

   _____

   _____

   _____

4. The spirit boy pointed to the water and said, "My grandfather's lodge is down there. Come." The child turned himself into a kingfisher and dove straight to the bottom.

   Afraid, Long Arrow thought, "How can I follow him and not be drowned?" But then he said to himself, "I knew all the time that this would not be easy. . . ." And he boldly jumped into the water. To his surprise, he found it did not make him wet, that it parted before him, that he could breathe and see.

   _____

   _____

   _____

"The Street of the Cañon" from *Mexican Village* by Josephina Niggli

Build Vocabulary

Spelling Strategy   For words ending in two consonants, keep both consonants when adding a suffix starting with either a vowel or a consonant. For example, *-ly* added to the word *nonchalant* forms the Word Bank word *nonchalantly*.

Using the Suffix *-ly*

In your reading you will often encounter words that end with the suffix *-ly*. Many words that end in *-ly* are adverbs—words that modify verbs, adjectives, or other adverbs. Adverbs can make writing clearer and more descriptive by telling exactly how something is done or said. For example, when Josephina Niggli writes that Pepe Gonzalez asks a question *audaciously*, you know he is speaking in a bold manner to make people believe he is comfortable in his surroundings.

A. DIRECTIONS: Complete each of the sentences with the best *-ly* word from the following list.

extravagantly   cautiously   abruptly

1. The stranger from Hidalgo walked _____ down the long, dark streets of the village.

2. Pepe Gonzalez adjusted his package and entered the _____ decorated party.

3. Pepe left the party _____, before anyone could identify him as an enemy.

Using the Word Bank

B. DIRECTIONS: Match each word in the left column with its definition in the right column. Write the letter of the definition on the line next to the word it defines.

_____ 1. officious   a. overly ready to serve; obliging

_____ 2. mottled   b. casually; indifferently

_____ 3. nonchalantly   c. arrogantly

_____ 4. audaciously   d. believability

_____ 5. imperiously   e. in a bold manner

_____ 6. plausibility   f. marked with spots of different shades

Understanding Antonyms

C. DIRECTIONS: Circle the letter of the word that is most nearly *opposite* in meaning to the word in capital letters. Because some of the choices are close in meaning, consider all the choices before deciding which is best.

1. NONCHALANTLY
   a. casually
   b. anxiously
   c. arrogantly
   d. carefully

2. AUDACIOUSLY
   a. timidly
   b. slowly
   c. quietly
   d. boldly

3. PLAUSIBILITY
   a. belief
   b. possibility
   c. workability
   d. impossibility

4. IMPERIOUSLY
   a. softly
   b. humbly
   c. rudely
   d. openly

"The Street of the Cañon" from *Mexican Village* by Josephina Niggli

Build Grammar Skills: Prepositional Phrase or Infinitive?

Do not confuse prepositional phrases with infinitives. An **infinitive** is a form of a verb that generally appears with the word *to* and acts as a noun, an adjective, or an adverb. The word *to* is also a preposition and can begin a prepositional phrase. A **prepositional phrase** contains a preposition, an object of the preposition, and its modifiers.

> **Infinitive:** Along the shadowy, moonlit streets, he dared *to walk*. (The word *walk* is a verb.)
> **Prepositional phrase:** He was on his way *to San Juan Iglesias*. (*San Juan Iglesias* is the object of the preposition *to*.)

Remember, an infinitive always ends with a verb. A prepositional phrase always ends with a noun or pronoun.

A. Practice: Underline the infinitive or the prepositional phrase beginning with *to* in each sentence. Then, on the line, write whether it is an infinitive or a prepositional phrase.

_____ 1. The streets were empty because all of the people, from the lowest-paid cowboy to the mayor, were attending a birthday celebration.

_____ 2. The stranger squared his shoulders and walked jauntily across the street to the laughter-filled house.

_____ 3. The room was filled with his enemies; to enter took great audacity.

_____ 4. Prepared to flee if anyone recognized him, he carefully examined every smiling face.

_____ 5. At Don Roméo Calderón's insistence, he drank a toast to Calderón's beautiful daughter, Sarita.

_____ 6. Then, he walked across the room and asked Sarita's chaperone to dance.

_____ 7. It was obvious that the stranger liked to flirt.

_____ 8. Sarita blushed to the roots of her hair and shyly lowered her white lids.

B. Writing Application: Write four sentences about "The Street of the Cañon." In the first two sentences, include an infinitive. In the second two, include a prepositional phrase that begins with *to*.

1. _____

_____

2. _____

_____

3. _____

_____

4. _____

_____

"The Street of the Cañon" from *Mexican Village* by Josephina Niggli

Reading Strategy: Predicting

You can **predict** the events of a story in the same way that you can predict events in your own life. As you read, you are continually gathering information about characters and situations. Using this information, you can make educated guesses about how the events of a story are going to unfold.

DIRECTIONS: Use the chart below to record your predictions about the events and characters in the story as you read. Update your predictions as new information becomes available.

Question	Clues	Predictions
Who is the stranger walking through the dark streets?		
Why is the stranger going to the party?		
What is the package the stranger clutches tightly?		
Why is the stranger concerned about being recognized?		
Where has the stranger seen the young woman before, and why does he dance with her?		
Why does the stranger leave so abruptly?		

Name _____ Date _____

"The Street of the Cañon" from *Mexican Village* by Josephina Niggli

Literary Analysis: Third-Person Point of View

When you read, you are able to see places and events through the eyes of a character or of the narrator, who may or may not be a character in the story. A story told by an outside narrator is told in the third person. In a **third-person limited point of view,** a writer reveals only one character's thoughts. The reader learns things only as the character learns them. In a story told from a **third-person omniscient point of view**—as is "The Street of the Cañon"—the narrator is all knowing, and readers witness events through the eyes of several characters.

DIRECTIONS: Read the following passages from "The Street of the Cañon," and identify whose point of view is being presented in each passage. Then explain why the characters' thoughts in the passage are important to the story.

1. He walked swiftly along, heading always for the distant sound of guitar and flute. If he met anyone now, who could say from which direction he had come? He might be a trader from Monterrey, or a buyer of cow's milk from farther North in the valley of the Three Marys. Who would guess that an Hidalgo man dared to walk alone in the moonlit streets of San Juan Iglesias?

Point of view: _____

_____

_____

_____

2. The last time he had seen that face it had been white and tense with rage, and lips clenched tight to prevent an outgushing stream of angry words.

Point of view: _____

_____

_____

_____

3. The girl was standing on tiptoe trying vainly to see what was happening. She was hardly aware of the stranger's whispering voice although she remembered the words that he said. "Sunday night— once around the plaza."

Point of view: _____

_____

_____

_____

4. [No voice said, "The stranger,"] but with one fluid movement every head in the patio turned toward the girl in the doorway. She also turned, her eyes wide with something that she realized to her own amazement was more apprehension than anger.

Point of view: _____

_____

_____

_____

"A Storm in the Mountains" by Alexander Solzhenitsyn

"In the Orchard" by Henrik Ibsen

"A Tree Telling of Orpheus" by Denise Levertov

Build Vocabulary

Spelling Strategy Most words of more than one syllable that end with a long *e* sound are spelled with a *y*, as is the Word Bank word *sultry*. There are exceptions, such as compound words like *carefree* or words whose accent is on the final syllable, such as *agree*, but in general, if a word ends with a long *e* sound and the word is more than one syllable, you can usually safely spell it with a *y*.

Using Latin Terms

In the first century A.D., when the Romans expanded their empire into what is now Great Britain, they brought their language with them, and Latin began contributing to English. Three hundred years later, when Emperor Constantine I made Rome a Christian empire, Latin became the written language of Christianity. In the Dark Ages, Latin survived in monasteries and abbeys, the few remaining European centers of written knowledge. As the languages of Europe evolved and borrowed from each other, Latin was an essential ingredient in the mix. Not only do vast numbers of words have Latin roots, but many come directly from the ancient tongue. Usually italicized, these terms maintain their meaning almost exactly, and appear often in legal or governmental contexts.

A. DIRECTIONS: Use a dictionary to find the meanings of the following Latin terms in common use today. Write the meaning of each italicized term in the space provided.

1. Orpheus' head, neck, arms, *etc.*, look like parts of a tree to the speaker of Levertov's poem.

_____

2. Ibsen probably does not object to work *per se*, but would not want it to cost us the love of the moment.

_____

3. The poem expresses its theme of *carpe diem* gently but reminds us that time will "shut the garden gate."

_____

Using the Word Bank

B. DIRECTIONS: In the blank, write the letter of the word or phrase most nearly *similar* in meaning to the Word Bank word.

_____ 1. sultry	_____ 2. asunder	_____ 3. terra firma
a. shady	a. beneath	a. dread
b. steamy	b. blaring	b. mainland
c. sturdy	c. varied	c. majesty
d glum	d. apart	d. firm ground

"A Storm in the Mountains" by Alexander Solzhenitsyn
"In the Orchard" by Henrik Ibsen
"A Tree Telling of Orpheus" by Denise Levertov

Build Grammar Skills: Gerunds

A **gerund** is a verb form ending in -*ing* that acts as a noun. A gerund may be the subject of a sentence, a predicate nominative, a direct or indirect object, the object of a preposition, or an appositive.

Subject	The storm's *flashing* blinded us.
Direct Object	Our new tent makes *camping* a pleasure.
Indirect Object	That storm gave *camping* a new dimension.
Predicate Nominative	My favorite activity is *climbing*.
Object of a Preposition	As many times as I've done it, I never tire of *climbing*.
Appositive	After the storm passed, we pursued our favorite activity, *climbing*.

A. Practice: Underline the gerund in each sentence. Then, on the line provided, identify its function in the sentence. Write *subject, predicate nominative, direct object, indirect object, object of a preposition,* or *appositive.*

_____ 1. When the rippling began, I took it for sea-wind, coming to our valley with rumors of salt, of treeless horizons.

_____ 2. And what I felt was no longer a dry tingling.

_____ 3. It was a wave that bathed me as if rain rose from below and around me instead of falling.

_____ 4. When he leaned on my trunk, I could not stop my trembling.

_____ 5. The balm, his singing, soaked in through my roots and flowed to the tips of my branches.

_____ 6. His music gave living a new significance.

B. Writing Application: Follow the directions in parentheses to write four sentences with gerunds.

1. (Use the gerund *singing* as a predicate nominative.)

_____

2. (Use the gerund *dancing* as a subject.)

_____

3. (Use the gerund *trembling* as the object of a preposition.)

_____

4. (Use the gerund *longing* as a direct object.)

_____

"A Storm in the Mountains" by Alexander Solzhenitsyn
"In the Orchard" by Henrik Ibsen
"A Tree Telling of Orpheus" by Denise Levertov

Reading Strategy: Engaging the Senses

As writers create worlds for us, their images speak to our senses. Denise Levertov invites you to be a tree and imagine the thrill of Orpheus' music "almost as if/fire had been lit below" your branches. If you engage your senses fully, you combine your own memory of the feeling of fire with the poet's words, and the sensory image succeeds in making you feel as if you were indeed that tree.

In order to appreciate this effect fully, it helps not only to identify which sense is being appealed to, but also the way in which your own experience relates to the sensory image. What connections do you make to sensory images in these selections? How do they help you engage your senses fully?

DIRECTIONS: In the left column are passages from the selections. In the center column, write what sense is being appealed to by the passage. In the right column, write what connection to your own experience the sensory image makes. Be as specific as you can in describing how the connection helps you engage your senses.

	Sense the Image Appeals To	Personal Connection to Image
Everything was black—no peaks, no valleys, no horizon to be seen . . . (Solzhenitsyn)		
The voice of the thunder filled the gorge, drowning the ceaseless roar of the rivers. (Solzhenitsyn)		
Will you let the scarecrow clapping/Drown all happy words and sounds? (Ibsen)		
With my living, with my singing/I will tear the hedges down. (Ibsen)		
When the rippling began,/ I took it for sea-wind, coming to our valley with rumors of salt. (Levertov)		
. . . two/moving stems, the short trunk, the two/arm-branches, flexible, each with five leafless/twigs at their ends. (Levertov)		

"A Storm in the Mountains" by Alexander Solzhenitsyn

"In the Orchard" by Henrik Ibsen

"A Tree Telling of Orpheus" by Denise Levertov

Literary Analysis: Speaker

The **speaker** of a poem or piece of prose may be an imaginary personality constructed by the author, or it may be the author addressing readers directly. Even if the speaker does not address the audience directly, the author may represent the voice as his or her own.

The speaker may be the author's persona created for the purpose of narration. Although not a character in the events, the speaker is not exactly the author either, especially in works of fiction. Much literary criticism is devoted to the complex relationship between the speaker and the flesh-and-blood author.

The speaker may be a character. Sometimes the character who is speaking is described, and sometimes the character merely speaks in a voice consistent with who that character may be. At other times, a speaker who is a character uses the pronouns *I, me, my.*

DIRECTIONS: Consider the qualities of the speakers of the three pieces in this selection, and answer the following questions. Write your answers in the space provided.

1. Name three things you learn about the speaker of "A Storm in the Mountains" from things he says about his situation.

   _____

   _____

2. When do you learn that the speaker was not alone during the storm and that it took place in the past?

   _____

   _____

3. Do you think Ibsen represents himself as the speaker of "In the Orchard"? Why or why not?

   _____

   _____

4. The speaker of "In the Orchard" uses the word *you* several times. Do you feel the speaker is addressing you directly? Why or why not?

   _____

   _____

5. The speaker in "A Tree Telling of Orpheus" is a tree. Name three places in the poem where convincing images help you believe a tree is speaking.

   _____

   _____

6. Who could be the audience for the speaking tree of Levertov's poem? Explain your choice.

   _____

   _____

Name _____ Date _____

"The Open Window" by Saki

Build Vocabulary

Spelling Strategy   The sound *shun* in a suffix is usually spelled *sion*, *tion*, or *ssion*. For example, the word *delude* becomes the Word Bank word *delusion*. The word *operate* drops its final *e* and becomes *operation*, and the word *possess* becomes *possession*.

Words From Names

In "The Open Window," a character walks across a lawn carrying a white mackintosh, which is a waterproof raincoat. This item is named after a real person—Charles Macintosh (1766–1843)—who invented waterproof clothing. Like the word mackintosh, many words in the English language are derived from the names of people and places.

A. DIRECTIONS: Each word in the following list comes from the name of a person or place. Read the sentences that follow the list, filling in each blank with the most appropriate word from the list.

   Braille   Spartan   sandwich   Machiavellian

1. People who are severe, restrained, and highly disciplined can be described as having _____ traits, characteristic of people from a powerful military city in ancient Greece.

2. People who are blind can read and write using _____, a system of printing and writing which uses patterns of raised dots. This system is named for the blind teacher who invented it.

3. The _____ was invented by the earl of a town in England so that he would not have to stop playing games in order to eat his meals.

4. A leader who is _____ is crafty, ruthless, and willing to sacrifice moral principles to achieve political goals—behavior advocated by an Italian political philosopher of the Renaissance in his famous book *The Prince*.

Using the Word Bank

B. DIRECTIONS: In the blank, write the letter of the definition next to the word it defines.

_____   1. delusion   a. a waterproof raincoat

_____   2. imminent   b. despised; outcast

_____   3. mackintosh   c. likely to happen soon; threatening

_____   4. pariah   d. a false belief held in spite of evidence to the contrary

C. DIRECTIONS: Circle the letter of the pair of words that best expresses a relationship *similar* to that expressed in the pair in capital letters.

1. PARIAH : DESPISED ::
   a. injure : hurt
   b. friend : enemy
   c. beloved : adored
   d. generous : friend

2. DELUSION : TRUTH ::
   a. chaos : order
   b. enjoy : dislike
   c. tiny : enormous
   d. calm : tranquility

3. MACKINTOSH : RAIN ::
   a. shoes : feet
   b. shovel : snow
   c. boat : water
   d. visor : sunlight

"The Open Window" by Saki

Build Grammar Skills: Placement of *Only* and *Just*

You should always place the modifiers **only** and **just** immediately before the words they modify. Changing their placement in a sentence directly affects the meaning of the sentence. In the following example from the story, notice that *just* modifies the word *give*:

> I shall *just* give you letters of introduction to all the people I know there.

In this example, *just* is modifying the phrase "give you letters of introduction." If you change the placement of *just*, the meaning of the sentence changes. For example:

> I shall give *just* you letters of introduction to all the people I know there.

> I shall give you *just* letters of introduction to all the people I know there.

In the first sentence, *just* modifies *you*. In the second, *just* modifies *letters of introduction*.

A. Practice: Explain how the different placement of the word *just* or *only* changes the meaning of each of the following sentences.

1. (a) Framton Nuttel wished for only rest and relaxation.
   (b) Framton Nuttel only wished for rest and relaxation.

   _____

   _____

2. (a) The young woman sat down and just began telling a story to Framton Nuttel.
   (b) The young woman sat down and began telling just a story to Framton Nuttel.

   _____

   _____

3. (a) Before his visit, Mr. Nuttel knew only Mrs. Sappleton's name and address.
   (b) Before his visit, Mr. Nuttel only knew Mrs. Sappleton's name and address.

   _____

   _____

4. (a) Mr. Nuttel spent only a short time at the rural retreat.
   (b) Mr. Nuttel only spent a short time at the rural retreat.

   _____

   _____

B. Writing Application: Rewrite each of the following sentences, inserting the modifier *only* or *just*. Try not to change or make unclear the original meaning of the sentence.

1. He thought it was truth but it was a story.

   _____

2. Poor Mr. Nuttel wanted to rest, but he was in for a shock.

   _____

3. The niece was trying to have some fun.

   _____

"**The Open Window**" by Saki

Reading Strategy: Identifying Relationships

When you read a story, **identify the relationships** within it. For example, look for the causes and effects of important actions, keep clear in your mind the sequence of events, and identify which events are of greater or lesser importance. This will help you understand the "nuts and bolts" of the story and let you devote your energy to more challenging tasks, such as determining the theme.

DIRECTIONS: For each action listed in the organizer below, give one cause or effect. Then, in the upper right-hand corner, number the four events in sequential order.

Action:

Framton Nuttel discusses his ailments in great detail.

Effect:

Action:

Framton Nuttel grabs his hat and stick and runs out the door.

Cause:

Action:

Framton Nuttel goes to the country for rest and fresh air.

Cause:

Action:

Vera tells Framton Nuttel the story of her aunt's "great tragedy."

Effect:

Which of the above events are of greater importance? Which are less important? Explain your answers.

_____

_____

_____

_____

_____

_____

"The Open Window" by Saki

Literary Analysis: Plot Structure

Plot is the sequence of a story's events. Most short stories are composed of some or all of the following plot elements—exposition, inciting incident, central conflict, climax, and resolution. **Exposition** introduces the setting, characters, and situation of the story. The story's **inciting incident** introduces the **central conflict,** which then develops until it reaches the **climax**—the story's high point of interest or suspense. The story ends with some kind of **resolution** to the conflict.

DIRECTIONS: As you read "The Open Window," refer to the following plot diagram. Decide what details and events in "The Open Window" make up each of its plot elements.

Plot Diagram

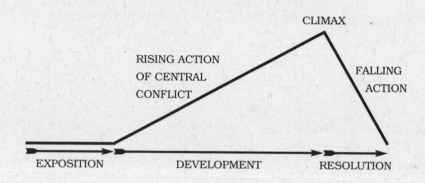

1. What details are given in the exposition of "The Open Window"?

   _____

   _____

2. What is the central conflict of the story?

   _____

   _____

3. What events lead to the story's climax?

   _____

   _____

4. What is the story's climax?

   _____

   _____

5. Describe the story's resolution.

   _____

   _____

"Leiningen Versus the Ants" by Carl Stephenson

Build Vocabulary

Spelling Strategy   Place *i* before *e* except after *c* or when sounded like *a* as in *neighbor* and *weigh*. Two exceptions to this rule are *weir* and *weird*, both of which are pronounced with a long *e* sound.

Using Latin Plural Forms

Words in English that are borrowed from Latin retain their Latin plural forms. The plural of *alluvium* is *alluvia*. Words from Latin change endings as follows to form plurals:

-um becomes *-a*

-on becomes *-a*

-us becomes *-i*

-a becomes *-ae*

A. DIRECTIONS: Write the plural form of each word.

1. stimulus _____   4. phenomenon _____

2. medium _____   5. fungus _____

3. formula _____   6. larva _____

Using the Word Bank

B. DIRECTIONS: Match each word in the left column with its definition in the right column. In the blank, write the letter of the definition next to the word it defines.

____   1. peons   a. laborers in Spanish America

____   2. flout   b. food

____   3. weir   c. material deposited by moving water

____   4. provender   d. show contempt for

____   5. alluvium   e. a low dam

____   6. fomentations   f. warm moist substances applied to treat an injury

C. DIRECTIONS: In the blank, write the letter of the word that best completes the meaning of the sentence.

____   1. The medicine man's ____ helped heal Leiningen's wounds.
          a. peons
          b. provender
          c. alluvium
          d. fomentations

____   2. Any plant or animal in the ants' path became their ____.
          a. peons
          b. weir
          c. provender
          d. alluvium

"Leiningen Versus the Ants" by Carl Stephenson

Build Grammar Skills: Subject and Verb Agreement

Verbs should agree in number and person with their subjects: Singular subjects take singular verbs, and plural subjects take plural verbs. When making a verb agree with its subject, you need to identify the subject and determine its number. Some subjects are difficult to locate. For example, in sentences beginning with *there is* or *there are*, the subject usually follows the verb. Often the subject is separated from its verb by a phrase or clause. Be careful not to confuse the object of a preposition for the subject.

OP
Examples: <u>One</u> of the defense measures <u>is</u> a water-filled ditch.

OP
There <u>is</u> a <u>cordon</u> of ants around the trench.

A. Practice: Circle the verb in parentheses that agrees with the subject.

1. Traveling toward his plantation (is, are) ten miles of ants.

2. There (is, are) no admonitions that will induce Leiningen to leave his land.

3. The official tells him that every single one of the ants (is, are) fiendish.

4. Leiningen, with the help of his men, (have, has) built two defenses against their arrival.

5. Only the vast moving shadow, spreading over the hills, (is, are) visible.

6. Many of the men who (stands, stand) behind the ditch (begins, begin) to worry.

B. Writing Application: Revise each sentence, correcting errors in subject-verb agreement by changing the form of the verb. If a sentence contains no errors, write *Correct.*

1. Both the brain of Leiningen and the brains of the Indians begins to stir with the unpleasant foreboding that inside every single one of that deluge of insects dwell a thought.

   _____

   _____

2. An immense flood of ants pour in a glimmering black cataract down the far slope of the ditch and drown in the sluggish creeping flow. _____

   _____

3. They are followed by troop after troop, who clamber over their sinking comrades, and then themselves serve as dying bridges to the reserves who hurry on in their rear. _____

   _____

   _____

Name _____ Date _____

"Leiningen Versus the Ants" by Carl Stephenson

Reading Strategy: Predicting Based on Plot Details

You will become a more active and involved reader if you can predict what will happen next in a story. **Base your predictions on plot details,** and follow the developing story to make subsequent predictions. You can also use what you know about similar types of stories to inform your predictions.

DIRECTIONS: Make two different predictions based on the question asked about each plot detail.

Plot Detail	Question	Prediction #1	Prediction #2
1. The outer and inner moats are described in great detail.	How will the moats figure in the plot?		
2. The ants reach the edge of the ditch.	How will the ants cross the ditch?		
3. Leiningen sleeps while the workers defend the perimeter.	What will Leiningen find when he returns the next morning?		
4. Leiningen orders the man at the weir to alternately raise and lower the water level.	How might this plan go wrong?		
5. Leiningen and his men retreat within the inner moat.	What is the next plan of action?		
6. Two men die a quick, horrible death while trying to escape.	What will happen next?		

Name _____ Date _____

"Leiningen Versus the Ants" by Carl Stephenson

Literary Analysis: Conflict

Short stories, like real life, contain conflicts. A **conflict** may be internal or external. Most stories contain a combination of both.

A. DIRECTIONS: Complete the following chart by describing how each conflict is either external or internal.

Conflict	Internal	External
Example: The ants approach the plantation.		This is the beginning of a battle between man and nature.
1. The ants find a way to cross the outer moat.		
2. After losing the first round of the battle, the peons must decide whether to stay with Leiningen or leave.		
3. The ants cross the second moat on a bed of ash.		
4. Leiningen decides to go to the dam himself, risking his own life.		

B. DIRECTIONS: Imagine that you are one of the peons employed by Leiningen. Will you stay to fight the ants or leave? Describe in a paragraph how you would solve this internal conflict.

_____

_____

_____

_____

_____

_____

_____

"By the Waters of Babylon" by Stephen Vincent Benét

Build Vocabulary

Spelling Strategy   When adding a suffix to a word that ends in *y* preceded by a consonant, change the *y* to *i* and then add the suffix. For the word *purify*, for example, change the *y*
to *i* before adding the *-ed* ending: *purify* + *-ed* = *purified*. However, keep the *y* when adding
-ing: *purifying*.

Using Conjunctive Adverbs

Conjunctive adverbs show a relationship between ideas and often connect independent
clauses. The Word Bank words *moreover* and *nevertheless* are just two examples of conjunctive
adverbs. Generally, a semicolon precedes a conjunctive adverb.

A. DIRECTIONS: Complete each sentence with one of the following conjunctive adverbs: *further-
more, otherwise, still, therefore.*

1. John is the son of a priest; _____, he is allowed to go into the Dead Places.

2. Metal may be taken from the Dead Places; _____, no objects may be touched.

3. In his dream, John sees a great Dead Place where gods walk; _____, he believes he
   must travel east and cross the river.

4. John fears what he might find in the great Dead Place; _____, he feels he must make
   the journey.

Using the Word Bank

B. DIRECTIONS: Circle the letter of the best synonym for each word bank word.

1. purified   a) burned   b) cleansed   c) blessed

2. bowels   a) organs   b) rivers   c) insides

3. moreover   a) additionally   b) twice   c) instead

4. nevertheless   a) impossible   b) also   c) however

Understanding Sentence Completions

C. DIRECTIONS: In the blank, write the letter of the pair of words that best completes the meaning of the sentence.

_____   1. John's vision compels him to
          travel east; _____, he feels a fire in
          his _____ to make the journey.
          a. bowels—nevertheless
          b. bowels—moreover
          c. moreover—bowels
          d. nevertheless—bowels

_____   2. Priests are allowed to take metal
          from the dead place; _____, they
          and the metal must be _____.
          a. purified—moreover
          b. purified—nevertheless
          c. moreover—purified
          d. nevertheless—purified

"By the Waters of Babylon" by Stephen Vincent Benét

Build Grammar Skills: Vary Sentence Beginnings

If all your sentences begin the same way, your writing becomes monotonous and is less likely to engage readers. **Varying sentence beginnings** can strengthen your writing and make it more interesting to read. Generally, avoid having more than three sentences in a row start the same way. The following examples show some of the ways you can vary sentence beginnings.

Beginning With an Adverb: Afterwards, both the man and the metal must be purified!

Beginning With a Prepositional Phrase: After a time, I myself was allowed to go into the dead houses and search for metal.

Beginning With a Participial Phrase: Taking no food, I waited again on the flat rock.

Beginning With a Subordinate Clause: When the night came, I made my fire and roasted meat.

A. Practice: Identify the type of beginning of each sentence as adverb, prepositional phrase, participial phrase, or subordinate clause.

1. Nevertheless, it was strange. _____

2. Raising my eyes, I saw the place of the gods. _____

3. If I went to the place of the gods, I would surely die. _____

4. After a while, my eyes were opened and I saw. _____

5. When I was very near, my raft struck and turned over. _____

6. Ascending the stairs, I reached a door. _____

B. Writing Application: Rewrite the following paragraph, using a variety of sentence beginnings to make it more engaging. Feel free to combine some sentences.

John is the son of a priest. He has a dream. He goes on a journey. He crosses the river. He visits the place of the gods. The wild dogs see John. He runs away. He finds safety in a building. He enters a room. He discovers the remains of a man. He understands what happened to the people of the city.

_____

_____

_____

_____

_____

_____

_____

_____

Name _____ Date _____

"By the Waters of Babylon" by Stephen Vincent Benét

Reading Strategy: Drawing Conclusions

As you begin reading "By the Waters of Babylon," you encounter mysterious settings and events. The narrator does not explain how the Dead Places came to be or what caused the Great Burning. You, as an involved reader, must analyze facts and details in the story to **draw conclusions** about the story's setting and background.

DIRECTIONS: Complete the chart by providing details and writing reasonable conclusions that can be drawn from those details.

Question	Detail #1	Detail #2	Conclusion
1. What are the old writings?			
2. What are the god-roads?			
3. What is the great river that John crosses?			
4. What is the strong magic that John observes at night in the Place of the Gods?			
5. What was the Great Burning?			
6. When does the story take place?			

"By the Waters of Babylon" by Stephen Vincent Benét

Literary Analysis: First-Person Point of View

Point of view is the position or perspective from which the events of a story are seen. When you read a story told from the **first-person point of view,** you experience the story through the eyes of a character who uses the first-person pronouns *I, me, my.* Through that first-person narrator, you—the reader—experience everything that happens in the story and know the character's thoughts and feelings.

A. DIRECTIONS: Write your answers to the following questions.

1. Name two details that help you identify John as the first-person narrator of "By the Waters of Babylon."

   _____

2. What mood does the first-person point of view create in this story?

   _____

3. What does John know that you do not know?

   _____

4. What information do you have that John does not?

   _____

5. Does seeing things through John's eyes make you look at the world around you in a different way? Why or why not?

   _____

   _____

B. DIRECTIONS: Write a paragraph in which you respond to the use of first-person point of view in "By the Waters of Babylon." What did you enjoy about this point of view? What did you dislike or find frustrating?

_____

_____

_____

_____

_____

_____

_____

_____

_____

_____

"**A Problem**" by Anton Chekhov
"**Luck**" by Mark Twain

Build Vocabulary

Spelling Strategy   Words that end in silent *e* drop the *e* before adding a suffix beginning with a vowel. For example, the silent *e* in the word *sublime* is dropped when the suffix *-ity* is added to form the Word Bank word *sublimity*.

Using the Root *-ver-*

The Word Bank word *veracity*, which means "truthfulness" or "honesty," contains the root *-ver-*, which comes from the Latin adjective *verax*, meaning "speaking the truth" or "truthful."

A. DIRECTIONS: Determine the meaning of the italicized word in each sentence by using context clues and what you know about the Latin root *-ver-*. Write your definition on the line below.

1. Meeting a *veracious* individual can be a refreshing and reaffirming experience.

   _____

2. The judge asked the witness to *verify* her statement.

   _____

3. *Verification* of Chekhov's declining health could be seen in his exhausted appearance.

   _____

Using the Word Bank

B. DIRECTIONS: In the blank, write the letter of the definition next to the word it defines.

____ 1. zenith   a. the expression on a person's face
____ 2. countenance   b. without slyness or cunning; frank
____ 3. veracity   c. a noble or exalted state
____ 4. guileless   d. having to do with rheumatism
____ 5. prodigious   e. the highest point
____ 6. sublimity   f. truthfulness; honesty
____ 7. taciturn   g. a small entrance hall or room
____ 8. rheumatic   h. enormous
____ 9. vestibule   i. silent

Using Antonyms

C. DIRECTIONS: In the blank, write the letter of the word most nearly *opposite* in meaning to the Word Bank word.

____ 1. prodigious   ____ 2. veracity   ____ 3. guileless
   a. petite   a. sublimity   a. innocent
   b. noticeable   b. dishonesty   b. frank
   c. elaborate   c. silence   c. truthful
   d. enormous   d. cunning   d. sly

"**A Problem**" by Anton Chekhov
"**Luck**" by Mark Twain

Build Grammar Skills: Restrictive and Nonrestrictive Adjective Clauses

An **adjective clause** is a group of words that contains a subject and verb and begins with a relative pronoun such as *who, that,* or *which.* An adjective clause modifies a noun or a pronoun and usually follows the word it modifies.

adjective clause
The Twain story *that appears in this unit* is "Luck."

Adjective clauses may be restrictive or nonrestrictive. A **restrictive adjective clause** is necessary, or essential, to complete the meaning of the noun or pronoun it modifies. It is not set off with a comma. A **nonrestrictive adjective clause** is not needed to make the meaning of a sentence clear, but adds details to the sentence. A nonrestrictive clause is always set off with commas.

Restrictive adjective clause
Chekhov's stories always include characters *who fascinate me.*

Nonrestrictive adjective clause
"A Problem," *which was written by Chekhov,* features the troubling character Sasha Uskov.

A. Practice: Underline the adjective clause that appears in each sentence. Then identify each clause as restrictive or nonrestrictive by writing *R* or *N* on the lines provided. .

_____ 1. Sasha Uskov, the young man of twenty-five who was the cause of all the commotion, had arrived some time before.

_____ 2. Ivan Markovitch was weeping and muttering something which it was impossible to catch through the door.

_____ 3. He went through . . . and got compliments too, while others, who knew a thousand times more than he, got plucked.

_____ 4. Consider what I did—I who so loved repose and inaction.

B. Writing Application: Complete each of the following sentences with either a restrictive or nonrestrictive adjective clause. Remember to set off nonrestrictive adjective clauses with commas.

1. Ivan Markovitch _____ defends Sasha's actions as the errors of an unlucky youth.

2. Another of Sasha's uncles argues in favor of defending the family's honor
_____.

3. The numerous blunders _____ are all interpreted as acts of genius.

4. The clergyman _____ confesses to the narrator, "Privately— he's an absolute fool."

5. At the banquet _____ the narrator hears all about Scoresby from his old acquaintance.

"**A Problem**" by Anton Chekhov
"**Luck**" by Mark Twain

Reading Strategy: Identifying With a Character

When you **identify with a character,** you put yourself in the character's place and share his or her thoughts, feelings, and experiences. In "A Problem," Sasha Uskov and his uncle, Ivan Markovitch, respond differently to troubling events. In "Luck," the narrator and the clergyman react to their discoveries. Imagine yourself in each character's place as he deals with different situations. How would you feel? How would you act? Answering these questions as you read will help you to better understand the characters and the part each plays in the stories.

DIRECTIONS: In the following chart, make notes about the character's reaction to the specified situations. Then, try to put yourself in that character's place and describe what you might say, do, or feel in the same situations. Explain why you might have these reactions.

"A Problem"

Situation	What Sasha Uskov says, does, or feels.	What you might say, do or feel and why.
1. Sasha Uskov waits to learn if his family will keep him out of trouble, or let him bear the consequences of his actions.		
Situation	What Ivan Markovitch says, does, or feels.	What you might say, do, or feel and why.
2. After Ivan Markovitch narrowly convinces the family to give Sasha another chance, Sasha accosts him and demands a hundred rubles.		

"Luck"

Situation	What the narrator says, does, or feels.	What you might say, do or feel and why.
3. As the narrator is admiring a man he holds in high esteem, the clergyman leans down and tells him that the man is "an absolute fool."		
Situation	What the clergyman says, does, or feels.	What you might say, do, or feel and why.
4. The clergyman unwittingly helps Scoresby pass a test. As a result, Scoresby is promoted to a position of great responsibility.		

"**A Problem**" by Anton Chekhov
"**Luck**" by Mark Twain

Literary Analysis: Static and Dynamic Characters

In fiction there are two types of characters: static and dynamic. A **static character** does not change during the course of a story—no matter what experiences the character encounters, his or her personality, attitudes, and beliefs are the same at the end of the story as they were at the beginning. In these two stories, Sasha Uskov and Arthur Scoresby are static characters.

A **dynamic character,** on the other hand, does change during the course of the story. He or she is affected by events in the story and, sometimes, learns and grows because of those events. Ivan Markovitch in Chekhov's story is an example of a dynamic character because a certain event drastically alters Markovitch's opinion of his paternal nephew.

DIRECTIONS: Complete the following charts, which contrast one static and one dynamic character from each story. Identify the evidence, whether from direct or indirect characterization, that illustrates the static or dynamic nature of each character. For the clergyman, you will find evidence only from direct characterization.

"A Problem"

Character	Type	Evidence from Story
Sasha Uskov	Static	Direct characterization 1. 2. Indirect characterization 1. 2.
Ivan Markovitch	Dynamic	Direct characterization 1. 2. Indirect characterization 1. 2.

"Luck"

Character	Type	Evidence from Story
Arthur Scoresby	Static	Direct characterization 1. 2. Indirect characterization 1. 2.
Clergyman	Dynamic	Direct characterization 1. 2. 3. 4.

Name _____ Date _____

"There Will Come Soft Rains" by Ray Bradbury
"The Garden of Stubborn Cats" by Italo Calvino

Build Vocabulary

Spelling Strategy   In English, many adjectives are formed with the suffix -ic, such as the Word Bank words *titanic* and *psychopathic*. The -ic suffix, which descended from Greek and Latin, has several variations, including -ique and -ick.

Using Words From Greek Myths

Who's your nemesis? Do you have arachnophobia? Many words in common use today derive from ancient Greek tales of gods and their sometimes complicated relationships with mortals. For example, Prometheus, one of the Titans (from which the Word Bank word *titanic* derives), got into trouble with Zeus for helping human beings. A Promethean idea is a good thing nevertheless.

A. DIRECTIONS: Use an encyclopedia, a dictionary, or another form of reference to discover the source in Greek mythology of the following terms. Then define each term in the space provided, and identify the myth from which it derives.

1. Promethean _____

_____

2. nemesis _____

_____

3. arachnophobia _____

_____

4. narcissism _____

_____

Using the Word Bank

B. DIRECTIONS: Circle the letter of the word most similar in meaning to the Word Bank word.

1. warrens
   a. documents
   b. cautions
   c. burrows
   d. guarantee

2. titanic
   a. metallic
   b. immense
   c. nautical
   d. ferocious

3. paranoia
   a. distrust
   b. occult
   c. immobility
   d. boundary

4. tremulous
   a. trembling
   b. vast
   c. prestigious
   d. frozen

5. psychopathic
   a. sensitive
   b. clairvoyant
   c. knowledgeable
   d. deranged

6. supernal
   a. better
   b. extrasensory
   c. subsequent
   d. heavenly

7. itinerary
   a. sanctuary
   b. necessary
   c. course
   d. utensil

8. transoms
   a. bribes
   b. windows
   c. vagrants
   d. visitors

"There Will Come Soft Rains" by Ray Bradbury
"The Garden of Stubborn Cats" by Italo Calvino

Build Grammar Skills: Parallel Structure

Parallel structure is the use of patterns or repetition of grammatical structures. Parallel structure adds rhythm and balance to writing by expressing ideas of equal importance in similar ways. It is created by using the same grammatical form in all of those parts of the sentence that have the same function and importance. Parallel structure should always be used *within* a sentence.

Parallel Phrases: There were cats *strolling in the garden, climbing up the trees, wandering across roofs, sleeping in the sun.*

Parallel Clauses: *No one heard the messages, no one ate the food, and no one noticed the whirring, robot mice* frantically cleaning the abandoned house.

For full sentences, varying style may add interest, but parallel structure can be used to emphasize important points and to create links between related ideas.

Parallel Sentences: *Bridge tables sprouted from patio walls. Playing cards fluttered onto pads in a shower of pips. Glasses manifested on an oaken bench.*

A. Practice: Underline the parallel elements in each of the following passages.

1. An aluminum wedge scraped them into the sink, where hot water whirled them down a metal throat which digested and flushed them away to the distant sea.

2. They thudded against chairs, whirling their mustached runners, kneading the rug nap, sucking gently at hidden dust.

3. Now the fire lay in beds, stood in windows, changed the colors of drapes!

4. Marcovaldo laid his place among the packing-cases in the warehouse, chewed his snack, smoked a half-cigar, and wandered around, alone and idle, waiting for work to resume.

B. Writing Application: Rewrite the following sentences so that all elements are parallel.

1. If they could see, if they could understand, if humans had programmed them for communicating, what story would the robots tell? _____

_____

2. The city had grown. It had taken over the plazas. Gardens are being filled in by it. It had pushed the cats out of their usual places. _____

_____

3. The Marchesa insisted that the cats were destroying her life, that they were keeping her prisoner, that plans were being ruined. _____

_____

4. Nobody had seen the Marchesa. No smoke came from her chimney. Her face wasn't peering out her window. No sign of life presented itself. _____

_____

"There Will Come Soft Rains" by Ray Bradbury
"The Garden of Stubborn Cats" by Italo Calvino

Reading Strategy: Clarifying

Writers manage information carefully to keep readers interested. Sometimes they arrange details about setting and plot in order to allow an effect to unfold. "Where are we, and what is going on?" readers should ask. These questions apply in different ways to "There Will Come Soft Rains" and "The Garden of Stubborn Cats." In order to answer the questions, readers must **clarify** details as they arise. Sometimes, you must reread or look back to understand what you have just read. Sometimes you must read on until you get needed information.

DIRECTIONS: Each of the following passages from "There Will Come Soft Rains" and "The Garden of Stubborn Cats" requires clarification. For each passage, list other details that help you clarify the meaning. The details may appear in the story either before or after the passage.

1. The morning house lay empty.

_____

2. The house stood alone in a city of rubble and ashes. This was the one house left.

_____

3. The entire west face of the house was black, save for five places.

_____

_____

4. The house shuddered, oak bone on bone, its bared skeleton cringing from the heat, its wire, its nerves revealed as if a surgeon had torn the skin off to let the red veins and capillaries quiver in the scalded air.

_____

_____

5. The city of cats and the city of men exist one inside the other, but they are not the same city.

_____

_____

6. Or, more precisely, above the partridges and quails the dishes whirled, and above the dishes, the white gloves, and poised on the waiters' patent-leather shoes, the gleaming parquet floor, from which hung dwarf potted palms and tablecloths and crystal and buckets like bells with the champagne bottle for their clapper . . .

_____

_____

7. Marcovaldo realized he had finally reached the heart of the cats' realm, their secret island.

_____

_____

8. "They keep me prisoner, they do, those cats."

_____

"There Will Come Soft Rains" by Ray Bradbury
"The Garden of Stubborn Cats" by Italo Calvino

Literary Analysis: Setting

The **setting** of a literary work is the time and place in which the events of the work occur. A story may have an overall setting as well as specific settings. There may be more than one setting as the action moves from place to place, and from one time to another. In Shakespeare's *Romeo and Juliet,* for example, the overall setting is Verona, Italy, in the sixteenth century, but the specific time and place changes from scene to scene.

Some stories, such as "There Will Come Soft Rains" and "The Garden of Stubborn Cats," are dependent on different aspects of setting. Although Bradbury's story is set in a specific location, it is more dependent upon the time for its impact. In Calvino's story, place is the key to the mystery in the garden.

You should pay attention to details about the setting, just as you pay attention to other information in the story. What details give you information about the time and place of a story, and what is the effect of those details? Use the following charts to organize what you learn about the settings of these selections as you read.

DIRECTIONS: In the "Setting" column, fill in the overall time, overall place, specific time, and specific place, as and if you discover them. In the "Evidence" column, fill in the detail from the story that gives you the information for the setting. In the "Impact" column, write how overall and specific times and places matter to the story. What effect, if any, does each have on the story?

"There Will Come Soft Rains"			
Type	**Setting**	**Evidence**	**Impact**
Overall Time:			
Overall Place:			
Specific Time:			
Specific Place:			

"The Garden of Stubborn Cats"			
Type	**Setting**	**Evidence**	**Impact**
Overall Time:			
Overall Place:			
Specific Time:			
Specific Place:			

"The Princess and All the Kingdom" by Pär Lagerkvist
"The Censors" by Luisa Valenzuela

Build Vocabulary

Spelling Strategy   When adding a suffix that begins with a consonant to a word that ends in a consonant, do not double the word's final consonant. From the Word Bank, *staid + ness = staidness*. Also, *invest**ment*** and *decided**ly*** illustrate this rule.

Using the Prefix *ultra-*

A. DIRECTIONS: The addition of *ultra, ulter,* or *ulti* at the beginning of a word extends the meaning of the word; *ultra* means "further," "beyond," or, in some cases, "extreme." Explain the meanings of the following words, keeping in mind the effect of the "ultra" portion of each word.

1. ultraminiature _____

2. ultramodern _____

3. ultranationalism _____

Using the Word Bank

B. DIRECTIONS: Complete each sentence to demonstrate your understanding of the italicized Word Bank word.

1. "My goal was to get a part-time job. I didn't tell anyone I wanted to start earning money for college." The second sentence represents an *ulterior* motive for getting a job because
   _____ .

2. The old chancellor was *venerable* because of his _____ .

3. The young man views the kingdom and its treasures as a *sordid* gain because
   _____ .

4. The building's exterior contrasted with the interior's *staidness.* The exterior was festive; the interior was _____ .

5. The young man's kisses were *ardent*, which indicates that he probably felt
   _____ about the princess.

C. DIRECTIONS: Circle the letter of the word or phrase that is most nearly *opposite* to the Word Bank word.

1. staidness	2. venerable	3. ardent
a. sweetness	a. not respected	a. indifferent
b. emotionality	b. lengthy	b. extremely enthusiastic
c. mobility	c. lacking substance	c. in a determined manner
d. strictness	d. prehistoric	d. unaware

"The Princess and All the Kingdom" by Pär Lagerkvist
"The Censors" by Luisa Valenzuela

Build Grammar Skills: Consistency of Tenses

Verb tenses are used to indicate when events occurred or conditions existed. Tenses within a sentence need to be consistent with the time of the sentence. The time of a sentence is established by context and is generally indicated by clues such as *yesterday, when I was little, this morning, next year.* Verbs should also be consistent with other verbs in the sentence. For example, if you are writing about something that occurred in the past, make sure that all your verbs are in a past tense, even if you use a variety of past tenses (basic, progressive, perfect). Consistency with the time of the sentence takes precedence over consistency with other verbs, but the time must be very clear (An hour ago, I *was* hungry, but now I *am* full.)

> **Mixed Tenses:** Once upon a time there *was* a prince, who *goes* out to fight in order to win the princess.
>
> **Consistent Tense:** Once upon a time there *was* a prince, who *went* out to fight in order to win the princess.

A. Practice: Underline the verbs in each sentence. Then, identify whether or not the verb tenses are consistent. On the line, write *consistent* or *mixed.*

_____ 1. At last he stands outside the city where the princess lived in her royal castle.

_____ 2. When the princess saw how proud and handsome he was and thought of how he has dared his life for her sake, she will not withstand his power but gave him her hand.

_____ 3. The whole city decked itself out for the festival and the wedding was celebrated with rejoicing, pomp, and splendor.

_____ 4. Here are the keys of the kingdom which open the treasuries where everything that now belongs to you will be kept.

_____ 5. I have not fought for sordid gain; I had fought merely to win her whom I love.

B. Writing Application: Rewrite the following sentences to make the verb tenses consistent within each sentence.

1. Yesterday, when Juan received the letter, he sits down and wrote a letter to Mariana.

   _____

   _____

2. If the censors get this letter, they will examine it, they look at everything, and even smell and felt the paper.

   _____

   _____

3. These things happen the minute you were careless, as one often is.

   _____

   _____

"**The Princess and All the Kingdom**" by Pär Lagerkvist
"**The Censors**" by Luisa Valenzuela

Reading Strategy: Challenging the Writer's Message

When reading, you should look for the writer's message and consider it carefully. In fiction, the writer's message is usually revealed through a narrator's words or through a main character's words or actions. The message may be stated directly or indirectly. Once you discover the message, state it in your own words. Then test the message to see whether it applies to your own life, and whether it is something with which you agree or disagree.

DIRECTIONS: Answer the questions in the following chart to uncover the messages in these selections.

"The Princess and All the Kingdom"

What is the message?
How is the message revealed in the story?
Does the message apply to my life? _____   If so, in what way?   If not, explain why.

"The Censors"

What is the message?
How is the message revealed in the story?
Does the message apply to my life? _____   If so, in what way?   If not, explain why.

"The Princess and All the Kingdom" by Pär Lagerkvist

"The Censors" by Luisa Valenzuela

Literary Analysis: Universal Themes

Most of us have read stories in which the underdog wins—the kid who tries the hardest succeeds, even if that kid isn't the smartest or the fastest or the "best." The stories may differ, but the theme is the same: Those who try hard or do their best will succeed. Although in stories and in real life the success may take different forms, this is an example of a **universal theme.** It is an idea that could be applied to most people's lives, regardless of their age, culture, or circumstances.

Both Pär Lagerkvist and Luisa Valenzuela deal with universal themes in their stories. Lagerkvist, writing in the 1950's, chose to put his in the form of a fairy tale. Valenzuela disguised her theme in a modern-day short story that is a commentary on her country's political system.

DIRECTIONS: For each of the following story descriptions, identify the theme and state specifically why it is universal.

1. Three strangers enter a small village. The village people hide all their food, not wanting to offer any hospitality. The three strangers borrow a pot in which to make "soup" by boiling three stones. They then trick the village people into volunteering to contribute their hidden vegetables and other food to add to the stone soup. The end result is a delicious soup and a happy gathering among the strangers and the village people.

Theme: _____

Explanation:_____

_____

2. An industrious character decides to plant a garden. She asks for help preparing the ground, but her friends do not help. She asks for help planting the seeds, but her friends prefer to watch. This continues through the weeding, harvesting, and preserving of the good things from her garden. When she cooks up a delicious pot of stew, her friends volunteer to help her eat it, but she tells them that because they would not help her plant, weed, or harvest, they cannot enjoy the final product.

Theme: _____

Explanation:_____

_____

3. Two characters, say a rabbit and a turtle, challenge each other to a race. The rabbit is sure of himself and begins the race with a rush, but then dawdles along the way. The turtle, knowing he is slow, sets a pace and keeps it up all the way along the course. The rabbit realizes his error too late, and the turtle wins.

Theme: _____

Explanation:_____

_____

"The Marginal World" by Rachel Carson

Build Vocabulary

Spelling Strategy   Words ending in silent e keep the e before a suffix beginning with a consonant. For example, the word *subjective* ends in silent e. When adding the suffix -*ly* to form the Word Bank word *subjectively*, the silent e remains.

Using the Suffix -*able*

A. DIRECTIONS: The suffix -*able* (sometimes -*ible*) means "capable of" or "capable of being." For example, the Word Bank word *mutable*, which contains the suffix -*able,* means "capable of change." Provide a definition for the following words, then give an example of something that each word describes. For example, for *mutable* you might write *weather* since weather is capable of change.

1. vulnerable _____

2. manageable _____

3. irreversible _____

4. invariable _____

Using the Word Bank

B. DIRECTIONS: Match each word in the left column with its definition in the right column.

____ 1. marginal   a. appearances; evidences

____ 2. primeval   b. personally

____ 3. mutable   c. real nature of something

____ 4. manifestations   d. ancient; primitive

____ 5. cosmic   e. capable of change

____ 6. ephemeral   f. passing quickly

____ 7. subjectively   g. occupying the borderland

____ 8. essence   h. relating to the universe

Recognizing Antonyms

C. DIRECTIONS: Choose the word or phrase that is most nearly *opposite* in meaning to the Word Bank word. Circle the letter of your choice.

1. ephemeral
   a. formidable
   b. transient
   c. durable
   d. passing quickly

2. primeval
   a. vigorous
   b. modern
   c. primitive
   d. ancient

3. cosmic
   a. relating to the universe
   b. ethereal
   c. heavenly
   d. earthly

Name _____ Date _____

Build Grammar Skills: Recognizing Degrees of Comparison

Most adjectives and adverbs have three different forms to show **degrees of comparison**—the *positive*, the *comparative*, and the *superlative*. Use the positive form to modify another word, the comparative form to compare two things, and the superlative form to compare more than two things.

Positive: Ocean plants are *hardy*.
The crab moved *swiftly* over the sand.

Comparative: Ocean plants are *hardier* than house plants.
The crab moved *more swiftly* than the lobster.

Superlative: Plants that live between the tide lines are the *hardiest* of all.
The sanderlings moved *most swiftly* of all.

In general, add *-er* to form the comparative degree and *-est* to form the superlative degree. Use *more* and *most* (or *less* and *least*) to form the comparative and superlative degrees in the following situations: with adverbs ending in *-ly*; with modifiers of three or more syllables; in cases when adding *-er* and *-est* to one- and two-syllable modifiers would sound awkward.

A. Practice: Underline the modifier in each sentence. Identify its degree by writing *Positive*, *Comparative*, or *Superlative* on the line.

_____1. Only the most adaptable can survive in such a region, yet the area is crowded with plants and animals.

_____2. I cannot think of a more beautiful place than the pool hidden within a cave that one can visit only when the level of the sea drops below its entrance.

_____3. There had been ominous showers in the night, with rain like handfuls of gravel flung on the roof.

_____4. In the moment when I looked into the cave, a starfish hung down, suspended by the merest thread.

B. Writing Application: Follow the directions below to write four sentences about "The Marginal World," using different degrees of comparison.

1. Use the comparative form of *tough*.

_____

2. Use the superlative form of *delicately*.

_____

3. Use the positive form of *strong*.

_____

4. Use the comparative form of *urgent*.

_____

"**The Marginal World**" by Rachel Carson

Reading Strategy: Recognizing Patterns of Organization

Writers of nonfiction organize their writing in a number of ways. **Patterns of organization** include explaining events in chronological order; developing ideas in order of importance; comparing and contrasting ideas, events, or things; explaining causes and effects; using spatial order to describe where things are in relation to one another; and so on. In "The Marginal World," Carson organizes her essay by describing the edge of the sea in different places at different times of day. She also uses other patterns of organization within her essay, such as compare and contrast order and cause and effect order. Noticing how the material is presented and developed can help you better understand it.

DIRECTIONS: Complete the chart by finding an example from the selection for each pattern of organization. Write the passages in the space provided.

Patterns of Organization	
Chronological Order	
Comparison and Contrast	
Classification	
Spatial Order	

"The Marginal World" by Rachel Carson

Literary Analysis: Expository Essay

An **expository essay** is a short nonfiction work written in order to inform. This is done by explaining, defining, or interpreting an idea, an event, or a process. The most effective expository essays are coherent and unified; in other words, all of the elements of the essay fit together in a logical, organized way. An expository essay can be organized in a number of ways: chronological order, order of importance, comparison and contrast, cause and effect, parts to a whole, pro and con, and so on. In her essay "The Marginal World," Rachel Carson describes parts of the intertidal zone of the ocean and explains the cause-and-effect relationships that affect the survival of the plants and animals in that "magical zone."

DIRECTIONS: Answer each of the following questions about Rachel Carson's expository essay.

1. With what concept or idea does Carson begin her essay?

   _____

   _____

2. Summarize why each of the three places "stands apart" in Carson's mind.

   _____

   _____

   _____

   _____

   _____

3. What details does Carson use to illustrate how each of the three places "stands apart"?

   _____

   _____

   _____

   _____

   _____

4. What pattern of organization does Carson use to explain the adaptability of snails?

   _____

5. What main point does Carson develop and support throughout her essay?

   _____

   _____

   _____

from *The Way to Rainy Mountain* by N. Scott Momaday

from "Nobel Lecture" by Alexander Solzhenitsyn

"Keep Memory Alive" by Elie Wiesel

Build Vocabulary

Spelling Strategy   Most adverbs end in *-ly*. When adding the suffix *-ly* to a word that ends in *-ble*, drop the *-le* and replace it with *-ly*. The Word Bank word *inexorably* is *inexorable* + *ly*. *Discernibly* and *capably* are also formed in this way.

Using Forms of *Reciprocity*

A. DIRECTIONS: Use the following exercise to distinguish between the forms of reciprocity. Match each word in the left column with its definition in the right column.

____   1. reciprocity   a. to do in return

____   2. reciprocal   b. a mutual exchange

____   3. reciprocate   c. mutual action or dependence

____   4. reciprocation   d. mutual

Using the Word Bank

B. DIRECTIONS: Complete each of the following sentences to demonstrate your understanding of the italicized Word Bank word.

1. Another way to say that natural wonders *engender* awe in humans is to say that natural wonders _____ .

2. When Momaday says that the Kiowas' well-being was *tenuous*, he means _____ _____ .

3. Solzhenitsyn's idea of *reciprocity* is _____ _____ .

4. If people are able to *assimilate* an idea into their way of thinking, that idea _____ _____ .

5. Someone who does something *inexorably* does it _____ .

6. Practicing *oratory* involves _____ .

7. If a historian claims that one event *transcends* another in importance, it means _____ _____ .

from *The Way to Rainy Mountain* by N. Scott Momaday
from "Nobel Lecture" by Alexander Solzhenitsyn
"Keep Memory Alive" by Elie Wiesel

Build Grammar Skills: Irregular Comparative and Superlative Degrees

A few commonly used adjectives and adverbs form their comparative and superlative degrees in unpredictable ways. The **irregular comparative and superlative degrees** of these modifiers must be memorized.

IRREGULAR MODIFIERS		
Positive	**Comparative**	**Superlative**
bad	worse	worst
badly	worse	worst
far (distance)	farther	farthest
far (extent)	further	furthest
good	better	best
ill	worse	worst
late	later	last or latest
little (amount)	less	least
many	more	most
much	more	most
well	better	best

A. Practice: Complete each sentence with the correct form of the adjective or adverb in parentheses.

1. Momaday's grandmother lived during the _____ of the good times in Kiowa history. (late)

2. They were some of the _____ horsemen ever known. (good)

3. Much _____ down, in the land of the Crows, the plain is yellow. (far)

4. They traveled _____ eastward and reached the plains. (far)

5. Despite _____ translations, his books found a responsive audience. (bad)

6. Between them there is the closest, the _____ profound bond. (much)

B. Writing Application: Follow the directions to write three sentences about "Keep Memory Alive."

1. Use the superlative form of *bad*.

_____

2. Use the comparative form of *late*.

_____

3. Use the superlative form of *much*.

_____

from *The Way to Rainy Mountain* by N. Scott Momaday
from "Nobel Lecture" by Alexander Solzhenitsyn
"Keep Memory Alive" by Elie Wiesel

Reading Strategy: Analyze Author's Purpose

Behind all writing there is a purpose. In their Nobel acceptance speeches, both Solzhenitsyn and Wiesel chose to persuade. In general, noticing details and knowing the background of the author may help you understand and analyze his or her purpose in writing a particular work.

DIRECTIONS: Following are some passages from the selections in this group. For each passage, tell why you think the author included those details or ideas. Then tell how the passage contributes to the author's larger purpose of reflection or informing (for Momaday) or persuasion (for Solzhenitsyn and Wiesel).

from *The Way to Rainy Mountain*

1. A single knoll rises out of the plain in Oklahoma, north and west of the Wichita Range. For my people, the Kiowas, it is an old landmark, and they gave it the name Rainy Mountain. The hardest weather in the world is there. Winter brings blizzards, hot tornadic winds arise in the spring, and in summer the prairie is an anvil's edge.

_____

_____

_____

_____

from "Nobel Lecture"

2. As I have understood it and experienced it myself, world literature is no longer an abstraction or a generalized concept invented by literary critics, but a common body and common spirit, a living, heartfelt unity reflecting the growing spiritual unity of mankind.

_____

_____

_____

from "Keep Memory Alive"

3. It all happened so fast. The ghetto. The deportation. The sealed cattle car. The fiery altar upon which the history of our people and the future of mankind were meant to be sacrificed.

_____

_____

_____

_____

from *The Way to Rainy Mountain* by N. Scott Momaday

from "Nobel Lecture" by Alexander Solzhenitsyn

"Keep Memory Alive" by Elie Wiesel

Literary Analysis: Reflective and Persuasive Essays

N. Scott Momaday's purpose in the passage from *The Way to Rainy Mountain*—or any writer's purpose in a **reflective essay**—is to share with readers a personal experience and its meaning. Momaday's unique perceptions and understanding of his own experience lead him to create a new experience for his readers. It is a writer's individual perspective that makes reflective writing engaging and fresh, even when the topic is a familiar one.

In a **persuasive essay**, the writer's purpose is to get the audience to agree with him or her. Effective persuasion should make points in a way that changes people's minds or makes them think or act in a different way. The art of persuasion is an appeal to reason.

DIRECTIONS: Refer to the selections by Momaday, Solzhenitsyn, and Wiesel as you answer the following questions.

1. Momaday writes about an event that many of his readers have experienced themselves— the loss, through death, of his grandmother. What is unique about Momaday's experience?

   _____

   _____

   _____

2. What is unique about the way Momaday acquaints readers with his grandmother?

   _____

   _____

   _____

3. In Solzhenitsyn's speech, the sentence "Writers and artists can do more: they can VAN-QUISH LIES!" sums up the idea with which he wants his listeners to agree. How does he build up to that point? With what reasonable statements or points does he support this statement?

   _____

   _____

   _____

   _____

4. What sentence in Wiesel's speech sums up the point with which he wants his listeners to agree? Show how Wiesel supports the sentence with reasonable, persuasive statements.

   _____

   _____

   _____

   _____

   _____

   _____

"A Child's Christmas in Wales" by Dylan Thomas
"Marian Anderson: Famous Concert Singer" by Langston Hughes

Build Vocabulary

Spelling Strategy If a word of more than one syllable ends in a single consonant following a single vowel, and the accent is not on the last syllable, do not double the final consonant before adding a suffix beginning with a vowel. For example, the suffix *-ed* added to *wallow* forms the Word Bank word *wallowed*, the suffix *-able* added to *consider* forms *considerable*, and the suffix *-ing* added to *remember* forms *remembering*.

Word Groups: Musical Words

In "Marian Anderson: Famous Concert Singer," Langston Hughes refers to *arias*—melodies from operas, usually for a solo voice—and Marian Anderson's *repertoire*—a stock of songs that a singer knows well and is ready to perform. There are many other words in the English language specifically related to the field of music.

A. Directions: Each word in the following list is a musical term that appears in "Marian Anderson: Famous Concert Singer." Complete each sentence with the most appropriate word.

hymns   bass   choral   octaves

1. Marian Anderson could sing in both soprano, the highest voice range, and _____, the lowest voice range.

2. The voice of Marian Anderson covered three entire _____, or intervals of eight tones.

3. Marian Anderson sang both individually and in _____ groups.

4. Before she was eight years old, Marian Anderson knew many _____ by heart.

Using the Word Bank

B. Directions: Match each word in the left column with its definition in the right column. Write the letter of the definition on the line next to the word it defines.

_____ 1. arias   a. walked

_____ 2. staunch   b. easily broken

_____ 3. repertoire   c. made of woven yarn or thread

_____ 4. sidle   d. move sideways

_____ 5. prey   e. abandoned

_____ 6. wallowed   f. loyal

_____ 7. crocheted   g. songs performed by a singer

_____ 8. brittle   h. vocal solos in an opera

_____ 9. trod   i. an animal hunted for food

_____ 10. forlorn   j. took great pleasure

"A Child's Christmas in Wales" by Dylan Thomas
"Marian Anderson: Famous Concert Singer" by Langston Hughes

Build Grammar Skills:
Restrictive and Nonrestrictive Appositives

An appositive is a noun or pronoun placed near another noun or pronoun to provide more information about it. An appositive phrase contains an appositive and any words that modify it. Appositives may be restrictive or nonrestrictive. A **restrictive appositive** is essential to the meaning of the sentence and is not set off by commas. A **nonrestrictive appositive** is not essential to the meaning of the sentence and is set off by commas. Read the following examples:

> **Restrictive Appositive:** The narrator's aunt *Hannah* stood in the snowbound back yard and sang.

The appositive *Hannah* is restrictive. It is necessary to identify which of the narrator's aunts is being described.

> **Nonrestrictive Appositive:** Marian Anderson's mother, *a church worker*, loved to croon the hymns of her faith.

The appositive *a church worker* is not essential in identifying Marian Anderson's mother.

A. Practice: Underline the appositive or appositive phrase in each sentence and identify it as restrictive or nonrestrictive.

1. We saw Miss Prothero, Jim's aunt, come downstairs and peer at the firemen.

2. My friend Jack suggested we sing "Good King Wenceslas."

3. The Philadelphia Choral society, an African American singing group, sponsored Marian Anderson's music studies after she graduated from high school.

4. The famous conductor Arturo Toscanini was amazed by Marian Anderson's singing.

B. Writing Application: Combine each of the following pairs of sentences by turning the second sentence into an appositive or an appositive phrase. Underline the appositive or the appositive phrase and then write restrictive or nonrestrictive above it.

1. I was with Mrs. Prothero's son in the garden. I was with the son whose name is Jim.

_____

2. I went out into the snow to call on my friends. I wanted to call on Jim, Dan, and Jack.

_____

3. Marian Anderson broke many stereotypes. Marian Anderson was a gifted singer.

_____

4. The writer wrote about Marian Anderson's talent in his *New York Times* article. The writer's name was Howard Taubman.

_____

5. In 1941 Marian Anderson received a public service award that allowed her to establish a scholarship fund for promising young musicians. The award was the Bok Award.

_____

"A Child's Christmas in Wales" by Dylan Thomas
"Marian Anderson: Famous Concert Singer" by Langston Hughes

Reading Strategy: Recognize Author's Attitude

Recognizing an **author's attitude**—the way in which he or she feels about a subject or about specific events—will help you to read with stronger understanding. In a biography, an author's attitude toward a subject is revealed through the details and events in a subject's life the author chooses to emphasize, and by the way he or she interprets these details and events. In an autobiography, an author's attitude toward events in his or her own life is revealed by the carefully chosen words and phrases used to describe these events.

DIRECTIONS: Read the following passages from "A Child's Christmas in Wales" and "Marian Anderson: Famous Concert Singer." Identify the author's attitude toward his subject and then list the specific words and phrases that express this attitude.

"A Child's Christmas in Wales"

1. "But all that the children could hear was a ringing of bells."

"You mean that the postman went rat-a-tat-tat and the doors rang?"

"I mean that the bells that the children could hear were inside them. . . . There were church bells, too . . . in the bat-black, snow-white belfries, tugged by bishops and storks. And they rang their tidings over the bandaged town, over the frozen foam of the powder and ice-cream hills, over the crackling sea. It seemed that all the churches boomed for joy under my window: and the weathercocks crew for Christmas, on our fence."

Attitude toward childhood Christmas:

_____

Words and phrases that express this attitude:

_____

"Marian Anderson: Famous Concert Singer"

2. When Marian Anderson again returned to America, she was a seasoned artist. News of her tremendous European successes had preceded her, so a big New York concert was planned. But a few days before she arrived at New York, . . . Marian fell and broke her ankle. She refused to allow this to interfere with her concert, however, nor did she even want people to know about it. . . . She propped herself in a curve of the piano before the curtains parted, and gave her New York concert standing on one foot!

Attitude toward Anderson as a performer:

_____

Words and phrases that express this attitude:

_____

_____

"A Child's Christmas in Wales" by Dylan Thomas
"Marian Anderson: Famous Concert Singer" by Langston Hughes

Literary Analysis: Biography and Autobiography

Both a biography and an autobiography are types of writing that give information about a person's life. A **biography** is a chronicle of a person's life written by another individual, whereas an **autobiography** is a person's chronicle of his or her own life.

A biographer gathers information about his or her subject from sources such as letters, journals, newspaper articles, and interviews with the subject or people who knew the subject. The biographer then organizes and interprets this information, deciding what should be emphasized and exactly what he or she wants to express about the life of the subject. A person writing an autobiography focuses on specific events in his or her own life and may share personal thoughts and feelings about these events. Often, a person writing an autobiography shares details about his or her life that others would never know, even after extensive research.

DIRECTIONS: Answer the following questions about the biography "Marian Anderson: Famous Concert Singer" and the autobiography "A Child's Christmas in Wales."

1. From what sources do you think Langston Hughes might have gathered his information about Marian Anderson? What specific sources does he name in the biography?

_____

_____

_____

2. What are some interesting details shared by Hughes about Marian Anderson's life? What do many of the details and events he chooses to share have in common?

_____

_____

_____

3. How does Hughes interpret the information he gathers? What does he want to express about Marian Anderson's life?

_____

_____

_____

4. Why do you think Thomas chooses to describe his own childhood Christmases? At what moments in the piece are you most aware of his feelings toward this time?

_____

_____

_____

5. What are some details Thomas reveals in his autobiographical account that only he would know?

_____

_____

_____

"Flood" by Annie Dillard

Build Vocabulary

Spelling Strategy When adding a suffix to a word ending in more than one consonant, never double the final consonant. For example, the words *usurp* and *repress* become the Word Bank words *usurped* and *repressed* when combined with the suffix *-ed*.

Using the Prefix *mal-*

In "Flood," Annie Dillard describes the malevolent hiss of a captured snapping turtle. The word *malevolent* contains the prefix *mal-*, which means "bad" or "evil." Therefore, a "malevolent hiss" is one that is intended as evil or harmful.

A. DIRECTIONS: Replace the italicized word or phrase in each sentence with a word from the following list:

malignant   malicious   malady   maladjusted

1. The floodwater seemed *evil and spiteful* as it destroyed everything in its path.

2. Some say dishonesty is a dangerous social *disorder*.

3. At first the new student seemed *unable to adapt*, but he soon became comfortable in his new surroundings.

4. Doctors found the disease to be *extremely harmful and dangerous*.

Using the Word Bank

B. DIRECTIONS: In the blank, write the letter of the definition next to the word it defines.

_____ 1. obliterates   a. evil or harmful

_____ 2. opacity   b. held back; restrained

_____ 3. usurped   c. roughly or clumsily handled

_____ 4. mauled   d. destroys; erases without a trace

_____ 5. malevolent   e. the quality of not letting light pass

_____ 6. repressed   f. taken power over; held by force

C. DIRECTIONS: Circle the letter of the pair of words that best expresses a relationship *similar* to that expressed in the pair in CAPITAL LETTERS.

1. OBLITERATES : DESTRUCTION ::
   a. revitalizes : encouragement
   b. willful : stubborn
   c. organizes : system
   d. elderly : youthfulness

2. USURPED : POWER ::
   a. won : prize
   b. grab : steal
   c. gather : organize
   d. prepare : events

3. MAULED : PROTECTED ::
   a. rested : relaxed
   b. shunned : welcomed
   c. immaculate : filth
   d. brief : tedious

Unit 7: Nonfiction

"**Flood**" by Annie Dillard

Build Grammar Skills: Commonly Confused Words: *Then* and *Than*

Words that are similar are sometimes confused. **Than** and **then** are two commonly confused words. Use *than* in comparisons between people, places, ideas, and events. *Then*, an adverb, usually refers to time.

It rained more today *than* yesterday. *Then*, this afternoon, a different rain came.

A. Practice: Complete each of the following sentences by writing the word *than* or *then* on the line.

1. It rained, and _____ the creek started to rise.

2. It looks more like a river _____ a creek.

3. The flooding looks worse now _____ it did a while ago.

4. The roaring wind sounds more like air _____ like water.

5. _____ the flood began to lessen.

6. Tree branches and other debris stream by faster _____ any express train.

7. _____ lattice fencing bobs along, and _____ a part of a gate.

8. The creek is more destructive when it floods _____ at any other time.

9. _____ the snapping turtle beelines down the bank, away from the children.

10. It _____ disappears into the swirling floodwater.

B. Writing Application: Write a paragraph about a time that you witnessed a memorable event in nature, such as a snowstorm, a hurricane, or an earthquake. Use the words *than* and *then* in your paragraph. Use each word at least twice.

_____

_____

_____

_____

_____

_____

_____

_____

_____

_____

_____

_____

"Flood" by Annie Dillard

Reading Strategy: Recognize Facts and Impressions

When a writer describes a personal experience in an essay, he or she often presents both facts and impressions. A fact is a provable, straightforward detail, whereas an impression is a particular feeling or image a writer remembers from an experience.

DIRECTIONS: As you read "Flood," identify and separate facts and impressions presented by Annie Dillard, using the following chart to help you.

Facts	Impressions
The creek's up.	The water was an opaque pale green, like pulverized jade, . . . like no earthly water.

"**Flood**" by Annie Dillard

Literary Analysis: Descriptive Essay

One purpose of a **descriptive essay** is to provide the reader with a mind's-eye picture of a particular place, a person, an event, or a natural phenomenon. For some readers the effect may be, "It is a place I have been"; for others, it may be, "That is a scene I wish I had actually witnessed." Annie Dillard has this kind of descriptive power:

> It's been gray sporadically, but not oppressively, and rainy for a week, and I would think: When is the real hot stuff coming, the mind-melting weeding weather? It was rainy again this morning, the same spring rain, and then this afternoon a different rain came: a pounding, three-minute shower. And when it was over, the cloud dissolved to haze. I can't see Tinker Mountain.

Dillard doesn't use just descriptive words—she uses *evocative* words, words that call forth the sense of sight, touch, hearing, smell, or taste that she wants us to be aware of.

Complete the following chart. In the right-hand column, write the sense to which each descriptive phrase in the left-hand column appeals.

Description	Sense to which it appeals
1. mind-melting weeding weather	1.
2. high water had touched my leg	2.
3. the long-haired girls strayed into giggling clumps	3.
4. the color is foul, a rusty cream	4.
5. The air smells damp and acrid, like fuel oil, or insecticide.	5.
6. [water] smashes under the bridge like a fist	6.

"Star Wars—A Trip to a Far Galaxy That's Fun and Funny . . ." by Vincent Canby
"Star Wars: Breakthrough Film Still Has the Force" by Roger Ebert

Build Vocabulary

Spelling Strategy   The Word Bank word *fastidious* ends in *-ous*, pronounced as *us*. The *-ous* suffix means "full of," as in *righteous*; "abounding in," as in *beauteous*; "by the nature of," as in *adventurous*; or "characterized by," as in *slanderous*.

Using Connotations

Good writers choose their words carefully to convey exactly the meaning they want. Words have **denotations**—precise definitions—one might find in a dictionary and **connotations**—extra meanings associated with or implied by a word.

A. Directions: Use a dictionary to check the denotations of each of the following pairs of words. Then explain the difference in connotations of each pair.

1. statesman, politician

_____

2. clever, intelligent

_____

3. staring, studying

_____

4. naïve, ignorant

_____

Using the Word Bank

B. Directions: Circle the letter of the word or phrase closest in meaning to the Word Bank word.

1. apotheosis
   a. disciple   b. pharmacy   c. deification   d. distance

2. eclectic
   a. of many sources   b. unconscious theft   c. poorly organized   d. religious ritual

3. facetiousness
   a. documentation   b. hypothesizing   c. jocularity   d. hypocrisy

4. adroit
   a. misguided   b. clever   c. inept   d. heavy

5. piously
   a. rapidly   b. corruptly   c. angrily   d. religiously

6. condescension
   a. haughtiness   b. recognition   c. decline   d. restoration

7. watershed
   a. disaster   b. turning point   c. dilemma   d. battleground

"Star Wars—A Trip to a Far Galaxy That's Fun and Funny . . ." by Vincent Canby
"Star Wars: Breakthrough Film Still Has the Force" by Roger Ebert

Build Grammar Skills: Commonly Confused Words:
Good and Well

Be sure not to confuse the words *good* and *well*. The adjective **good** modifies another word after linking verbs such as feel, look, smell, taste, and seem. Use **well** as an adverb (often describing how skillfully something is done) or as an adjective describing health.

Canby thinks the writer did a *good* job.　　　Ebert thinks the writer did his job *well*.
He feels *good* about its possibility of success.　Jabba looks as though he doesn't feel *well*.

A. Practice: Complete each of the following sentences by writing the word *good* or *well* on the line.

1. *Star Wars* was _____ received by critics and moviegoers alike.

2. The plot is thin, but it is _____ enough to hold interest.

3. Mr. Lucas gets high praise, as both writer and director, for a job _____ done.

4. Opposing the _____ guys are the imperial forces led by the Grand Moff Tarkin and his assistant, Lord Darth Vader.

5. You can't blame the film for what it did; you can only observe how _____ it did it.

6. By now the ritual of classic film revival is _____ established.

7. Space scenes had always been done with a fixed camera, and for a very _____ reason.

8. There is an especially _____ scene in an intergalactic bar where they serve customers who look like turtles, apes, pythons and various amalgams of same, but draw the line at robots.

9. The scene in the Death Star's garbage bin is also especially _____ done.

10. The actors treat their material with the proper combination of solemnity and _____ humor.

B. Writing Application: Follow the directions to use *good* or *well* in sentences about *Star Wars*.

1. Write a sentence about Canby's review using *well*.

_____
_____

2. Write a sentence about Canby's review using *good*.

_____
_____

3. Write a sentence about Ebert's review using *well*.

_____
_____

4. Write a sentence about Ebert's review using *good*.

_____
_____

"Star Wars—A Trip to a Far Galaxy That's Fun and Funny . . ." by Vincent Canby

"Star Wars: Breakthrough Film Still Has the Force" by Roger Ebert

Reading Strategy: Identify Evidence

Unit 7: Nonfiction

A reviewer, like anyone else, is entitled to his or her own opinion. For that opinion to be responsible and persuasive, though, it must be backed up by information and evidence. Evidence in writing supports or explains a statement or an opinion. The clearer and more concrete the evidence is, the better it is. An explanation of why battle scenes seem contrived, for example, is more convincing if it includes a concrete description like "Spaceships wouldn't fly like old-time biplanes" rather than a general statement like "It didn't seem real."

The more solid evidence a writer provides for his or her assertions, the more credibility he or she gains with readers. When the writer is credible, you are more likely to accept his or her opinion on subjective matters, such as whether or not a movie is worth your time and money.

DIRECTIONS: Find evidence in the selection for each of the following assertions. Write the evidence in the space provided.

1. Canby: The story of *Star Wars* could be written on the head of a pin and still leave room for the Bible.

   _____

2. Canby: The thin one, who looks like a sort of brass woodman, talks in the polished phrases of a valet . . .

   _____

3. Canby: The true stars of *Star Wars* are John Barry, who was responsible for the production design, and the people who were responsible for the incredible special effects . . .

   _____

4. Canby: It's difficult to judge the performances in a film like this.

   _____

5. Ebert: Like *Birth of a Nation* and *Citizen Kane*, *Star Wars* was a technical watershed that influenced many of the movies that came after.

   _____

6. Ebert: It located Hollywood's center of gravity at the intellectual and emotional level of a bright teenager.

   _____

7. Ebert: There's also an improved look to the city of Mos Eisley ("A wretched hive of scum and villainry," says Obi-Wan Kanobi).

   _____

8. Ebert: The films that will live forever are the simplest-seeming ones.

   _____

Name _____ Date _____

"Star Wars—A Trip to a Far Galaxy That's Fun and Funny . . ." by Vincent Canby
"Star Wars: Breakthrough Film Still Has the Force" by Roger Ebert

Literary Analysis: Critical Review

Typically, a **critical review** opens with an engaging line to interest the reader, then briefly summarizes the work being reviewed. The reviewer should not assume the reader has experienced the work, nor should the reviewer give away any surprises. The summary is just a starting point.

The reviewer then begins to reveal his or her comments. In movies, plots, characters, lighting, acting, and direction are elements to consider. A book review evaluates the style of narration. A music review could comment on technique and interpretation.

Most reviews close with an overall evaluation of the work. Effective criticism is unbiased, knowledgeable, detailed, specific in praise as well as censure, and has a clear sense of quality. What makes something good? You don't have to be an expert to write criticism, but you must demonstrate that you have experienced the work and have something worth saying about it. What is your opinion? Why did you form that opinion? If your writing answers these questions clearly, you will be a good critic and a good writer.

DIRECTIONS: Think about the qualities of a good critical review as demonstrated in the selections by Canby and Ebert. Then answer the following questions in the space provided.

1. What is the purpose of a critical review?

   _____

2. How can you tell that both Ebert and Canby have actually seen *Star Wars?*

   _____

3. What in Canby's and Ebert's reviews indicates to you that they are knowledgeable about film?

   _____

4. Why should the summary of the work in a critical review be brief?

   _____

   _____

5. Both Canby and Ebert praise *Star Wars.* What appear to be the criteria they are using to make their evaluations?

   _____

   _____

6. What does it mean for a review to be unbiased? Why is it important that a reviewer be unbiased?

   _____

   _____

7. List three or four qualities you think a good critic should have.

   _____

   _____

"Mothers & Daughters" by Tillie Olsen and Estelle Jussim

Build Vocabulary

Spelling Strategy   When -ness is added to a word ending in n, keep all the letters intact: *sullen* + *-ness* = *sullenness*.

Using Words Describing Color

Many words, such as *hue*, refer to differences in color. *Shade* refers to the degree of darkness of a particular color. A pale or delicate shade of a color is called a *tint*.

A. Directions: Match each word in the left column with the appropriate color in the right column. Write the letter of the color on the line next to the word used to describe that type of color.

_____ 1. hue   a. burgundy

_____ 2. shade   b. pink

_____ 3. tint   c. red

Using the Word Bank

B. Directions: Write **T** for true or **F** for false in the blank next to each sentence.

_____ 1. A painter would be concerned with *hue*.

_____ 2. A child might indicate *sullenness* by frowning or pouting.

_____ 3. An audience would clap politely to show its *fervor* for a performance.

_____ 4. Not all viewers will discover the photograph's *implicit* message.

Understanding Antonyms

C. Directions: Each of the following questions consists of a word in CAPITAL LETTERS followed by four lettered words or phrases. Circle the letter of the word or phrase that is most nearly *opposite* in meaning to the word in capital letters.

1. SULLENNESS
   a. enjoyment
   b. happy
   c. grateful
   d. resentment

2. FERVOR
   a. unexcited
   b. sadness
   c. boredom
   d. commotion

"Mothers & Daughters" by Tillie Olsen and Estelle Jussim

Build Grammar Skills: Correct Use of Adjectives and Adverbs

When choosing modifiers, avoid confusing adjectives and adverbs. Remember that adjectives modify nouns and pronouns, and adverbs modify verbs, adjectives, and other adverbs. A common mistake is the use of an adjective to modify a verb where an adverb would be correct.

The daughter is unconcerned with the camera. (The predicate adjective *unconcerned* modifies the subject *daughter*.)

The daughter is sullenly unconcerned. (The adverb *sullenly* modifies the predicate adjective *unconcerned*.)

A. Practice: Circle the adjective or adverb that correctly completes each sentence. Underline the word it modifies and label that word's part of speech.

1. The photograph shows a young family walking (swift, swiftly) down the road.

2. The mother and daughter pose (patient, patiently) for the photographer.

3. The teenager seems (reluctant, reluctantly) to embrace her mother.

4. The mother and daughter look (proud, proudly) as they stand before the flag in their matching outfits.

5. No photograph can capture a (permanent, permanently) ascribable mood.

B. Writing Application: Review the photographs that accompany "Mothers and Daughters" in your text. Write answers to the following questions including an appropriate adjective or adverb.

1. What does the landscape look like in the photograph accompanying "Observations by Tillie Olsen and Julie Olsen Edward"?

_____

2. In the photograph accompanying "Observations by Sage Sohier," how would you describe the way the mother is holding the cat?

_____

3. In what manner are the mother and daughter posing in the Bicentennial photograph accompanying "Observations by Eudora Welty"?

_____

4. How would you describe the grandmother's dress in the photograph titled "Tang Chung, Lisa Lu, Lucia and Loretta"?

_____

5. In the photograph accompanying "Observations by Estelle Jussim," what does the mother's demeanor suggest about her?

_____

"Mothers & Daughters" by Tillie Olsen and Estelle Jussim

Reading Strategy: Interpret Pictures

When you **interpret pictures**, you "read" their message from the elements within the pictures. Examining these elements can help you discover the meaning behind the pictures.

A. DIRECTIONS: Complete the chart by recording details about each photograph for the categories listed.

Photograph	Facial Expressions	Body Language	Distance Between Subjects	Background
1. *August*, New Mexico, 1979				
2. *Bicentennial Celebration*				
3. *Tang Chung, Lisa Lu, Lucia and Loretta*				
4. *Untitled* (Sage Sohier)				
5. *Untitled* (Bruce Horowitz)				

B. DIRECTIONS: Based on your completed chart, write your interpretation of the relationship between mothers and daughters in the photographs.

1. *August*, New Mexico, 1979

_____

2. *Bicentennial Celebration*

_____

3. *Tang Chung, Lisa Lu, Lucia and Loretta*

_____

4. *Untitled* (Sage Sohier)

_____

5. *Untitled* (Bruce Horowitz)

_____

"Mothers & Daughters" by Tillie Olsen and Estelle Jussim

Literary Analysis: Visual Essay

Pictures can speak ideas and truths that we find difficult to express in words. In a **visual essay,** photographs or other visual forms are combined with written text to convey meaning about a particular subject.

DIRECTIONS: Read each example of written text. Then answer the questions about the relationship between the text and the photographs.

> Here are mothers and daughters of lack and of privilege, in various dress, settings, environments; posing for photographs or (unconcerned with the camera) sharing tasks, ease, occasions, activities; holding, embracing, touching; or in terrible isolation.

1. Which of the five photographs reflect the positive aspects of mother-daughter relationships described by Tillie Olsen? Why do you think so?

   _____

   _____

   _____

2. Which of the five photographs most strongly conveys a sense of "terrible isolation" between mother and daughter? Explain your choice.

   _____

   _____

   _____

   _____

> [My mother] was teaching me one more, almost her last, lesson: emotions do not grow old. I knew that I would feel as she did, and I do.

3. How do Eudora Welty's words relate to the images in *Bicentennial Celebration* or *Tang Chung, Lisa Lu, Lucia and Loretta?*

   _____

   _____

   _____

   _____

> To portray two persons defined as mother and daughter is to define a relationship fraught with cultural and emotional overtones.

4. Which photographs illustrate Estelle Jussim's words? Why do you think so?

   _____

   _____

   _____

   _____

"Imitating Nature's Mineral Artistry" by Paul O'Neil
"Work That Counts" by Ernesto Ruelas Inzunza

Build Vocabulary

Spelling Strategy   The Word Bank word *topography* is one of many words in English derived from the Greek word *graphein,* meaning "to write" or "to record."

Using the Prefix *syn-*

A. DIRECTIONS: Following are words that contain the prefix *syn-*, meaning "together" or "with." Each is attached to a word root that comes from Greek, followed by a definition in parentheses. Determine the literal meaning of the English word. Then, consulting a dictionary if necessary, explain the full meaning that the word has taken on in English.

1. synergetic (*ergos* means "work") _____
   _____

2. synonym (*onyma* means "name") _____
   _____

3. syntax (*tassein* means "to arrange") _____
   _____

Using the Word Bank

B. DIRECTIONS: For each sentence, replace the italicized word or phrase with the appropriate word from the Word Bank. Rewrite the sentence in the space provided.

1. In nature, many kinds of *change of form* take place, each one more amazing than the last.
   _____
   _____

2. The failed experiment was *both accidental and beneficial* since it had an unexpected outcome that revealed new information.
   _____
   _____

3. The qualities of *man-made* gems are invisible to most consumers.
   _____
   _____

4. The girls were reluctant to *reveal* the topic of their science fair project.
   _____
   _____

5. For scientists as well as for gem dealers, *watchfulness* is a virtue.
   _____
   _____

Name _____ Date _____

Build Grammar Skills: Placement of Modifiers

Make sure that your modifiers are properly placed in each sentence of your writing. Other-wise, the meaning of the sentence may be unclear. A phrase or clause that acts as an adjective or adverb should be placed as close as possible to the word it modifies. A modifier placed too far away from the word it modifies is called a **misplaced modifier**. Because it is misplaced, the phrase or clause seems to modify the wrong word in the sentence.

Misplaced Modifier: Synthetic gems bear hallmarks of their laboratory origin, *artful as they are.*
Correctly Placed Modifier: *Artful as they are,* synthetic gems bear hallmarks of their laboratory
origin.

A. Practice: Read each sentence carefully, and check the placement of the italicized modifier. Then, underline the word that the phrase modifies. If the sentence is correct, write *C* on the line. If the sentence contains a misplaced modifier, write *MM*.

_____ 1. Technicians can now create conditions of heat and chemical activity similar to those that give birth to gemstones deep within the earth *in laboratories and factories.*

_____ 2. The result is synthetic gems, identical *in chemistry and crystalline structure* to their natural counterparts.

_____ 3. *Including ruby, sapphire and spinel,* the flame-fusion method has been used to grow crystals of about 100 minerals and gems.

_____ 4. The apparatus was loaded with a mixture of graphite powder and an iron com-pound, pressurized and heated with an electric current to more than 4,800° F *in a series of experiments.*

_____ 5. My eyes, *from dozens of tiny triangular faces of octahedral crystals that were stuck to the tantalum,* had caught the flashing light.

B. Writing Application: Revise the following sentences to eliminate any misplaced modifiers. If no change is needed, write *Correct.*

1. I finally have time to sit peacefully and tell my friend Jeros, who is new to hawk watching, the story of the discovery of the River of Raptors after sunset.

_____

_____

2. At eight this morning, about forty-five Swainson's hawks were just taking off from the nearby canyon where they had spent the night as Jeros and I climbed the observation tower.

_____

_____

3. Shortly afterward, we saw hundreds of them turning circles in the thermal columns of hot air, effortlessly gaining altitude.

_____

_____

"Imitating Nature's Mineral Artistry" by Paul O'Neil
"Work That Counts" by Ernesto Ruelas Inzunza

Reading Strategy: Relate Diagrams to Text

With a single diagram, the writer of a technical article may shed light on a process, a method, or a structure. A diagram may *add* meaning to a text by illustrating something that is just too difficult to explain effectively with words, or it may *enhance* information in the text by reinforcing the text's meaning. Whatever the relationship of the diagram to the text, readers get information in a visual way that helps them understand and remember.

DIRECTIONS: Refer to Diagram A and Diagram B in "Imitating Nature's Mineral Artistry" in your textbook as you answer these questions.

1. The text indicates that the chemical ingredients of ruby "sift from a hopper." How is this indicated in Diagram A?

_____

_____

2. In what ways does this diagram work *with* its caption to give readers a complete sense of the process?

_____

_____

_____

_____

3. In Diagram B, how does the illustration show that the crystals settle to the bottom of the crucible?

_____

_____

_____

_____

4. Do you think these diagrams explain processes that would be difficult to explain in the text, or do they enhance the text by providing an image of the process? Explain your answer.

_____

_____

_____

_____

"Imitating Nature's Mineral Artistry" by Paul O'Neil
"Work That Counts" by Ernesto Ruelas Inzunza

Literary Analysis: Technical Article

Unlike fiction, in which writers use expressive language, **technical articles** must be clear and to the point. To attain clarity, technical writers carefully and logically organize and present their information.

Technical writers need to be especially aware of their audience. They must have a sense of what their audience knows. If a scientist is writing for a scientific journal, she need not define basic scientific terms in her article. If she is writing a science column for a weekly news-magazine, however, she needs to define basic terms because a general audience has less scientific knowledge. Both O'Neil and Inzunza are writing for general audiences, so they are careful to define the specialized terms they use in their articles.

DIRECTIONS: Examine the characteristics of technical articles by completing the following table.

"Imitating Nature's Mineral Artistry"	"Work That Counts"
1. Briefly explain the process that is described in each technical article.	
2. From each article, cite two specialized terms and their definitions.	
3. Cite one comparison or analogy from each article that makes a concept more understandable.	
4. Describe the type of audience each article is written for, and explain the reasons for your answer.	

Antigone, **Prologue through Scene 2,** by Sophocles

Build Vocabulary

Spelling Strategy Words ending in silent *e* drop the *e* before a suffix beginning with a vowel: *sate + -ed = sated.*

Using the Prefix *trans-*

A. DIRECTIONS: Knowing that the prefix *trans-* means "through," "above," or "across," write a definition for each italicized word in the following sentences.

1. The *transatlantic* flight began in New York and ended in London.

   _____

2. Happily, Karl's experiences often *transcend* his rather low expectations.

   _____

3. Which shipping company will *transport* the produce?

   _____

4. After the election, the power of government *transferred* from one party to another.

   _____

Using the Word Bank

sated	anarchists	sententiously	sultry	transcends

B. DIRECTIONS: For each Word Bank word, choose the word or phrase that is most nearly *opposite* in meaning. In the blank, write the letter of your choice.

____ 1. sated
        a. angry   b. unfulfilled   c. desperate   d. content

____ 2. sententiously
        a. wordy   b. vaguely   c. in a roundabout way   d. nonsensically

____ 3. sultry
        a. frigid   b. oppressive   c. muggy   d. sweltering

____ 4. transcends
        a. exceeds   b. stagnates   c. oppresses   d. rises above

____ 5. anarchists
        a. terrorists   b. nihilists   c. mercenaries   d. authorities

Unit 8: Drama

Name _____ Date _____

Build Grammar Skills: Objective Pronouns

A pronoun takes the objective case when it is used as the object of a verb, preposition, or verbal. **Objective pronouns** include: *me, you, him, her, it, us,* and *them.* The chart below shows the uses of objective pronouns.

OBJECTIVE PRONOUNS	
Direct Object	No one shall bury *him*.
Indirect Object	Creon gave *him* a soldier's funeral.
Object of a Preposition	Come out here with *me*.
Object of a Participle	Oedipus died, everyone hating *him*.
Object of a Gerund	Burying *him* was her primary concern.
Object of an Infinitive	Creon is coming here to announce *it* publicly.

A. Practice: Circle the objective pronoun to complete each sentence. Identify how it is used in the sentence. Then, write *direct object, indirect object, object of a preposition, object of a participle, object of a gerund,* or *object of an infinitive* on the line.

_____ 1. Antigone wants her sister to help (she, her) bury their brother.

_____ 2. Ismene fears that the king will kill (they, them).

_____ 3. Antigone replies that in death "I shall be as dear to Polyneices as he to (I, me)."

_____ 4. Ismene, begging (she, her) to reconsider, declines to help.

_____ 5. Sentencing (they, them) to die is the king's immediate response.

_____ 6. Creon tells Antigone that her death gives (he, him) everything he wants.

B. Writing Application: Follow the directions to write four sentences with objective pronouns.

1. Use the pronoun *him* as the object of a preposition.

_____

_____

2. Use the pronoun *her* as an indirect object.

_____

_____

3. Use the pronoun *them* as the object of an infinitive.

_____

_____

4. Use the pronoun *it* as a object of a gerund.

_____

_____

Name _____ Date _____

Antigone, **Prologue through Scene 2,** by Sophocles

Reading Strategy: Question Characters' Motives

In *Antigone,* the actions of Antigone, Creon, and Ismene have serious and lasting consequences. Why do these characters behave as they do? The inner drive or impulse that makes a person act in a certain way is called **motive.** Like people, characters in a play also have motives. You can understand the action of a play if you identify the characters' motives.

DIRECTIONS: Explore the motives of Creon, Antigone, and Ismene by completing the following chart. Provide at least one piece of evidence to support each conclusion you draw.

Question	Motive	Supporting Evidence
1. What is Creon's motive for forbidding Polyneices' burial?		
2. What is Creon's motive for arresting Ismene as well?		
3. What is Ismene's motive for accepting guilt for Antigone's crime?		
4. What is Antigone's motive for refusing Ismene's help?		

Antigone, **Prologue through Scene 2,** by Sophocles

Literary Analysis: Protagonist and Antagonist

Like many Greek tragedies, *Antigone* focuses on a conflict that one character has with an authority figure, often a ruler or a god. In this play, as in other works of literature, the main character, called the **protagonist,** is the character at the center of the action. As readers, we identify with the protagonist and the crisis he or she faces. In this play, the protagonist is Antigone. The **antagonist** is the character or force that is in conflict with the protagonist. Antigone is in conflict with the antagonist Creon, who is both her uncle and the king.

A. DIRECTIONS: Write your answers to the following questions.

1. Explain how Antigone is the protagonist of the play.

   _____

   _____

2. Explain how Creon is in conflict with Antigone.

   _____

   _____

3. How does Antigone's sense of honor put her in conflict with Creon?

   _____

   _____

4. How does Creon's pride pit him against Antigone?

   _____

   _____

B. DIRECTIONS: Read the following quotations. Explain how the contrasting lines illustrate the conflict between protagonist and antagonist.

   ISMENE. [*To Antigone*] Go then, if you feel that you must./You are unwise./But a loyal friend indeed to those who love you.

   CREON. No one values friendship more highly than I; but we must remember that friends made at the risk of wrecking [the Ship of State] are not real friends at all.

   _____

   _____

   _____

   _____

   _____

   _____

   _____

   _____

   _____

Antigone, **Scenes 3 through 5,** by Sophocles

Build Vocabulary

Spelling Strategy   Place *i* before *e* except after *c* or when sounded like *a* as in *neighbor* and *weigh*. Examples: *fierce, receive, reign.*

Using the Root -*chor*-

A. DIRECTIONS: The word root -*chor*- comes from Terpsichore, the Greek Muse of dance and song. Complete each sentence with one of the following words: *chord, chorister, chorus, choreograph.*

1. The song's _____ is repeated three times.

2. The dance company has employed the former prima ballerina to

   _____ the new ballet.

3. Please play a single _____ to help the musicians find their pitch.

4. The lead _____ sang his solo beautifully.

Using the Word Bank

deference	vile	piety
blasphemy	lamentation	chorister

B. DIRECTIONS: Match each word in the left column with its definition in the right column. In the blank, write the letter of the definition next to the word it defines.

____ 1. blasphemy   a. an expression of grief; weeping

____ 2. chorister   b. disrespectful speech or action concerning God

____ 3. deference   c. extremely disgusting

____ 4. lamentation   d. a yielding in thought

____ 5. piety   e. a member of the chorus

____ 6. vile   f. holiness; respect for the divine

Unit 8: Drama

Antigone, **Scenes 3 through 5,** by Sophocles

Build Grammar Skills: Pronoun Case in Elliptical Clauses

In some English constructions, words that are understood can be omitted. **Elliptical clauses** introduced by *than* or *as* use the form of the pronoun that you would use if the understood words were present. The case of the pronoun depends upon whether the omitted words belong before or after the pronoun. If the words left out come *after* the pronoun, use a nominative pronoun because it is the subject of the omitted verb. If the words left out come *before* the pronoun, use an objective pronoun because the pronoun will be an object. In the examples that follow, the omitted words are given in brackets.

Words Left Out Before Pronoun	Creon sentenced Antigone to death; he gave Ismene the same sentence as her.
	Creon sentenced Antigone to death; he gave Ismene the same sentence as [he gave] her.
Words Left Out After Pronoun	Haimon was as infuriated as I at Creon's stubbornness.
	Haimon was as infuriated as I [was] at Creon's stubbornness.

A. Practice: Circle the correct pronoun, and write the word or phrase that best completes each sentence.

1. Creon believes that no one is more entitled than (he/him) _____ to decide Antigone's fate.

2. It infuriates Creon that Haimon shows Antigone more devotion than _____ (he/him).

3. Haimon tells Creon what the people are saying about him; clearly, Haimon believes as (they/them) _____ .

4. As a reader, I identified most with Antigone; in my opinion, no one suffered more than (her/she) _____ .

5. My friend appreciated the actors more than (I/me) _____ .

B. Writing Application: For each of the following phrases, write a sentence that contains an elliptical clause using a pronoun in the correct case. Write at least one sentence in which the omitted words belong *before* the pronoun.

1. as excited as

_____

2. more determined than

_____

3. longer message than

_____

4. as patient as

_____

5. more than

_____

Antigone, **Scenes 3 through 5,** by Sophocles

Reading Strategy: Identify With a Character

You can more fully experience a drama when you identify with a character. By putting yourself in the character's place, you imagine what he or she is feeling and thinking. Imagining yourself as a particular character in a drama can make you sympathize with that character. As a result, you can gain greater insight into the character's motivation and the play's meaning.

DIRECTIONS: For each character, list two actions, events, and/or lines that helped you identify with the character. Then state the insight you gained from identifying with the character.

Character	Identifying Elements	Resulting Insight
1. Antigone		
2. Creon		
3. Haimon		
4. Ismene		
5. Eurydice		

Unit 8: Drama

Antigone, **Scenes 3 through 5,** by Sophocles

Literary Analysis: Tragic Character

A **tragic character** is a dramatic figure who makes an error in judgment that accounts for his or her downfall. The error is often called a **tragic flaw.** Through choice and circumstance, the tragic character is caught up in a series of events that lead to disaster. In *Antigone,* both the protagonist (main character in conflict with forces or another character) and antagonist (figure in conflict with the main character) are tragic characters.

DIRECTIONS: Below are some passages from *Antigone.* Read each passage, go back to its context in the play if necessary, and then identify the tragic flaw and how it shows itself at that moment.

1. *(Scene 1 : ll. 44–65)* **Creon:** "... that is why I have made the following decision concerning the sons of Oedipus : ... :—Polyneices, I say, is to have no burial: no man is to touch him ... he shall lie on the plain, unburied ... no traitor is going to be honored with the loyal man."

   _____

   _____

   _____

   _____

2. *(Scene 2 : ll. 58–63)* **Antigone:** "I dared. ... Your edict, King, was strong, But all your strength is weakness itself against / The immortal unrecorded laws of God. They are ... Operative forever, beyond man utterly."

   _____

   _____

   _____

   _____

3. *(Scene 3 : ll. 94–96)* **Creon:** "You consider it right for a man of my years and experience / To go to school to a boy?"

   _____

   _____

   _____

   _____

4. *(Scene 4 : ll. 42–44)* **Antigone:** "I have been a stranger here in my own land: / All my life / The blasphemy of my birth has followed me."

   _____

   _____

   _____

   _____

The Tragedy of Julius Caesar, **Act I,** by William Shakespeare

Build Vocabulary

Spelling Strategy Many words in the English language end with a /jus/ sound. Whenever you run across one of these words, such as *prodigious*, *religious*, and *contagious*, the ending is almost always spelled *-gious*. An exception is *courageous*, which retains the *e* from its base form.

Using Forms of *portent*

A. DIRECTIONS: The Latin verb from which the word *portent* comes means literally "to stretch forward." Therefore, a portent is an event or sign whose meaning "stretches forward" into the future. Write sentences using forms of *portent* according to the instructions that follow.

1. Use the verb *portend* in a sentence about a weather forecast.

   _____

   _____

2. Use *portentous* in a sentence about the coming of the twenty-first century.

   _____

   _____

3. Use the noun *portent* in a sentence about an event that foreshadowed a *good* happening.

   _____

   _____

Using the Word Bank

replication	spare	infirmity
surly	portentous	prodigious

B. DIRECTIONS: Choose the lettered word or phrase that is most nearly *opposite* in meaning to the Word Bank word. In the blank, write the letter of your choice.

____ 1. spare
   a. lanky
   b. gaunt
   c. used
   d. corpulent

____ 2. surly
   a. friendly
   b. knotted
   c. not noticing
   d. apologetic

____ 3. prodigious
   a. meager
   b. immeasurable
   c. superstitious
   d. bad luck

____ 4. infirmity
   a. illness
   b. weakness
   c. strength
   d. attitude

____ 5. replication
   a. anger
   b. forgery
   c. duplicate
   d. original

____ 6. portentous
   a. loud
   b. indivisible
   c. insignificant
   d. overweight

The Tragedy of Julius Caesar, Act I   **197**

Name _____ Date _____

The Tragedy of Julius Caesar, **Act I,** by William Shakespeare

Build Grammar Skills: The Subjunctive Mood

The **subjunctive mood** expresses a condition that is contrary to fact, or a wish, suggestion, demand, or request. For example, when saying, "If I *were* president, . . ." you are expressing something contrary to fact, and therefore use the subjunctive *were* instead of *was.* The subjunctive mood of a verb is used in two kinds of situations.

The **present subjunctive** is used to express a suggestion or a necessity. This kind of expression always appears in a subordinate clause beginning with *that.* The independent clause always contains a word indicating a suggestion (*ask, request, suggest,* or *recommend*) or a necessity (*necessary* or *essential*).

> Brutus **requested that** Casca *tell* him what had happened.

> It is **essential that** Brutus and Cassius *talk* privately.

The **past subjunctive** is used to express a wish or a condition contrary to fact. The words *if, as if,* and *as though* express something that is not true—something that is contrary to fact. In this kind of expression, and in the expression of a wish, the verb *were* is usually used.

> If there **were** any more strange portents, the people might really be frightened.

> I wish I **were** able to speak more expressively.

A. Practice: Circle the verbs that are in the subjunctive mood in each of the following sentences. Also, underline any other words in the sentence that indicate that the subjunctive mood is being used.

1. It is necessary that the conspirators recruit as many accomplices as they can.

2. If you were Caesar, would you have accepted the crown?

3. Cassius responds as though Caesar were already king.

4. Cassius suggests that Brutus consider himself worthy of respect.

B. Writing Application: Complete each of the following sentences in the subjunctive mood.

1. If Caesar _____

_____

2. The conspirators recommend that _____

_____

3. It was as though _____

_____

4. Caesar asks that Antony _____

_____

Name _____ Date _____

The Tragedy of Julius Caesar, **Act I,** by William Shakespeare

Reading Strategy: Use Text Aids

Stage actors rely on stage directions to know what mood or movement a playwright intended. As readers, we sometimes need more than stage directions to discover meaning, particularly when reading the language of sixteenth-century England. Most versions of Shakespeare's works include **text aids**—explanations, usually written in the margins, of words, phrases, or customs that may be unfamiliar to modern-day readers.

The key to reading Shakespeare is to read slowly and carefully, remembering to pause where punctuation indicates, not necessarily at the end of each line. When you come upon a numbered text aid, read the explanation carefully, and then return to the text. Reread the sentence, applying the meaning or explanation you obtained from the text aid.

DIRECTIONS: Use the text aids to answer the following questions about what you read in Act I.

1. In Act I, lines 30–33, the cobbler states his reason for being in the street: "But indeed, sir, we make holiday to see Caesar and to rejoice in his triumph." What sort of triumph is Caesar having?

   _____

2. Flavius tells Marullus to remove decorations from the statues. Marullus questions him in lines 67 and 68, saying it is the feast of Lupercal. What and when is the feast of Lupercal?

   _____

   _____

3. At the opening of Act I, Scene ii, Antony is dressed "for the course," or for a footrace. Why is a footrace being held? Why does Caesar tell Antony to touch Calpurnia during the race?

   _____

   _____

4. What date is the ides of March? _____

5. In Act I, Scene iii, Cicero and Casca meet and talk. In lines 28–32, Casca says, ". . . When these prodigies/Do so conjointly meet, let not men say,/'These are their reasons, they are natural,'/for I believe they are portentous things/Unto the climate that they point upon." Restate these lines in your own words.

   _____

   _____

   _____

   _____

   _____

   _____

   _____

   _____

Name _____ Date _____

The Tragedy of Julius Caesar, **Act I,** by William Shakespeare

Literary Analysis: Exposition in Drama

In the plot of a literary work, usually the first section is devoted to introducing the characters and the situation. This section is called the **exposition,** and it occurs in drama just as it does in a short story or a novel. The audience—or the readers—meet characters, discover where the action takes place, and find out what's going on. The exposition sets the scene and the mood.

In Act I of *The Tragedy of Julius Caesar,* Scene i serves as the exposition. A conversation between two tribunes and some common people reveal details that set the stage for what follows in the rest of Act I, and beyond.

DIRECTIONS: Use the following chart to examine the information revealed in the exposition of *The Tragedy of Julius Caesar.*

Topic	What do you learn about the topic?	Where do you learn about the topic? Cite line numbers.
Physical setting		
Time setting		
Caesar		
Response to Caesar's triumph		

The Tragedy of Julius Caesar, Act II, by William Shakespeare

Build Vocabulary

Spelling Strategy When adding a suffix to a word ending in two consonants, the consonants are not changed. Thus the Word Bank word *imminent* becomes *imminently*, and *augment* becomes *augmenter, augmentation, augmentative,* or *augmented* without change to the final two consonants.

Using the Root -*spir*-

The Latin word *spirare*, meaning "to breathe," is the source of the word root -*spir*-. Most of the words in common use today that come from the root -*spir*- either derive from the literal sense of breathing, or from a figurative sense related to a life force. Breath itself was thought to be a vital force, and to have life was to have breath. Thus, the conspirators breathe together in their plan to murder Caesar.

A. Directions: Use a dictionary to determine whether each of the following words is related to the literal sense of breathing or the figurative sense of a life force. Write the meaning of each word in the space provided.

1. aspirate _____

2. aspire _____

3. spiracle _____

4. sprite _____

Using the Word Bank

augmented	entreated	conspiracy
resolution	exploit	imminent

B. Directions: Each item consists of a related pair of words in CAPITAL LETTERS, followed by four lettered pairs of words. Choose the lettered pair that best expresses a relationship similar to that expressed in the pair in capital letters. In the blank, write the letter of your choice.

____ 1. ENTREATED : PLEA ::
    a. begged : wanted
    b. beseeched : appeal
    c. weaken : wish
    d. beggar : supplicant

____ 2. RESOLUTION : ACCOMPLISHMENT ::
    a. fear : flight
    b. anger : hope
    c. uncertainty : perseverance
    d. exercise : strength

____ 3. IMMINENT : REMOTE ::
    a. immediate : future
    b. distant : aloof
    c. clear : obscure
    d. looming : appearing

____ 4. ADVENTURER : EXPLOIT ::
    a. driver : designer
    b. coward : courage
    c. flight : pilot
    d. traitor : treachery

____ 5. CONSPIRACY : PLOT ::
    a. speech : audience
    b. plan : action
    c. counsel : advice
    d. rebel : dissent

____ 6. AUGMENTED : GREW ::
    a. wore : eroded
    b. increased : decreased
    c. changed : lessened
    d. planned : executed

The Tragedy of Julius Caesar, **Act II,** by William Shakespeare

Build Grammar Skills: Commonly Confused Words:
Who vs. *Whom; Who's* vs. *Whose*

The pronouns *who, whom,* and *whose* refer to people. Remembering when to use them is less confusing if you understand how the words are used. As shown in the chart below, *who* is a nominative case pronoun, *whom* is an objective case pronoun, and *whose* is a possessive case pronoun.

Case	Pronoun	Use in Sentence	Example
Nominative	who	Subject or Predicate Nominative	*Who is* conspiring against Caesar?
Objective	whom	Direct Object, Object of a Participle, Object of a Gerund, Object of an Infinitive, or Object of a Preposition	*Whom* can he trust? Of *whom* is he suspicious?
Possessive	whose	To Show Ownership	*Whose* idea is it to kill him?

The words *whose* and *who's* sound alike, but be careful not to confuse them. *Who's* is the contraction of "who is."

   Possessive: *Whose* idea is it to kill him?   **Contraction:** *Who's* conspiring against Caesar?

A. Practice: Complete each sentence by writing *who, whom, who's* or *whose* on the line.

1. Cassius, _____ Caesar distrusts, is organizing the conspiracy against Caesar.

2. _____ side is Brutus on?

3. Brutus, _____ is Caesar's friend, worries about Caesar's ambition.

4. The conspirators, _____ want to win Brutus to their side, plant letters.

5. Brutus tells Lucius to see _____ knocking at the gate.

B. Writing Application: Follow the directions to write four sentences about *Julius Caesar*.

1 . Write a sentence using *whom* as the object of a preposition.

_____

2. Write a sentence using the possessive form of *who.*

_____

3. Write a sentence using *who* as the subject.

_____

4. Write a sentence using the contraction of *who is.*

_____

5. Write a sentence using *whom* as the object of an infinitive.

_____

The Tragedy of Julius Caesar, Act II, by William Shakespeare

Reading Strategy: Read Blank Verse

Often, readers of blank verse pause at line breaks as if they were commas, and treat the capital letters at the beginning of lines as if they were new sentences. In doing so, the meaning may be difficult to grasp.

Here are some tips for reading blank verse:

1. **Read by punctuation, not by line.** Consider Brutus' thoughts:

   Th' abuse of greatness is when it disjoins

   Remorse from power; and, to speak truth of Caesar,

   I have not known when his affections swayed

   More than his Reason.

If you ignore the line breaks and read by punctuation, the sentence is much easier to understand.

   Th' abuse of greatness is when it disjoins remorse from power; and, to speak truth of Caesar, I have not known when his affections swayed more than his Reason.

2. **"Translate" unfamiliar words and phrases.** When you grasp the sentence structure, investigate words you don't know and rearrange difficult sentences so that the meaning becomes clearer.

   The abuse of greatness is when it separates compassion from power, but, to tell the truth, I have not known when Caesar's emotions ruled his reason.

DIRECTIONS: In Scene i, line 113, Cassius proposes an oath to bind the conspirators. Brutus disagrees. Using the preceding tips, recast lines 114 through 128 as a modern paragraph that makes clear the grounds of Brutus' position.

_____

_____

_____

_____

_____

_____

_____

_____

_____

_____

_____

_____

_____

_____

_____

The Tragedy of Julius Caesar, Act II, by William Shakespeare

Literary Analysis: Blank Verse

Most of the speeches of major characters in Shakespeare's plays are written in **blank verse.** Blank verse is five iambic feet in length. An **iamb** is a two-syllable unit (called a foot) with a stress on the second syllable (aroúnd). Five iambs make up a line of **iambic pentameter,** which is the meter (or rhythm) of blank verse.

Typically, poetic analysis indicates these stresses by means of two marks, [˘] for unstressed syllables and [´] for stressed ones. Here is a line of iambic pentameter with the feet and the stressed syllables marked:

Yŏu sháll | cŏnféss | thăt yóu | ăre bóth | deceíved.

The iambic pentameter pattern varies for emphasis and phonetic considerations. You will find many examples of variation from perfectly metrical iambic pentameter in Shakespeare. Not every speech fits perfectly, and it would be sing-song and boring if it did. Sometimes, deliberate drama is created by variation. When Calpurnia warns Caesar of her dreams, she says

And ghosts did shriek and squeal about the streets

O Caesar, these things are beyond all use

And I do fear them.

The first line is in perfect pentameter, but the second line begins to crack the rhythm as Calpurnia begins to break. The brief *And I do fear them* is a warning and a cry of grief left hanging in the air.

A. DIRECTIONS: Mark the metrical notation using [˘] and [´] for unstressed and stressed syllables in the following passage. Place + in front of each line that is exactly five metrical feet, and − in front of each line that is not.

Here I will stand till Caesar pass along

And as a suitor will I give him this.

My heart laments that virtue cannot live

Out of the teeth of emulation.

If thou reads this, O Caesar, thou mayest live;

If not, the Fates with traitors do contrive.

B. DIRECTIONS: Answer the following questions about the meter of the preceding passage.

1. Which line breaks from pentameter the most? With what words does it break, and why?

_____

_____

2. What in the meter of the final line in the passage suggests that it is the closing line of Artemidorus's speech?

_____

_____

The Tragedy of Julius Caesar, **Act III**, by William Shakespeare

Build Vocabulary

Spelling Strategy   When adding a suffix that begins with a vowel to a word that ends in a single consonant preceded by two vowels, do not double the final consonant. For example, *repeal + ing = repealing.*

Using the Root -ora-

A. DIRECTIONS: The following English words are formed from the Latin root *-ora-*, meaning "to speak," "to plead," or "to pray." Define each of these words that contain the root *-ora-*. Check a dictionary if necessary.

1. oracle _____

2. orate _____

3. oration _____

Using the Word Bank

suit	spurn	confounded	mutiny
malice	oration	discourse	vile

B. DIRECTIONS: Match each word in the left-hand column with its definition in the right-hand column. In the blank, write the letter of the definition next to the word it defines.

____ 1. suit   a. desire for harm

____ 2. spurn   b. rebellion

____ 3. confounded   c. depraved

____ 4. mutiny   d. speech for a formal occasion

____ 5. malice   e. petition

____ 6. oration   f. to speak at length

____ 7. discourse   g. confused

____ 8. vile   h. kick disdainfully (*archaic*)

The Tragedy of Julius Caesar, Act III   **205**

Unit 8: Drama

Name _____   Date _____

The Tragedy of Julius Caesar, Act III, by William Shakespeare

Build Grammar Skills: Reflexive Pronouns

A **reflexive pronoun** ends in -*self* or -*selves* and points back to a noun or pronoun in the same sentence. *Myself, yourself, himself, herself,* and *itself* are singular reflexive pronouns; *ourselves, yourselves,* and *themselves* are plural reflexive pronouns. A reflexive pronoun always adds information to a sentence. It cannot be deleted without changing the meaning of the sentence. In the following sentence, the reflexive pronoun *themselves* tells whom the conspirators bathed.

The conspirators bathed *themselves* in Caesar's blood.

Do not confuse reflexive pronouns with intensive pronouns. An **intensive pronoun** also ends in -*self* or -*selves* but does not add information to a sentence. It simply emphasizes a noun or pronoun in the same sentence. If an intensive pronoun is removed, the sentence will still have the same meaning.

Only we, *ourselves,* will take responsibility for the deed. (The intensive pronoun *ourselves* emphasizes *we.*)

A. Practice: Underline the noun or pronoun to which the italicized pronoun refers. If the pronoun is intensive, write *Intensive*. If the pronoun it reflexive, tell what information it adds to the sentence.

1. If this be known, Cassius or Caesar never shall turn back, for I will slay *myself*.

   _____

2. If I *myself* must die, there is no hour so fit as Caesar's death hour.

   _____

3. Brutus declares that he will put *himself* into the pulpit first.

   _____

4. Do any of you consider *yourselves* so base that you would be a bondsman?

   _____

5. I have the same dagger for *myself*, when it shall please my country to need my death.

   _____

6. He says, for Brutus' sake, he finds *himself* indebted to us all.

   _____

B. Writing Application: Follow the directions to write two sentences using reflexive pronouns.

1. Use a singular reflexive pronoun.

   _____

   _____

2. Use a plural reflexive pronoun.

   _____

   _____

The Tragedy of Julius Caesar, **Act III**, by William Shakespeare

Reading Strategy: Paraphrase

To **paraphrase** a text or passage is to restate it in your own words. Paraphrasing can be a useful study tool. If you take the time to paraphrase passages from *The Tragedy of Julius Caesar*, you will better understand the significance of the play. Here is an example:

> **Shakespeare's text:** I blame you not for praising Caesar so;
>
> But what compact mean you to have with us?
>
> Will you be pricked in number of our friends,
>
> Or shall we on, and not depend on you?
>
> **Paraphrase:** I don't blame you for praising Caesar that way, but what agreement will you have with us? Are you one of us, or shall we proceed without you?

DIRECTIONS: Paraphrase the following passages from Act III. Remember that a paraphrase is a restatement of a passage in your own words.

1. Here is a mourning Rome, a dangerous Rome,
   No Rome of safety for Octavius yet. [Scene i, ll. 288–289]

   _____

   _____

2. They that have done this deed are honorable.
   What private griefs they have, alas, I know not,
   That made them do it. They are wise and honorable,
   And will, no doubt, with reasons answer you. [Scene ii, ll. 213–216]

   _____

   _____

   _____

3. Thy master is a wise and valiant Roman;
   I never thought him worse.
   Tell him, so please him come unto this place,
   He shall be satisfied and, by my honor,
   Depart untouched. [Scene i, ll. 138–142]

   _____

   _____

   _____

4. I know not, gentlemen, what you intend,
   Who else must be let blood, who else is rank.
   If I myself, there is no hour so fit
   As Caesar's death's hour, nor no instrument
   Of half that worth as those your swords, made rich
   With the most noble blood of all this world. [Scene i, ll. 151–156]

   _____

   _____

Name _____ Date _____

The Tragedy of Julius Caesar, Act III, by William Shakespeare

Literary Analysis: Dramatic Speeches

The characters in *The Tragedy of Julius Caesar* make several different kinds of speeches: asides, soliloquies, and monologues. A character may speak an **aside** to the audience or to himself, or even to one other character, but out of earshot of the other characters onstage. In Act III, Cassius speaks an aside to Brutus about whether they should let Mark Antony speak at Caesar's funeral. In a **soliloquy,** a character reveals his or her true thoughts and feelings, unheard by other characters, usually while alone onstage. Brutus speaks a soliloquy in Act II, as he thinks about Caesar's potential as a ruler. A **monologue** is a long, uninterrupted speech by one character, to which the other characters listen. Brutus speaks in a monologue to the other conspirators in Act II when he persuades them not to harm Mark Antony.

Complete the following chart by identifying the type of speech listed and explaining how each speech reveals the speaker's feelings.

Speech	Type	How does it reveal the speaker's feelings?
Example: Cassius, Scene I, lines 232–243	aside	Cassius is worried that Mark Antony's speech might persuade the plebeians to favor Caesar and turn against Cassius and Brutus.
1. Caesar, Scene i, lines 58–73		
2. Brutus, Scene i, lines 103–110		
3. Antony, Scene i, lines 254–275		
4. Antony, Scene ii, lines 261–262		

The Tragedy of Julius Caesar, Act IV, by William Shakespeare

Build Vocabulary

Spelling Strategy   Form the plural of words ending in *z, x, sh, ch, s,* or *y* by adding *-es* or *-ies* to their base words. For example, the plural form of the word *legacy* is the Word Bank word *legacies.*

Using the Root *-phil-*

The word *philosophy* contains the word root *-phil-,* which means "love," and *-sophy,* which means "wisdom" or "knowledge and thought." *Philosophy,* therefore, can be called a "love of wisdom, knowledge, or thought."

A. Directions: Replace the italicized word or phrase in each sentence with a word which contains the root *-phil-* from the following list:

bibliophile   philanthropy   Philadelphia   philology   philodendron

1. The community leader was recognized for her *kindness and charitable acts.*
   _____

2. *"The city of brotherly love"* is located in Pennsylvania, on the Delaware River.
   _____

3. We placed the *plant with heart-shaped leaves* in the kitchen window.
   _____

4. *The study of written records* is an area of study for people who love language.
   _____

5. The literature professor was a *lover of books* and often added new titles to her collection.
   _____

Using the Word Bank

legacies	slanderous	covert
chastisement	philosophy	

B. Directions: Write the Word Bank word that best completes the meaning of each of the following sentences.

1. Brutus and Cassius are unaware of Antony's _____ plans.

2. Throughout difficult circumstances, Brutus never loses sight of his personal
   _____.

3. Antony wants to decrease the _____ left to the Roman people by Caesar.

4. Cassius is angered by Brutus' _____ of his behavior.

5. Mark Antony's _____ comments seriously damage Brutus' reputation among the Roman people.

The Tragedy of Julius Caesar, Act IV   **209**

The Tragedy of Julius Caesar, **Act IV**, by William Shakespeare

Build Grammar Skills: Pronoun and Antecedent Agreement

An **antecedent** is a word or group of words that the pronoun replaces in a sentence—the word or words to which a pronoun refers. The antecedent of a pronoun may be a noun, another pronoun, or a phrase or clause acting as a noun. It can come before or after the pronoun, can be in another sentence, and might be more than one word. For a pronoun to make sense, it must agree with its antecedent in number (singular or plural) and gender (masculine, feminine, or neuter).

> *Publius* shall not live; with a spot Antony damns *him*.

In the above example, the singular, masculine pronoun *him* refers to the singular, masculine noun *Publius*.

> These *people* then shall die; *their* names are pricked.

Here, the plural, neuter possessive pronoun *their* refers to the plural, neuter noun *people*.

A. Practice: Underline each pronoun and circle its antecedent. Label the number (singular or plural) and gender (masculine, feminine, or neuter) of the antecedent.

1. Caesar has died and Antony, Octavius, and Ledipus must punish someone for his death.

2. Brutus and his generals wait for Cassius at their camp.

3. Cassius argues with Brutus and accuses him of taking bribes.

4. Portia has committed suicide and Brutus misses her.

5. The senators have heard that some of them will be put to death.

6. Caesar's ghost visits Brutus and tells him a secret.

B. Writing Application: Revise the following passage to correct any errors in pronoun-antecedent agreement.

> After Caesar's death, Antony, Lepidus, and Octavius take his position as rulers who share equal authority. Together the men plan which of your political opponents must be killed. However, Antony is manipulative and cunning. Before long, he sends Lepidus on an errand and immediately begins to criticize her to Octavius. Antony tells them that Lepidus is not fit to rule.

_____

_____

_____

_____

_____

_____

Name _____ Date _____

Reading Strategy: Read Between the Lines

Reading line by line helps you understand the basic events of a dramatic work. But by **reading between the lines,** you find deeper meaning in the words and actions of characters. Certain lines of dialogue and certain scenes may reveal clues about characters, their relationships, and events to come. For example, in Act IV, Brutus and Cassius are engaged in a lengthy argument. On the surface, this argument seems only a minor battle of wills. Reading between the lines, however, you can see that the argument reveals a great deal about the personalities of Brutus and Cassius and about their ability to conquer Antony and win over the people of Rome.

DIRECTIONS: Respond to the following questions, using your ability to read between the lines and understand people and situations in Act IV of *The Tragedy of Julius Caesar*.

1. At the beginning of Act IV, Antony, Octavius, and Lepidus discuss which Romans must die. Who are some of the people they specifically mention as being marked for death? What does this conversation reveal about their characters and their drive for power?

_____

_____

2. Referring to Lepidus, Octavius says, "You may do your will;/But he's a tried and valiant soldier." Antony then replies, "So is my horse, Octavius, . . ." What does Antony mean by this reply? How does he feel about Lepidus?

_____

_____

3. Brutus and Cassius call each other names and argue about who is the better soldier. Is this discussion important to the larger matter at hand—defeating Antony? Why do you think they are arguing in this way? What does this argument reveal about the leadership abilities of Brutus and Cassius, and about what the future probably holds for them?

_____

_____

_____

_____

4. How does Brutus react to news that his wife, Portia, is dead? What does his reaction reveal about his sincerity in trying to live according to his personal philosophy? Why is Cassius especially shocked to hear this news from Brutus? What does he mean when he says, "How scap'd I killing when I/cross'd you so?" What does this exchange reveal about how Cassius and Brutus differ in their emotional responses?

_____

_____

_____

_____

_____

The Tragedy of Julius Caesar, Act IV, by William Shakespeare

Literary Analysis: Conflict in Drama

Conflict is a struggle between opposing forces. Conflict may be **external,** such as between a person and nature or between two people or groups of people. For example, Brutus and Cassius have a bitter quarrel, beginning with Cassius' accusation that Brutus has wronged him by condemning Lucius Pella publicly. A conflict may be **internal**—that is, within a person who is struggling with a difficult decision. In Act II, for example, Caesar struggles with opposing desires within himself when considering whether to go to the Capitol despite all warnings.

Complete the following chart by indicating how each character views the conflict described on the left.

Conflict	How one character views it	How the other character views it
Example: Cassius accuses Brutus of having wronged him by ignoring his requests and publicly condemning Pella.	Cassius feels that Brutus is being overcritical of minor faults.	Brutus thinks that Cassius lowered himself in defending a man such as Pella.
1. Antony and Octavius argue over whether or not Lepidus is fit to be one of the three rulers of Rome.		
2. Brutus claims that Cassius has a reputation for taking bribes.		
3. Brutus and Cassius discuss whether or not they should march to Philippi.		

The Tragedy of Julius Caesar, **Act V**, by William Shakespeare

Build Vocabulary

Spelling Strategy   When a word ends in silent *e*, drop the *e* before adding a suffix beginning with a vowel. For example, if you add the suffix -*ed* to the word *misconstrue*, you form the Word Bank word *misconstrued*.

Using the Prefix *mis-*

In Act V, Titinius, reacting to Cassius' fatal error of judgment, exclaims, "Alas, thou hast misconstrued everything!" The word *misconstrued* contains the prefix *mis-*, which means "wrong" or "bad." Because the word *construed* means "interpreted" or "understood," *misconstrued* means "made the wrong interpretation."

A. DIRECTIONS: Complete each of the following sentences with the best word from the list. Use each word only once.

misfortune   miscalculates   misdeeds   misappropriate   misguided

1. As a leader, Brutus was noble and sincere but _____.

2. Cassius _____ a situation, and the error costs him his life.

3. Brutus seemed plagued by terrible _____.

4. The _____ of Antony and Cassius raise important questions about the use and abuse of power.

5. According to Antony, Brutus is the only person who did not _____ his power.

Using the Word Bank

presage	ensign	consorted	demeanor
disconsolate	misconstrued	envy	

B. DIRECTIONS: Match each word in the left column with its definition in the right column. In the blank, write the letter of the definition next to the word it defines.

____ 1. presage   a. accompanied

____ 2. ensign   b. distressed; hopeless

____ 3. consorted   c. jealousy; spite

____ 4. demeanor   d. flag; banner

____ 5. disconsolate   e. foretell

____ 6. misconstrued   f. conduct; behavior

____ 7. envy   g. made the wrong interpretation

Unit 8: Drama

The Tragedy of Julius Caesar, Act V, by William Shakespeare

Build Grammar Skills: Words of Direct Address

A drama is a story told mainly through the dialogue, or conversation, of its characters. In order to emphasize to whom or what a character is speaking, a playwright will often set off **words of direct address** with commas and occasionally an exclamation point. Look at these four examples from Act V:

> "Now, Brutus, thank yourself . . ."
> "Come, Antony; away!"
> "Go, Pindarus, get higher on that hill . . ."
> "O Cassius!/Far from this country Pindarus shall run, . . ."

A. Practice: Read each of the following passages from Act V of *The Tragedy of Julius Caesar.* Underline the word or words of direct address and insert commas in the correct locations.

1. Ho Lucilius hark, a word with you.

2. Give me thy hand Messala.

3. Yet countrymen O, yet hold up your heads!

4. Come poor remains of friends rest on this rock.

5. How died my master Strato?

6. Octavius then take him to follow thee.

B. Writing Application: Write a brief dialogue between Antony, Octavius, and Messala, in which they discuss the death of Brutus. Have the characters address each other directly. Punctuate their words of direct address with proper punctuation marks.

_____

_____

_____

_____

_____

_____

_____

_____

_____

_____

_____

_____

_____

_____

The Tragedy of Julius Caesar, Act V, by William Shakespeare

Reading Strategy: Identify Cause and Effect

Situations that unfold in a drama have both causes and effects. A **cause** is what makes something happen, and an **effect** is the result of that cause. In a play, incidents and characters' actions are linked together as a sequence of causes and effects. For example, the death of Caesar is the cause of Antony's decision to both secure his own power and retaliate against Caesar's killers. One effect of his plot is his war with Cassius and Brutus. This war, ultimately, is the cause of the play's tragic outcome. What other causes and effects occur in Act V, before the death of Brutus?

DIRECTIONS: Use the following boxes to track connected causes and effects that lead to the ending of *The Tragedy of Julius Caesar* in Act V.

Julius Caesar is killed.

Cause
↓
Effect

Antony vows to punish the people responsible for Caesar's death.

Cause
↓
Effect

Cause
↓
Effect

Cause
↓
Effect

Cause
↓
Effect

Cause ⟶

Cause
↑
Effect

Cause
↑
Effect

Cause
↑
Effect

Cause
↑
Effect

Effect

Unit 8: Drama

The Tragedy of Julius Caesar, Act V, by William Shakespeare

Literary Analysis: Tragedy

A **tragedy** has a central action and a main character who is considered noble but who has a character flaw, or weakness, that brings about his or her downfall. The downfall of that character illustrates the **theme** of the tragedy—the meaning of the central action and the main character's recognition of that meaning and its consequences. The theme of *The Tragedy of Julius Caesar* is perhaps best stated by Messala : "O Error, soon conceived, / Thou never com'st unto a happy birth, / But kill'st the mother that engend'red thee!" In other words, a grave error, once planned and committed, will never come to any good.

DIRECTIONS: Complete the following chart to explore the ways in which various events or statements contribute to the central theme of *The Tragedy of Julius Caesar.*

Statement or Event	Contribution to the Theme
Example: Caesar is assassinated.	This is the central action of the play, the grave error.
1. Antony and Octavius are engaged in a civil war against Cassius and Brutus.	
2. Cassius kills himself, with the help of Pindarus, because of a misunderstanding.	
3. Brutus says, "O Julius Caesar, thou art mighty yet! / Thy spirit walks abroad, and turns our swords / In our own proper entrails."	
4. Brutus says, "Farewell good Strato—Caesar, now be still; / I killed not thee with half so good a will."	
5. Brutus kills himself, with the help of Strato.	
6. Antony says about Brutus, "This was the noblest Roman of them all. All the conspirators save only he Did that they did in envy of great Caesar; He, only in a general honest thought And common good to all, made one of them."	

"The Stolen Child" by William Butler Yeats

Build Vocabulary

Spelling Strategy   When adding a suffix to a word that ends in more than one consonant, never double the final consonant. For example, *wound + ed = wounded*; *gloss + es =*
the Word Bank word *glosses*.

Using Words With Multiple Meanings

A. DIRECTIONS: Words with multiple meanings allow writers to increase impact by suggesting
two or more possibilities of meaning with a single word. For each of the following sentences,
identify two meanings of the italicized word, and explain how both meanings contribute to the
effect of the sentence.

1. She grew up in *mean* circumstances and was cautious all her life.

_____

_____

_____

2. In the *green* days of youth, we do not know what awaits us.

_____

_____

_____

3. Pouring money into maintenance, she discovered her old car to be everything *dear*.

_____

_____

_____

4. He feared his *rough* hands would upset the baby.

_____

_____

_____

Using the Word Bank

herons	glosses	slumbering

B. DIRECTIONS: Each item consists of a word from the Word Bank followed by four lettered
words or phrases. Choose the word or phrase most nearly similar in meaning to the Word Bank
word. Circle the letter of your choice.

1. herons	2. glosses	3. slumbering
a. descendents	a. tumbles	a. sleeping
b. swallows	b. polishes	b. bungling
c. messengers	c. leers	c. slogging
d. egrets	d. battles	d. weakening

The Stolen Child **217**

"The Stolen Child" by William Butler Yeats

Build Grammar Skills: Correct Usage of
Their, There and They're

When writing, it is important to use the correct words to express your meaning. The words *their*, *there* and *they're* are sometimes confused because they sound the same. However, each word is used differently. The word **their** is the possessive form of *they*. **There** often refers to a location. **They're** is the contraction of *they are*. The following examples demonstrate the correct use of *their*, *there* and *they're*.

> **Their:** The fairies want to take you to *their* world.
> **There:** Do not follow them *there*.
> **They're:** *They're* not to be trusted.

A. Practice: Complete each sentence by circling the correct word in parentheses.

1. (Their/There/They're) on the leafy island, the fairies have hidden (their, there, they're) vats full of berries.

2. (Their/There/They're) determined to lure the child into (their, there, they're) fairy world.

3. (Their/There/They're), they suggest, the child will be free from the woes of the human world.

4. However, (their, there, they're) suspicious characters.

5. We suspect that (their, there, they're) not acting in the best interest of the child.

6. (Their/There/They're) actions regarding the trout seem especially menacing.

7. Also, (their, there, they're) insisting that the child give up all human comforts.

8. Although the child is entering a new world, he has no guarantee of happiness (their, there, they're).

9. Once the fairies have him, (their, there, they're) not likely to let him go.

10. I would not advise any child to go (their, there, they're).

B. Writing Application: Follow the directions below to write three sentences using the words *their*, *there* and *they're*.

1. Use the word *their* in a sentence.

_____

_____

2. Use the word *there* in a sentence.

_____

_____

3. Use the word *they're* in a sentence.

_____

_____

"The Stolen Child" by William Butler Yeats

Reading Strategy: Respond

Reading poetry is a subjective experience. A poem can evoke different feelings in different readers. Think about what this poem means to you. What feelings does it evoke in you? How do the images and actions in the poem affect you? How do you feel about the ideas suggested by the poem?

DIRECTIONS: Use the graphic organizer to analyze your responses to the following images, events, and ideas in "The Stolen Child." Write your responses in the spaces provided.

Image/Actions/Idea	Response
Image: moonlight softly illuminating grey sands	
Image: the lowing of the calves on the warm hillside and the kettle on the hob	
Action: the fairies whisper to the sleeping trout, giving them unquiet dreams	
Action: the child goes away with the fairies	
Idea: the tradeoff that the child makes by going with the fairies: giving up all human comforts	

Unit 9: Poetry

"The Stolen Child" by William Butler Yeats

Literary Analysis: Atmosphere

When you enter a room, the feeling you get from your surroundings is the **atmosphere.** Literature, too, has atmosphere. Writers make choices about the scenes they represent and the words and images they use to represent them.

To discover how Yeats produces the overall effect, it is helpful to analyze, specifically, some of the language that produces the scenes and images. Use the graphic organizer to help you see how Yeats creates atmosphere in "A Stolen Child."

DIRECTIONS: In the first column are words and phrases from "A Stolen Child." In the second column, identify the scene, action, or image the words and phrases depict. In the third column, describe the feeling the image or action gives you. Then, go back to the first column and circle the particular words that gave you the feeling you experienced.

Words	Description	Feeling
1. Where flapping herons wake / The drowsy water rats;		
2. We foot it all the night / Weaving olden dances,		
3. And whispering in their ears / Give them unquiet dreams;		
4. The solemn-eyed: He'll hear no more . . .		
5. From a world more full of / weeping than he can understand.		

"In Flanders Fields" by John McCrae
"The Kraken" by Alfred, Lord Tennyson
"Reapers" by Jean Toomer
"Meeting at Night" by Robert Browning
"Prayer of First Dancers" Traditional Navajo Chant

Build Vocabulary

Spelling Strategy   The suffix -al is often used to turn nouns into related adjectives. For example, the noun *abyss* and its alternate form *abysm* refer to an extreme depth or a bottomless chasm. The adjective form of *abyss* and *abysm* is the Word Bank word *abysmal*, which means "bottomless" or "profoundly deep."

Using the Prefix *mil-*

Alfred, Lord Tennyson describes "huge sponges of millennial growth and height" that surround the Kraken. The word *millennial* contains the prefix *mil-*, which comes from the Latin word *mille*, meaning "one thousand." *Millennial* means "of or relating to a thousand-year period" and, in Tennyson's poem, suggests that the sponges are so large that they might have been growing for a thousand years.

A. Directions: In each sentence, replace the italicized word or phrase with a word from the following list. Write the word on the line provided.

milligrams   millionaire   millisecond

1. She paused for what seemed liked one *one thousandth of a second.* _____

2. The doctor prescribed five *one thousandths of a gram* of medicine. _____

3. Only a *person worth a least a million dollars* could afford to buy that estate. _____

Using the Word Bank

abysmal	millennial

B. Directions: Fill in each of the following blanks with the appropriate Word Bank word.

1. The Kraken sleeps far away, deep in the _____ sea.

2. Geologists described _____ changes in the earth's surface.

3. We studied the _____ growth of trees in an ancient forest.

4. Divers could not retrieve many pieces of the boat, which sank to the bottom of the _____ body of water.

5. Citizens prepared to celebrate their country's _____ anniversary.

Flanders Fields/Kraken/Reapers/Meeting at Night/First Dancers   **221**

"**In Flanders Fields**" by John McCrae
"**The Kraken**" by Alfred, Lord Tennyson
"**Reapers**" by Jean Toomer
"**Meeting at Night**" by Robert Browning
"**Prayer of First Dancers**" Traditional Navajo Chant

Build Grammar Skills: Correct Usage of *Between* and *Among*

Be sure not confuse the words *between* and *among*. Use **between** when referring to two people or things. Use **among** when talking about groups of three or more. The following examples show the correct use of *between* and *among*.

Among: *Among* the poems in this book, Tennyson's are my favorite.
Between: What is the difference *between* his early poems and his later ones?

A. Practice: Complete each sentence by writing the word *between* or *among* on the line.

1. As a poet, he was _____ the best in the country.

2. _____ the many sound devices used in "Meeting at Night," which is used most frequently?

3. What is the difference _____ consonance and assonance?

4. The dancers in "Prayer of First Dancers" will be welcome _____ the villagers.

5. In "Meeting at Night," the meeting _____ the speaker and the person inside the farmhouse is joyful.

6. In "Reapers," the field rat was caught _____ the blade and the ground.

B. Writing Application: Answer the following questions. Use the word *between* or *among* in each response.

1. What do the poets Tennyson and Browning have in common?

_____

_____

2. What do the poems "In Flanders Fields," "The Kraken" and "Prayer of First Dancers" have in common?

_____

_____

3. How far is it from the beach to the farm in "Meeting at Night"?

_____

_____

4. Where was the field rat nesting before being startled in "Reapers"?

_____

_____

"In Flanders Fields" by John McCrae
"The Kraken" by Alfred, Lord Tennyson
"Reapers" by Jean Toomer
"Meeting at Night" by Robert Browning
"Prayer of First Dancers" Traditional Navajo Chant

Reading Strategy: Listen

To fully appreciate a poem, it is often helpful to read the poem aloud. When you hear a poem read aloud, **listen** for rhythm and for rhymes and other repeated sounds. A poet will often incorporate rhythm and repeated sounds into a poem to create a particular mood, to reflect an important idea, or to draw attention to key lines. Listening to the poetry you are reading can help you to gain new insights into a poet's purpose.

DIRECTIONS: Read the following excerpts from "Meeting at Night" and "Prayer of First Dancers" aloud. Then make notes on the lines provided about rhythm, rhyme, and any other repeated sounds. Describe how you think these sounds relate to the meanings of the pieces.

"Meeting at Night"

1. The gray sea and the long black land; / And the yellow half-moon large and low; / And the startled little waves that leap / In fiery ringlets from their sleep, / As I gain the cove with pushing prow, / And quench its speed i' the slushy sand.

   _____
   _____
   _____
   _____
   _____

"Prayer of First Dancers"

2. With the far darkness made of the dark / cloud over your head, come to us / soaring. / With the far darkness made of the / he-rain over your head, come to us / soaring. / With the far darkness made of the dark / mist over your head, come to us / soaring. / With the far darkness made of the she-rain over your head, come to us / soaring. / With the zigzag lightning flung out on / high over your head, come to us / soaring. / With the rainbow hanging high over your head, come to us / soaring.

   _____
   _____
   _____
   _____
   _____
   _____

© Prentice-Hall, Inc.
Flanders Fields/Kraken/Reapers/Meeting at Night/First Dancers **223**

Unit 9: Poetry

"In Flanders Fields" by John McCrae
"The Kraken" by Alfred, Lord Tennyson
"Reapers" by Jean Toomer
"Meeting at Night" by Robert Browning
"Prayer of First Dancers" Traditional Navajo Chant

Literary Analysis: Musical Devices

Poets often use **musical devices** to create sounds in their poems. These sounds are used to create a particular mood, emphasize meaning, or draw attention to important lines in a poem. The most common musical devices found in poetry include **alliteration,** the repetition of the first sound of several words in a line; **onomatopoeia,** the use of words that imitate actual sounds; **assonance,** the repetition of similar vowel sounds; **consonance,** the repetition of similar consonant sounds; **meter,** the organization of rhythms in a poem; and **repetition and rhyme,** the repeating of certain key sounds, words, and phrases.

DIRECTIONS: Read the following excerpts from the poems you've read, identifying musical devices used in each poem.

1. What words create consonance in the following excerpt from "The Kraken"? What sounds are repeated in these words?

   From many a wondrous grot and secret cell / Unnumbered and enormous polypi / Winnow with giant arms the slumbering green

   _____

   _____

2. What words create assonance in the following excerpt from "The Kraken"? What sound is repeated in these words?

   Battening upon huge seaworms in his sleep: / Until the latter fire shall heat the deep: / Then once by man and angels to be seen.

   _____

   _____

3. What words create alliteration in the following excerpt from "Reapers"? What sound is repeated in these words?

   Black reapers with the sound of steel on stones / Are sharpening scythes.

   _____

   _____

4. Name two examples of onomatopoeia in the following two lines from "Meeting at Night." What sounds are these words imitating?

   . . . And quench its speed i' the slushy sand . . .

   . . . And blue spurt of a lighted match.

   _____

   _____

"The Wind—tapped like a tired Man" by Emily Dickinson
"A Pace Like That" by Yehuda Amichai
"Metaphor" by Eve Merriam
"Right Hand" by Philip Fried

Build Vocabulary

Spelling Strategy   When writing words ending in silent e, drop the e before adding an ending beginning with a vowel. For example, the ending -ed added to the word *diffuse* forms the Word Bank word *diffused*.

Using the Root -*tac*-

In "Right Hand," the speaker describes how his grandfather "ironed countless *taciturn* trousers." The root of the word *taciturn* is -*tac*-. Both the root -*tac*- and its variation -*tic*- mean "silent." The word *taciturn* means "silent or uncommunicative".

A. DIRECTIONS: For each sentence, fill in the blank with the most appropriate word from the following list.

tacitly   reticence   taciturn

1. With a handshake, they _____ agreed to work together peacefully.

2. Our _____ neighbor remained a stranger to many people.

3. His _____ kept him from taking risks.

Using the Word Bank

decipher	countenance	tremulous	flurriedly	taciturn
eloquent	guttural	diffused	garrulity	

B. DIRECTIONS: Match each word in the left column with its definition in the right column. Write the letter of the definition on the line next to the word it defines.

____ 1. decipher   a. vividly expressive

____ 2. countenance   b. produced from the throat; rasping

____ 3. tremulous   c. silent; uncommunicative

____ 4. flurriedly   d. talkativeness

____ 5. taciturn   e. trembling

____ 6. eloquent   f. spread out; dispersed

____ 7. guttural   g. the face; facial features

____ 8. diffused   h. translate

____ 9. garrulity   i. in a flustered way

Wind/Pace/Metaphor/Hand   **225**

Unit 9: Poetry

"The Wind—tapped like a tired Man" by Emily Dickinson
"A Pace Like That" by Yehuda Amichai
"Metaphor" by Eve Merriam
"Right Hand" by Philip Fried

Build Grammar Skills: Elliptical Clauses

In an **elliptical clause**, one or more words are omitted because they are implied or understood. For example:

> I remembered the way *(that)* Grandfather ironed trousers.

> When *(you are)* awakening, think of morning as a blank sheet of paper.

In the first sentence, the complete clause is *that Grandfather ironed trousers*, but the word *that* is omitted because it can be understood. In the second sentence, the complete clause is *When you are awakening*, but the words *you are* can be omitted.

A. Practice: For each of the following sentences, underline the elliptical clause. On the line provided, write the omitted word or words.

1. Listen to the way the wind taps on your door. _____

2. Did you see the tree I planted? _____

3. I know the night will fold up and file away my paper. _____

4. Grandfather is a person I admire. _____

5. When ironing, Grandfather was fascinating. _____

B. Writing Application: Rewrite the following paragraph, omitting certain words to create elliptical clauses.

> Poems often present details of nature that poets observe in their everyday lives. In "The Wind—tapped like a tired Man," the speaker recognizes that the wind is like a tired man. While she was home one day, the speaker invited the wind inside and observed its unique look and sound. In "A Pace Like That," the speaker describes a lemon tree that he admires. He knows that he must live his life at a slower pace in order to see the growth of its branches and leaves.

_____

_____

_____

_____

_____

_____

_____

_____

_____

"The Wind—tapped like a tired Man" by Emily Dickinson
"A Pace Like That" by Yehuda Amichai
"Metaphor" by Eve Merriam
"Right Hand" by Philip Fried

Reading Strategy: Paraphrase

When you **paraphrase** the lines of a poem, you restate what they say in your own words. Paraphrasing can clarify and help you to understand complex or abstract sections of the poems you read. To paraphrase, you can rewrite each sentence of a poem, or you can list important ideas from a poem and then express these ideas in your own words. If a poet presents a comparison between two items, you can describe in your own words the similarities between the two items.

Here's an example using the first two lines of the poem "Metaphor."

Morning is / a new sheet of paper / for you to write on.
Whatever you want to say, / all day, / until night / folds it up / and files it away

Paraphrase: The start of a day is a new beginning filled with possibilities. You can start fresh, filling your day with new experiences. When night comes, the day ends and all the day's experiences are stored away.

DIRECTIONS: Paraphrase each of the following excerpts from "The Wind—tapped like a tired Man" and "A Pace Like That."

1. The Wind—tapped like a tired Man— / And like a Host—"Come in" / I boldly answered—entered then / My residence within

   A Rapid—footless Guest— / To offer whom a Chair / Were as impossible as hand / A Sofa to the Air— . . .

   _____
   _____
   _____
   _____
   _____

2. The longer you live, the more people there are / who comment on your actions. Like a worker / in a manhole: at the opening above him / people stand around giving free advice / and yelling instructions, / but he's all alone down there in his depths.

   _____
   _____
   _____
   _____
   _____

© Prentice-Hall, Inc.

"The Wind—tapped like a tired Man" by Emily Dickinson
"A Pace Like That" by Yehuda Amichai
"Metaphor" by Eve Merriam
"Right Hand" by Philip Fried

Literary Analysis: Figurative Language

Figurative language is writing or speech not meant to be interpreted literally. There are specific types of figurative language, called figures of speech. A **simile** is a comparison using the words *like* or *as*. A **metaphor** is a comparison in which one thing is spoken or written about as if it were another. **Personification** is a figure of speech in which an object, animal, or idea is described as if it had human characteristics. Writers use figures of speech to present ideas in new ways and to create vivid images for readers.

DIRECTIONS: Answer the following questions based on excerpts from the poems.

"The Wind—tapped like a tired Man"

1. He visited—still flitting— / Then like a timid Man / Again, He tapped—'twas flurriedly— / And I became alone—

How does Emily Dickinson use personification in this final stanza? What specific human characteristics are being described? How does this instance of personification make the poem more vivid for readers?

_____

_____

"A Pace Like That"

2. I want a pace like that. / Not like reading a newspaper / but the way a child learns to read, / or the way you quietly decipher the inscription / on an ancient tombstone.

What similes does Yehuda Amichai use to describe the pace at which he wants to live? Why is this comparison effective?

_____

_____

"Metaphor"

3. Morning is / a new sheet of paper / for you to write on.

What metaphor does Eve Merriam present in this stanza? Why is this comparison effective?

_____

_____

"Right Hand"

4. Grandfather carried his voice in the seamed/palm of his right hand, the one/that had ironed countless taciturn trousers.
What an eloquent hand, it broke into grins/and self-assured narration whenever/it opened— . . . .

What metaphor does Philip Fried present in this excerpt? Why is this comparison effective?

_____

_____

"La Belle Dame sans Merci" by John Keats
"Danny Deever" by Rudyard Kipling

Build Vocabulary

Spelling Strategy Some compound words, such as the Word Bank word *quickstep*, are spelled as a single word. Others are spelled as separate words (*attorney general*) or hyphenated (*great-grandson*). When using a compound word, check a dictionary for the correct spelling.

Using the Root -*journ*-

A. Directions: The root -*journ*- comes from the old French transcription of the Latin word for day. Words using this root have some connection to the concept of a day. Use a dictionary to check the meaning of each of the following words; then explain how the word contains the sense of *day* in its meaning. Write each answer in the space provided.

1. journey

_____

_____

2. journalism

_____

_____

3. adjourn

_____

_____

4. journeyman

_____

_____

Using the Word Bank

sedge	thrall	sojourn	quickstep	whimpers

B. Directions: Match each word in the left column with its definition in the right column. Write the letter of the definition on the line next to the word it defines.

____ 1. sedge   a. slavery

____ 2. thrall   b. stay temporarily

____ 3. sojourn   c. pace used in military marching

____ 4. quickstep   d. grassy plant

____ 5. whimpers   e. makes a low whining sound

"La Belle Dame sans Merci" by John Keats
"Danny Deever" by Rudyard Kipling

Build Grammar Skills: Hyphens

Hyphens connect words. They connect words that break between lines; they connect certain prefixes that aren't part of a word (*pro-democracy)*; and they often connect two or more words that function as one.

> **Compound Noun:** John Keats could have been a *doctor-poet*, but chose to pursue only poetry.
> **Compound Modifier:** Keats's *well-known* poems celebrate and mourn the impermanence of beauty.
> **Compound Number:** Keats died in Rome when he was twenty-five.

Compound modifiers are usually hyphenated if they appear before the noun they modify. They are not hyphenated when they appear after the noun they modify.

> Keats's poems are well known.

A. Practice: In the blank to the left of each of the following sentences, write *N* if the hyphenated word is a compound noun, or *M* if the hyphenated word is a compound modifier.

____ 1. Rudyard Kipling's father was a scholar-artist in India.

____ 2. The six-year-old Kipling was left in England by his parents..

____ 3. Kipling's early stories chronicle the struggle for self-respect.

B. Writing Application: Rewrite each of the following sentences, placing hyphens where necessary.

1. When he was twenty three, Keats fell hopelessly in love.

   _____

   _____

2. His best loved odes reveal the depth of his thought and passion.

   _____

   _____

3. Keats left letters that give a close up look at his life.

   _____

   _____

Name _____ Date _____

"La Belle Dame sans Merci" by John Keats
"Danny Deever" by Rudyard Kipling

Reading Strategy: Identify the Speaker

One of the ways a reader gets information about the plot is by paying attention to the speaker. In a poem, the speaker may be a character or just a narrative presence—perhaps the poet.

Sometimes the speaker of a poem is clearly identified, and sometimes you may have to figure out who is speaking. Once you **identify the speaker,** consider the information the speaker provides in order to determine an attitude, a personality, or a point of view.

DIRECTIONS: Read "La Belle Dame sans Merci" and "Danny Deever," paying attention to the identity of the speaker in each poem. Answer the following questions about the speakers in the poems.

1. How many speakers can you identify in "La Belle Dame sans Merci"?

_____

2. What descriptive information can you give about each speaker?

_____

_____

3. What parts of the poem do you identify with each speaker?

_____

_____

4. Describe the role the first speaker performs in the poem.

_____

5. How do you know when the poem shifts from one speaker to another?

_____

6. How many speakers can you identify in "Danny Deever"?

_____

7. What details from each speaker tell you about his personality?

_____

_____

_____

8. What opinion does each speaker seem to have about the events in "Danny Deever"?

_____

_____

_____

"La Belle Dame sans Merci" by John Keats
"Danny Deever" by Rudyard Kipling

Literary Analysis: Narrative and Dramatic Poetry

A **narrative poem** tells a story. Narrative poems are often longer than other poems and usu-ally have a plot or sequence of events, as well as setting and characters.

In a **dramatic poem,** whether or not there is a developed sequence of events, the main ac-tion is conveyed through the words of the speakers. Dialogue draws the reader into the action and reveals events and the personalities of the characters who relate them.

A. DIRECTIONS: Summarize the narrative of "La Belle Dame sans Merci" by paraphrasing the plot development. The first three stanzas have been paraphrased as an example.

1. Example: What's bothering you, knight? You are alone and ailing this quiet autumn day.

2. _____
_____

3. _____
_____

4. _____
_____

5. _____
_____

B. DIRECTIONS: Read each of the following lines from "Danny Deever." Identify the speaker and explain what the line reveals about the action and the speaker.

1. "I'm dreadin' what I've got to watch . . ." _____
_____
_____

2. "They've taken off his buttons an' cut his stripes away . . . " _____
_____
_____

3. "'Is cot was right-'and cot to mine . . . " _____
_____
_____

4. "Nine 'undred of 'is county and the regiment's disgrace . . . " _____
_____
_____

5. "It's Danny fightin' 'ard for life . . . "_____
_____
_____

"The Guitar" by Federico García Lorca
"Making a Fist" by Naomi Shihab Nye
"Jade Flower Palace" by Tu Fu
"The Moon at the Fortified Pass" by Li Po
"What Are Friends For" by Rosellen Brown
"Some Like Poetry" by Wisɫawa Szymborska

Build Vocabulary

Spelling Strategy The adjective suffix -ful means "full of." Remember that this suffix ends with just one l, not two: wist + -ful = wistful.

Using the Root -path-

A. DIRECTIONS: Knowing that the Greek root -path- means "feeling" or "suffering," write T for *true* or F for *false* on the blanks that precede the following sentences. Check a dictionary if you are uncertain of the meaning of a word.

_____ 1. A person might show *empathy* with a cold stare.

_____ 2. A visitor to a cemetery might feel *pathos*.

_____ 3. Warm smiles and hugs indicate *antipathy*.

_____ 4. *Pathology* students learn the art of road building.

_____ 5. Disaster victims often stir feelings of *sympathy*.

_____ 6. An audience would give much praise to a *pathetic* speaker.

Using the Word Bank

monotonously	pathos	wistful

B. DIRECTIONS: For each Word Bank word, choose the word or phrase that is most similar in meaning. Circle the letter of your choice.

1. monotonously
   a. singly
   b. sing-song
   c. tediously
   d. loudly

2. pathos
   a. sympathy
   b. joyfully
   c. contented
   d. pleasurable

3. wistful
   a. portly
   b. yearning
   c. startling
   d. indecisive

"The Guitar" by Federico García Lorca
"Making a Fist" by Naomi Shihab Nye
"Jade Flower Palace" by Tu Fu
"The Moon at the Fortified Pass" by Li Po
"What Are Friends For" by Rosellen Brown
"Some Like Poetry" by Wisława Szymborska

Build Grammar Skills: Placement of *Only*

In order to make the meaning of a sentence clear, avoid placing the word *only* in a position where it appears to modify more than one word in the sentence. Instead, place *only* as close as possible to the word or group of words it modifies. As the examples show, the same sentence can have many meanings depending on the placement of *only*.

Only he plays sorrowful tunes on the guitar. (No one besides him plays sorrowful tunes.)
He plays **only** sorrowful tunes on the guitar. (He plays nothing but sorrowful tunes.)
He plays sorrowful tunes **only** on the guitar. (He does not play those tunes on any other instrument.)
He plays sorrowful tunes on the **only** guitar. (There is no other guitar.)

A. Practice: Read each sentence below to determine if its meaning is clear. (The intended meaning appears in parentheses.) If the meaning of the sentence is not clear, rewrite the sentence, moving *only* as close as possible to the word or group of words it modifies. If the meaning of the sentence is clear, write *Correct*.

1. A stone horse only is left of his glory. (Nothing is left besides a stone horse.)

   _____

2. I sit on the grass and only start a poem. (I do not complete the poem.)

   _____

3. Only the soldiers turn around, looking toward the border. (The soldiers do not look anywhere else.)

   _____

4. Friends only make her bitter. (No one else has this effect on her.)

   _____

B. Writing Application: Write two sentences using the word *only*. Be sure that each sentence reflects the meaning indicated in parentheses.

1. (He does not like any other kind.)

   _____

   _____

2. (No one else likes to do that.)

   _____

   _____

"The Guitar" by Federico García Lorca
"Making a Fist" by Naomi Shihab Nye
"Jade Flower Palace" by Tu Fu
"The Moon at the Fortified Pass" by Li Po
"What Are Friends For" by Rosellen Brown
"Some Like Poetry" by Wisława Szymborska

Reading Strategy: Read in Sentences

Reading poetry in sentences, rather than line by line, is key to understanding a poem's meaning. Use the poem's punctuation as your guide. Rather than stopping at the end of a line, stop only at a comma, colon, semicolon, or dash. Look at the stops in the following lines from "The Guitar."

> It weeps
> For distant things,
> Warm southern sands
> Desiring white camellias.

DIRECTIONS: Write your answers to the following questions.

1. Line 25 of "The Guitar" ends with an exclamation point—"Oh guitar!" How does this punctuation affect your reading of the poem?

_____

_____

2. How many sentences or complete thoughts are expressed in the following lines from "Jade Flower Palace"?

> The stream swirls. The wind moans in
> The pines. Gray rats scurry over
> Broken tiles. What prince, long ago,
> Built this palace, standing in
> Ruins beside the cliffs? . . .

_____

3. Each line in "What Are Friends For" ends with a stop—a period, comma, or dash. Is it reasonable to conclude that each line expresses a single thought? Why or why not?

_____

_____

4. Of all the stanzas in "Some Like Poetry," the second stanza, "Like—," has the most lines that express complete thoughts. How does the punctuation affect the meaning and impact of these lines?

_____

_____

Name _____ Date _____

"**The Guitar**" by Federico García Lorca

"**Making a Fist**" by Naomi Shihab Nye

"**Jade Flower Palace**" by Tu Fu

"**The Moon at the Fortified Pass**" by Li Po

"**What Are Friends For**" by Rosellen Brown

"**Some Like Poetry**" by Wisława Szymborska

Literary Analysis: Lyric Poetry

A **lyric poem** expresses the observations and feelings of a single speaker. Lyric poetry was originally written to be accompanied by music; its musicality is one of its distinctive features. Because it aims to capture the feeling of a single moment, a lyric poem never tells a full story. Unlike narrative poetry, lyric poetry zeros in on an experience or creates and explores a single effect. It can be written in a traditional form or in free verse.

DIRECTIONS: For each poem listed in the chart, indicate the form in which the poem is written (traditional or free verse), the poem's subject, the speaker's feelings about the subject, and the overall effect created.

Poem	Form	Subject	Speaker's Feelings	Overall Effect
1. "The Guitar"				
2. "Making a Fist"				
3. "Jade Flower Palace"				
4. "The Moon at the Fortified Pass"				
5. "What Are Friends For"				
6. "Some Like Poetry"				

Sonnet 18 by William Shakespeare
"The Waking" by Theodore Roethke
Tanka by Ki Tsurayuki and Priest Jakuren
Haiku by Matsuo Bashō and Kobayashi Issa

Build Vocabulary

Spelling Strategy If a word of more than one syllable ends in a single consonant coming after a single vowel and the accent *is not on the last syllable*, do *not* double the final consonant before a suffix beginning with a vowel: *temper + -ate = temperate.*

Using Forms of *temperate*

A. Directions: Circle the best answer to each of the following questions.

1. Which location would have the most *temperate* weather?
   Siberia   Amazonian rain forest   North Carolina

2. Which individual would most likely demonstrate *temperance* in her conduct?
   a judge   an actor   a coach

3. Which item can be *tempered*?
   water   steel   salt

4. Which of the following is an *intemperate* action?
   making regular deposits in a savings account   eating an entire bag of chips

   watching less than an hour of television per day

Using the Word Bank

camellia	temperate	eternal	lapping

B. Directions: Complete each sentence by writing the correct Word Bank word in the blank.

1. A _____ breeze blows off the southern waters.

2. The thirsty dog was _____ the water.

3. The _____ is my favorite flower.

4. He swore that his love was _____.

Unit 9: Poetry

Sonnet 18 by William Shakespeare
"The Waking" by Theodore Roethke
Tanka by Ki Tsurayuki and Priest Jakuren
Haiku by Matsuo Bashō and Kobayashi Issa

Build Grammar Skills: Correct Usage of *To*, *Too* and *Two*

Be sure not to confuse the words *to, too* and *two*. Use **to** as part of an infinitive or when you mean "in the direction of." Use **too** when you mean "also" or "excessively." Use **two** when you are refering to the number that follows *one*. The following examples show the correct use of *to, too* and *two*.

To: I am going *to* a poetry reading.

Too: Why don't you come, *too*?

Two: The *two* of us will have fun.

A. Practice: Complete each of the following sentences by writing *to, too* and *two* on the line.

1. I agree with Shakespeare: summer always seems _____ end _____ quickly.

2. Sometimes the days are _____ hot, but that doesn't bother me _____ much.

3. I had to read "The Waking" at least _____ times before I understood it.

4. If "waking" is life, then I, _____, will take it slow.

5. What point is the author of "The Waking" trying _____ make when he says that he learns by going where he has _____ go?

6. Which of the _____ Tankas did you like best?

7. I wonder if Priest Jakuren ever went _____ the cypress-mountain during his travels.

8. I noticed when reading the _____ Haikus that they both have _____ do with water falling _____ earth.

B. Writing Application: Rewrite the following paragraph, revising for correct usage of *to, too* and *two*.

Last week my classmates and I went to a poetry festival at a local park. It wasn't to far, so we all walked to the park together. A podium stood in the center of a small open air theater. We walked into the theater and past the podium to too booths set up nearby. They offered crafts and food for people too buy between readings. I was supposed too read one of my poems, but I felt to nervous, so Gary offered to read it for me. Two other classmates were reading, to.

_____

_____

_____

_____

_____

_____

_____

Sonnet 18 by William Shakespeare
"The Waking" by Theodore Roethke
Tanka by Ki Tsurayuki and Priest Jakuren
Haiku by Matsuo Bashō and Kobayashi Issa

Reading Strategy: Envision the Imagery

When you **envision the imagery**, or create a mental picture of images that poets use, you can better understand the messages that poets convey. Use your memory and imagination to envision sensory details in the poems. For instance, when Shakespeare writes of "the darling buds of May," you might create a mental picture of brilliantly colored flower buds and bright sunshine. Use associations to envision images that are not as familiar. If you have never seen a camellia, the flower mentioned in Bashō's haiku, you might associate another flower that has a cuplike blossom, such as a buttercup.

DIRECTIONS: Write at least one association for each image listed. Then use the associations to draw conclusions about the poet's meaning. Write your conclusions in the spaces provided in the chart.

Image	Association	Poet's Meaning
1. Sometime too hot the eye of heaven shines.		
2. The lowly worm climbs up a winding stair		
3. That winter night / The river blew so cold		
4. On the cypress-mountain, / Autumn evening		
5. Falling upon earth, / Pure water spills . . .		
6. A gentle spring rain		

Unit 9: Poetry

Sonnet 18 by William Shakespeare
"The Waking" by Theodore Roethke
Tanka by Ki Tsurayuki and Priest Jakuren
Haiku by Matsuo Bashō and Kobayashi Issa

Literary Analysis: Poetic Forms

A **haiku** is a lyric, unrhymed poem of three lines of five, seven, and five syllables. A **tanka** consists of five unrhymed lines of five, seven, five, seven, and seven syllables. Both forms include simple, straightforward images. A haiku always includes an image from nature.

A **sonnet** is a fourteen-line poem written in iambic pentameter (five unaccented syllables each followed by an accented one). There are two types of sonnets, Shakespearean and Petrarchan. A Shakespearean sonnet contains three quatrains (*abab cdcd efef*) followed by a rhymed couplet (*gg*).

A **villanelle** is a lyric poem written in three-line stanzas, ending with a four-line stanza. It has two refrain lines that appear in the first and third line of the first stanza; they appear alternately as the third line of subsequent stanzas and finally as the last two lines of the poem.

DIRECTIONS: List the poetic form used by each poet, and supply two examples from each poem that illustrate the form.

Poet	Poetic Form	Examples of Form
1. Shakespeare		
2. Roethke		
3. Tsurayuki		
4. Priest Jakuren		
5. Bashō		
6. Issa		

from *Don Quixote* by Miguel de Cervantes

Build Vocabulary

Spelling Strategy   If a word ends in *y*, and you want to add a suffix beginning with *ing*, *ist*, or *ish*, keep the *y* and simply add the ending; for example, *sally + ing = sallying*; *boy + ish = boyish*; and *essay + ist = essayist*.

Using the Root *-son-*

A. DIRECTIONS: The root *-son-* comes from a Latin word meaning "sound." The Word Bank word *sonorous* derives from this origin, as do other words containing *-son-*. Use a dictionary to check the meaning of each of the following words; then explain how it relates to sound. Write each answer in the space provided.

1. sonar _____

2. resonate _____

3. sonata _____

4. sonogram _____

Using the Word Bank

lucidity	adulation	interminable	affable	sallying
requisite	sonorous	veracious	vanquish	extolled

B. DIRECTIONS: Circle the letter of the word closest in meaning to the Word Bank word.

1. lucidity
   a. evil   b. clarity   c. brightness   d. dream

2. adulation
   a. maturity   b. praise   c. vibration   d. infidelity

3. interminable
   a. interior   b. fatal   c. endless   d. disconnected

4. affable
   a. amazing   b. fragile   c. obese   d. friendly

5. sallying
   a. venturing   b. navigating   c. courting   d. farming

6. requisite
   a. curious   b. chosen   c. required   d. ask

7. sonorous
   a. sleepy   b. respiratory   c. snoring   d. loud

8. veracious
   a. ravenous   b. truthful   c. malicious   d. wandering

9. vanquish
   a. defeat   b. celebrate   c. dissolve   d. satisfy

10. extolled
   a. charged   b. dismissed   c. deceased   d. praised

from *Don Quixote* by Miguel de Cervantes

Build Grammar Skills: Capitals for
Proper Nouns and Adjectives

All proper nouns and proper adjectives begin with capital letters. **Proper nouns** name *specific* people, places, things, and ideas.

    Specific Person: Don Quixote   **Specific Place:** La Mancha   **Specific Thing:** Friday

In proper nouns consisting of two or more words, do not capitalize any articles, the words *and, but, or,* and *nor,* or prepositions with fewer than four letters.

    Emperor of Trebizond   Knight of the Burning Sword

Proper adjectives are formed from proper nouns.

    Turkey—Turkish   Spain—Spanish   Algiers—Algerian

When proper adjectives are combined with common nouns, do not capitalize the common nouns.

    Turkish soldier   Trinitarian friars   Spanish writer

A. Practice: Use proofreading marks to indicate the correct capitalization of proper nouns and proper adjectives in each sentence. Mark the sentences as shown in the following example.

    don quixote's favorite books were those written by the famous feliciano de silva.

1. Many an argument did he have with the priest of his village (a learned man, and a graduate

   of sigüenza) as to which had been the better knight, palmerin of england or amadis of gaul.

2. sigüenza was one of a group of "minor universities" granting degrees that were often

   laughed at by spanish humorists.

B. Writing Application: Write complete sentences to answer the following questions. In each sentence, use at least one proper noun or one proper adjective. If necessary, refer to the selection for information to help you write your sentences.

1. What consumed three quarters of Don Quixote's income?

   _____

   _____

2. Who was Cid Ruy Diaz?

   _____

3. What did Don Quixote say about Cid Ruy Diaz?

   _____

   _____

4. What did Don Quixote imagine himself vanquishing and sending to his lady as a present?

   _____

   _____

Name _____ Date _____

Reading Strategy: Compare and Contrast

When Miguel de Cervantes penned his tale of the woeful knight, he knew that his readers would consider his work in the light of what they already knew. In fact, Cervantes depended upon readers making such comparisons for much of the comedy of the novel.

As you read Don Quixote, look for places you can **compare and contrast** the world in the book to the world you know. For example, Quixote's best efforts at equipping himself as a knight become comic as the daft old man comes up with a cardboard helmet, rusty armor, and a broken-down nag for a steed.

DIRECTIONS: Use the following chart to help you compare and contrast parts of the story. List qualities of the topic in the first column to compare or contrast to the topic in the second column. In the third column, write how or why the comparison or contrast is comic.

Compare . . .	To . . .	Producing . . .
Sancho Panza	Don Quixote	Comic Effect
Quixote's Vision	Reality	Comic Effect
Era of Knighthood	Modern Era	Comic Effect
Narrator's Language	Plain Speech	Comic Effect

from *Don Quixote* by Miguel de Cervantes

Literary Analysis: Parody

The *Reader's Encyclopedia* defines parody as

. . . a comic or satirical imitation of a piece of writing, exaggerating its style and content, and playing especially on any weakness in structure or meaning of the original.

DIRECTIONS: The language of *Don Quixote* is an exaggerated version of the language of the romance novels of chivalry. To see how absurdly embellished the language really is, rewrite each of the following passages in simple, straightforward language.

1. But there were none he liked so well as those written by the famous Feliciano de Silva, for their lucidity of style and complicated conceits were as pearls in his sight, particularly when in his reading he came upon outpourings of adulation and courtly challenges.

_____

_____

_____

_____

_____

_____

2. He fancied that it was right and requisite, no less for his own greater renown than in the service of his country, that he should make a knight-errant of himself, roaming the world over in full armor and on horseback in quest of adventures.

_____

_____

_____

_____

_____

3. Those are giants, and if you are afraid, away with you out of here and betake yourself to prayer, while I engage them in fierce and unequal combat.

_____

_____

_____

_____

_____

_____

"Morte d'Arthur" by Alfred, Lord Tennyson
"Arthur Becomes King of Britain" from *The Once and Future King*
by T. H. White

Build Vocabulary

Spelling Strategy   When the sound /shun/ occurs at the end of a word of three or more syllables, the sound is always produced by the letters *tion*, as in *lamentation*.

Using the Suffix *-ous*

A. DIRECTIONS: Use what you already know about the suffix *-ous*, meaning "full of" or "possessing the qualities of," to define the italicized word in each sentence.

1. The sights were *marvelous* to behold.

   _____

2. T. H. White takes a *humorous* approach to the legend.

   _____

3. Wart's first attempt to pull out the sword was *disastrous*.

   _____

4. The animals made a *thunderous* noise when Wart succeeded.

   _____

stickler	sumptuous	palfrey	lamentation	swarthy

Using the Word Bank

B. DIRECTIONS: Match each word in the left column with its definition in the right column. In the blank, write the letter of the definition next to the word it defines.

____   1. stickler   a. an uncompromising person

____   2. palfrey   b. having a dark complexion

____   3. lamentation   c. a saddle horse

____   4. swarthy   d. magnificent

____   5. sumptuous   e. mourning

"Morte d'Arthur" by Alfred, Lord Tennyson
"Arthur Becomes King of Britain" from *The Once and Future King*
by T. H. White

Build Grammar Skills: Quotation Marks With Other Punctuation

Some writers find it difficult to remember when to place punctuation marks inside quotation marks and when to place them outside quotation marks. The following rules will help you.

Rule	Example
Always place a comma or a period inside the final quotation mark.	Tennyson's most famous excerpt from *Idylls of the King* is "Morte d' Arthur."
Always place a semicolon or colon outside the final quotation mark.	First I read "Morte d' Arthur"; then, a few years later, I read the entire epic.
Place a question mark or exclamation mark inside the final quotation mark if the end mark is part of the quotation.	At the start of White's "Arthur Becomes King of Britain," a character asks, "What's the matter with the King?"
Place a question mark or exclamation mark outside the final quotation mark if the end mark is not part of the quotation.	Have you read "Arthur Becomes King of Britain"?

A. Practice: Read each of the following passages from "Morte d'Arthur." If the passage is punctuated correctly, write *C* on the line. If it is punctuated incorrectly, write *I* on the line. Adjust the punctuation to the incorrect sentences and circle your corrections.

_____ 1. Francis, laughing, clapped his hand on Everard's shoulder, with "I hold by him". "And I", quoth Everard, "by the wassail-bowl".

_____ 2. "Why yes," I said, "we knew your gift that way at college; but another which you had—I mean of verse (for so we held it then), what came of that?"

_____ 3. Then those that stood upon the hills behind repeated—"Come again, and thrice as fair;" and, further inland, voices echoed—"Come with all good things, and war shall be no more."

B. Writing Application: All quotation marks have been removed from the dialogue in the following passage from "Arthur Becomes King of Britain." Rewrite the passage, adding quotation marks where necessary. Be sure to follow the rules of punctuation.

Our blessed monarch, said the Nurse tearfully, never had no hair. Anybody that studied the loyal family knowed that.
Good gracious! exclaimed Sir Ector. But he must have had a next-of-kin?
That's just it, cried King Pellinore in high excitement.

_____

_____

_____

_____

"Morte d'Arthur" by Alfred, Lord Tennyson
"Arthur Becomes King of Britain" from *The Once and Future King*
by T. H. White

Reading Strategy: Recognize Author's Attitude

Did you find yourself thinking that King Pellinore is a bit silly or foolish? That is certainly how White presents him in the story. The way an author depicts a character or a situation can reveal to readers how the author feels about his or her subject. Notice how these words spoken by King Pellinore make him appear a bit foolish.

> "Well, there has appeared a sort of sword in a stone, what, in a sort of a church. Not in the church, if you see what I mean, and not in the stone, but that sort of thing, what, like you might say."

White portrays Pellinore as a somewhat silly, eccentric old man. Readers can recognize White's attitude toward other characters from the following kinds of details:

- White's description of the characters
- the characters' thoughts and actions
- how characters speak and what they say
- how other characters respond to a character

DIRECTIONS: Read each passage. Then describe the attitude that the author reveals about the topic of the passage.

1. About truth and knighthood:

> "Thou has betrayed thy nature and thy name,
> Not rendering true answer, as beseemed
> Thy fealty, nor like a noble knight; . . "
>
> ["Morte d'Arthur," ll. 124–126]

_____

2. About the death of the legendary King Arthur:

> " . . . To the island-valley of Avilion;
> Where falls not hail, or rain, or any snow,
> Nor ever wind blows loudly, but it lies
> Deep-meadowed, happy, fair with orchard lawns
> And bowery hollows crowned with summer sea,
> Where I will heal me of my grievous wound."
>
> ["Morte d'Arthur," ll. 310–315]

_____

3. About young Arthur:

> "Poor Kay," he said. "All that shilling stuff was only because he was scared and miserable, and now he has good cause to be. Well, he shall have a sword of some sort if I have to break into the Tower of London."
>
> [from "Arthur Becomes King of Britain"]

_____

"Morte d'Arthur" by Alfred, Lord Tennyson
"Arthur Becomes King of Britain" from *The Once and Future King*
by T. H. White

Literary Analysis: Legend

The legend of King Arthur owes its popularity—even its very existence—to many writers who have enlarged, changed, and added to the seed of a very old story. Much of what we imagine about Arthur is based on the stories Sir Thomas Mallory wrote in the 1400s. His elaborate tales of knighthood, bravery, and magic in a medieval setting are the foundation for many of our modern ideas about Arthur. In fact, the real Arthur, if he existed, would have lived in quite primitive conditions. Mallory's Arthur lived in a massive stone castle and held relatively modern ideals, similar to those that Mallory might have held.

Mallory, Tennyson, White, and other "users" of the legend all lend to Arthur their own ideas about how kings should act and how knights should show their loyalty. People who write stories about legends almost always do this. Keep in mind that legends are not sources of historical information. When we read legends we learn about the culture of the *writer*, not necessarily about the culture of the *subject* of the legend.

DIRECTIONS: Answer the following questions about the legends of King Arthur you have just read.

1. What ideas about religion are expressed in Tennyson's poem?

   _____

   _____

   What do those ideas indicate about Tennyson and his nineteenth-century values?

   _____

   _____

   _____

2. How does White describe the experience of Wart removing the sword from the stone?

   _____

   _____

   What effect does this portrayal have on the event?

   _____

   _____

   _____

3. How do both Tennyson and White help ensure that the legend will live on? (Hint: Note the title of T. H. White's book.)

   _____

   _____

   _____

"Rama's Initiation" from the *Ramayana* by R. K. Narayan

Build Vocabulary

Spelling Strategy Words ending in y preceded by a consonant form their plurals by dropping the y and adding *ies: austerity + -ies = austerities.*

Using the Root *-min-*

A. Directions: Remembering that the root *-min-* means "small," complete each sentence below with a word from the following list.

minimize   minute   minor

1. A person under the age of eighteen is considered a _____.

2. Embarrassed officials tried to _____ the seriousness of the crime.

3. The baby alligator seemed _____ compared to the size of its parent.

Using the Word Bank

austerities	decrepitude	sublime	august	secular
obeisance	exuberance	diminutive	esoteric	

B. Directions: For each Word Bank word, choose the word or phrase that is most nearly *opposite* in meaning. Circle the letter of your choice.

1. austerities
   a. denials   b. indulgences   c. selfish   d. freedom

2. decrepitude
   a. youthfulness   b. renovate   c. decaying   d. futuristic

3. sublime
   a. vulgar   b. majestic   c. baseness   d. pauper

4. august
   a. respectable   b. outrage   c. undignified   d. energetic

5. secular
   a. rectangular   b. sacred   c. royal   d. scientific

6. obeisance
   a. shaking hands   b. praying   c. bowing   d. defiance

7. exuberance
   a. depression   b. agitation   c. elation   d. confusion

8. diminutive
   a. bulk   b. growth   c. thin   d. gigantic

9. esoteric
   a. appealing   b. popular   c. inviting   d. suave

"Rama's Initiation" from the *Ramayana* by R. K. Narayan

Build Grammar Skills: Commas After Introductory Clauses

Commas are used more than any other internal punctuation mark. They tell readers when to pause in a sentence. Using commas correctly helps readers better understand your meaning. When you write, remember to use commas after introductory clauses.

When the message was relayed to the King, he got up and hurried forward to receive the visitor.

A. Practice: Decide where a comma is needed in each of the following sentences. On the line, write the word that goes before the comma, the comma, and the word that goes after it. If no comma is needed, write *Correct*.

1. After Viswamithra had gone half way he realized that the visitor was leaving unceremoniously and was not even shown the courtesy of being escorted to the door.

   _____

2. Once they were all seated again Vasishtha addressed the King: "There must be a divine purpose working through this seer, who may know but will not explain."

   _____

3. When the sun came over the mountain peak they reached a pleasant grove over which hung, like a canopy, fragrant smoke from numerous sacrificial fires.

   _____

4. When they mediated on and recited these incantations, the arid atmosphere was transformed for the rest of their passage and they felt as if they were wading through a cool stream with a southern summer breeze blowing in their faces.

   _____

5. Before Viswamithra could answer she arrived, the ground rocking under her feet and a storm preceding her.

   _____

B. Writing Application: Write five sentences about "Rama's Initiation." Use an introductory clause in each sentence.

1. _____

   _____

2. _____

   _____

3. _____

   _____

4. _____

   _____

5. _____

   _____

"Rama's Initiation" from the *Ramayana* by R. K. Narayan

Reading Strategy: Drawing Inferences About Culture

As you were reading this episode from the *Ramayana*, you were **making inferences about the culture** of ancient India. When you draw upon details in the story and combine that information with your own experiences, you can make inferences about the beliefs, customs, and values of the culture that created and revered the hero Rama.

DIRECTIONS: List details from the selection and refer to your own experience as you write your answers to the following questions.

1. What does the *Ramayana* reveal about the role of women in ancient India?

_____

_____

_____

_____

_____

2. What does the *Ramayana* reveal about the role of religion in everyday life in ancient India?

_____

_____

_____

_____

_____

3. What does the *Ramayana* reveal about the gods and goddesses in Hinduism?

_____

_____

_____

_____

_____

4. What does the *Ramayana* reveal about the roles and responsibilities of royalty in ancient India?

_____

_____

_____

_____

_____

"Rama's Initiation" from the *Ramayana* by R. K. Narayan

Literary Analysis: Epic Hero

The dictionary *Literary Terms* defines the word **hero** as follows :

(1) Traditionally, a character who has such admirable traits as courage, idealism, and fortitude. (2) The earliest heroes, as revealed in myth and literature, were frequently favored by the gods or were themselves semi-divine; such were Achilles and Odysseus. (3) The deified hero symbolized the possibility of overcoming human limitations in a hostile universe ruled by the certainty of death. (4) Moreover, the hero embodied the cultural values of his time and functioned as a defender of his society.

DIRECTIONS: Think about Rama as he is portrayed in "Rama's Initiation." Find episodes or descriptions in the story that demonstrate Rama's fulfillment of each element of the definition above. Write your answers on the lines provided.

1. _____
_____
_____
_____
_____

2. _____
_____
_____
_____
_____

3. _____
_____
_____
_____
_____

4. _____
_____
_____
_____
_____

from *Sundiata: An Epic of Old Mali,* retold by D. T. Niane

Build Vocabulary

Spelling Strategy For words ending in two consonants, keep both consonants when adding a suffix starting with either a vowel or a consonant. For example, the suffix *-ity* added to the word *infirm* forms the Word Bank word *infirmity*.

Using the Root *-firm-*

At the beginning of this selection, Sogolon Kedjou is concerned about the *infirmity* her son seems to have. The word *infirmity* contains the word root *-firm-*, which comes from the Latin word *firmare*, meaning "to strengthen." Knowing that the prefix *in-* means "lacking" or "without," you can figure out that the word *infirmity* means "without strength" or "physical weakness."

A. Directions: For each sentence, fill in the blank with the most appropriate word containing the root *-firm-* from the following list.

affirmation
infirmary
confirmation
firmament

1. Students who are not feeling well can rest in the _____ .

2. I called for a(n) _____ of my appointment on Friday.

3. The award is a(n) _____ of her value as a teacher.

4. There were no clouds interrupting the solid blue _____ .

Using the Word Bank

fathom	taciturn	malicious	infirmity
innuendo	diabolical	estranged	affront

B. Directions: Match each word in the left column with its definition in the right column. In the blank, write the letter of the definition next to the word it defines.

____ 1. fathom   a. quiet; aloof

____ 2. taciturn   b. ailment

____ 3. malicious   c. understand; grasp

____ 4. infirmity   d. humiliation; mockery

____ 5. innuendo   e. spiteful

____ 6. diabolical   f. alienated

____ 7. estranged   g. suggestion; insinuation

____ 8. affront   h. demonic

from *Sundiata: An Epic of Old Mali*, retold by D. T. Niane

Build Grammar Skills: Semicolons

A **semicolon** tells the reader to pause longer than for a comma but without the finality of a period. Use a semicolon to join independent clauses not already joined by a conjunction.

Conjunction: Griots call themselves the memory of the people, and they travel from village to village.
Semicolon: Griots call themselves the memory of the people; they travel from village to village.

Use a semicolon to join independent clauses separated by either a conjunctive adverb or a transitional expression.

Conjunctive Adverb: Doua defended the king's will; *nevertheless*, the king's wishes were ignored.
Transitional Expression: Sassouma plotted to win her son the throne; *as a result*, he became king.

Use semicolons to avoid confusion when independent clauses or items in a series already contain commas.

Independent Clause: Sologon asked Sassouma for some baobab leaf, a condiment; and Sassouma humiliated her.
Items in a series: The king's sons included Mari Djata, the son of Sologon; Dankaran Touman, the son of Sassouma; and Boukari, the son of Namandjé.

A. Practice: Read the following sentences. Decide which commas, if any, should be replaced with semicolons. For each semicolon, write the word that goes before the semicolon, the semicolon, and the word that goes after it. If the sentence is correct, write *Correct*.

1. No matter how great the destiny promised for Mari Djata might be, the throne could not be given to someone who had no power in his legs, if the jinn loved him, let them begin by giving him the use of his legs.

   _____

2. The king's will reserved the throne for Mari Djata, however, the council of elders took no account of Naré Maghan's wishes.

   _____

3. Naré Maghan met with Nounfaïri, the blacksmith seer of Niani, and Nounfaïri's words, along with Doua's confidence, gave the king some assurance.

   _____

B. Writing Application: Use semicolons to combine each set of sentences into one sentence.

1. The king believed that Mari Djata would be king, as was foretold. He believed that Balla Fasséké, the son of Doua, would be Mari Djata's griot, just as Doua had been his own griot. He believed that Boukari, son of Namadjé, would be Mari Djata's right hand.

   _____

   _____

   _____

2. The king had confidence in Mari Djata's destiny, despite his infirmity. Unfortunately, the people of Niani did not.

   _____

   _____

from *Sundiata: An Epic of Old Mali,* retold by D. T. Niane

Reading Strategy: Storyteller's Purpose

A **storyteller's purpose** is his or her reason for relating a story to readers or listeners. For the griots of ancient Mali, telling and retelling the epic *Sundiata* served a variety of purposes. They used the story to teach people about important historical events, to entertain people, and to persuade people to support certain beliefs and accept certain standards of behavior.

DIRECTIONS: For each of the following passages from the selection, explain which of the author's purposes—to inform, entertain, or persuade—is illustrated. Some of the passages may serve more than one purpose. Explain your reasoning.

1. God has mysteries which none can fathom. . . . Each man finds his way already marked out for him and he can change nothing of it.

   _____

   _____

   _____

2. Sogolon's son was spoken of with nothing but irony and scorn. . . . No matter how great the destiny promised for Mari Djata might be, the throne could not be given to someone who had no power in his legs. . . . Such were the remarks that Sogolon heard every day. The queen mother, Sassouma Bérété, was the source of all this gossip.

   _____

   _____

   _____

3. A deathly silence had gripped all those present. Sogolon Djata closed his eyes, held tight, the muscles in his arms tensed. . . . Sogolon Kedjou was all eyes and watched her son's legs, which were trembling as though from an electric shock. Djata was sweating and the sweat ran from his brow. In a great effort he straightened up and was on his feet at one go. . . .

   _____

   _____

   _____

4. "Oh day, what a beautiful day, Oh day, day of joy; Allah Almighty, you never created a finer day. So my son is going to walk!"

   _____

   _____

   _____

5. With all his might the son of Sogolon tore up the tree and put it on his shoulders. . . ."Mother, here are some baobab leaves for you From henceforth it will be outside your hut that the women of Niani will come to stock up."

   _____

   _____

   _____

Name _____ Date _____

from *Sundiata: An Epic of Old Mali,* retold by D. T. Niane

Literary Analysis: Epic Conflict

Conflict in a story may take place in one of three ways:

- between characters
- between a character and society
- between a character and himself or herself

The hero often endures all three kinds of conflict at various points in an epic. It is the hero's ability to confront and overcome obstacles that marks him or her as heroic.

DIRECTIONS: Think about the excerpt you have read from *Sundiata.* When does Sogolon Djata meet each of the three kinds of conflict? How does he overcome the obstacle? Write an example of each kind of conflict (there may be more than one example in the story), and explain the hero's efforts to resolve it.

	Example of Conflict	Resolution of Conflict
Conflict between Sogolon Djata and a second character		
Conflict between Sogolon Djata and society		
Conflict between Sogolon Djata and himself		